# How To Do (Just About) Everything Right the First Time

# Publisher's Note

The editors of FC&A have taken careful measures to ensure the accuracy and usefulness of the information in this book. While every attempt has been made to assure accuracy, errors may occur. We advise readers to carefully review and understand the ideas and tips presented and to seek the advice of a qualified professional before attempting to use them. The publisher and editors disclaim all liability (including any injuries, damages or losses) resulting from the use of the information in this book.

The health information in this book is for information only and is not intended to be a medical guide for self-treatment. It does not constitute medical advice and should not be construed as such or used in place of your doctor's medical advice.

*"And Jesus said to him, 'If you can?' All things are possible to him who believes."*

*Mark 9:23*

FC&A Publishing®
103 Clover Green
Peachtree City, GA 30269

Produced by the staff of FC&A

ISBN 978-1-932470-79-6

# Table of contents

# Car talk from the pros

# Real estate tricks and traps

# Look your best for less

# Perfect pastimes

# Stretch your food dollars

**Don't get cheated by the scanner.** Price scanners at the grocery store help speed up checkout, lower costs by cutting labor, and create a detailed receipt of what you buy. They're also meant to help stores charge the correct price, but sometimes customers find mistakes. The U.S. Federal Trade Commission (FTC) keeps records of how accurate price scanners are. A 1998 study of scanners found one of every 30 items was mispriced. Half were undercharges, and half were overcharges. But overall the FTC found most stores got the price right 98 percent of the time — a passing grade. Here's what the FTC suggests you do to avoid being ripped off.

+ Keep an eye on the display screen as the prices appear. Speak up if you see a problem, and ask about the store's policy on overcharging. You should get the price corrected, and some stores offer a bonus or free item.

+ Write shelf prices on your items as you put them into the shopping cart.

+ Take a copy of the store's ad flier for items on special. The cashier may need to enter these discounts by hand.

+ Check your receipt, and ask the cashier to make corrections. If you've left the checkout line when you find an error, you may need to complain at the customer service desk.

If you see a pattern of scanner errors at your favorite supermarket, talk to the manager. You can also contact your state's attorney general's office or the FTC at 877-382-4357.

**Cut shopping trips to save money.** If you're not at the store, you're not spending money. That's one key to spending less on groceries from Steve and Annette Economides, supersavers and authors of *America's Cheapest Family Gets You Right on the Money*. The Economides family — including five growing children — spends about $350 a month on groceries, toiletries, and cleaning supplies. The trick is to plan ahead, store food in the freezer, and limit shopping to once a month.

"The more often you go to the store, the more often you will walk past displays, endcaps of special items, and the ever-enticing goodies in the checkout lane," say the Economideses. "The more often you pass these locations, the more likely you'll be to spend more than you intended."

You may worry that fresh fruits, vegetables, and dairy products won't last a month, but they can. The Economides plan is to eat fruits like grapes and bananas first, then start on longer-lasting pears, apples, and oranges. Shred cheese before you freeze it since it's hard to slice after it thaws. Be sure to pour off a little milk from the container before you put it in the freezer. This little bit of effort pays off by saving time and money.

"The less you shop, the more you save," say the Economideses.

## Handy guide saves money and time

There's no need to dirty a measuring cup if you know how much is in your can of soup or vegetables. Some older recipes may call for cans by their number. Refer to this handy table so you won't buy more than you need or open extra cans.

| Can size | Weight inside | Volume of food |
|----------|---------------|----------------|
| Buffet | 8 ounces | 1 cup |
| No. 1 | 10–12 ounces | about 1 1/2 cups |
| No. 300 | 14–16 ounces | 1 3/4 cups |
| No. 303 | 16–17 ounces | 2 cups |
| No. 2 | 20 ounces | 2 1/2 cups |
| No. 3 | 48 ounces | 5 3/4 cups |

**Make haste without wasting dollars.** Nobody likes spending a lot at the supermarket — either time or money. But finding the best deals seems to take all day. Try these tricks to speed up your bargain hunting.

+ Make a list, and check it at least twice. Look at the store's weekly ads before you leave home so you won't spend time standing at the shelves comparing prices. You can find supermarket weekly sales fliers online or in the newspaper.

+ Swim upstream. Most people move counterclockwise through the grocery store. If you go in the opposite direction, you'll spend less time waiting behind slowpokes in the aisles.

+ Get there early. If a sale starts on Sunday, you may find items sold out by Friday. You may get a rain check on the sale item, but that means another trip to the store.

+ Stay home. You can order all kinds of groceries, including specialty items your local store doesn't carry, by shopping online. Your goodies will be delivered right to your door. See what's available at *www.netgrocer.com*, *www.schwans.com*, or *www.amazon.com*.

**Weigh options for best deals.** One supermarket in your town may have the lowest prices on frozen foods, while another has lovely fresh produce. Maybe a third store offers the best specials on canned goods. There's no such thing as a perfect supermarket, so you may need to visit several stores to find the quality you want at the best price. But once you're familiar with each store, don't spend your weekends making the rounds. Plan ahead and check store flyers for specials so you can take turns at your favorite stores yet still limit your shopping to once a week or less.

**7 ways to shrink your grocery bills.** Try these tricks to slash spending on groceries.

✦ Use a list, and stick to it. That's the number one way to save. Everything you really need should be on your list. If it's not, leave it at the store for next time.

✦ Never shop for groceries when you're hungry. Enough said.

✦ Leave children and spouses at home so you can focus on finding bargains.

✦ Buy items you use often in large quantities when they're on sale. But never buy an item simply because it's on sale.

✦ Don't be fooled by fancy wrappers or clever advertising. Instead, check unit prices, like price per ounce, to compare brands. When you find the best price is on a generic or store brand, grab it.

✦ Shop at several stores so you'll know which ones have the best deals. If you know there is a bargain across town, ask your favorite store to match the price.

✦ Skip the expensive meats at the deli counter. Instead, look in the meat section for a chub, or large chunk of turkey, ham, or bologna, and take it to the butcher or deli counter to be sliced. They'll do it for free.

### Keep your brain sharp with fruit juice

Shopping with a list is better than relying on memory, no matter what your age. But don't forget to put fruit juice on your list. Some studies show drinking fruit and vegetable juices with lots of natural antioxidants called polyphenols may delay the onset of Alzheimer's disease. Purple grape juice is one of the best sources of polyphenols. Three glasses a week seem to do the trick.

## Let Labelman help you lose

There's a new mascot who can help you sort out food labels. Labelman, created by the U.S. Food and Drug Administration, will guide you through online training to use the nutrition facts label on food packages for weight control. Navigate to *www.cfsan.fda.gov,* select "Food Labeling and Nutrition" under "Program Areas," then click on the "Make Your Calories Count" button.

**Secret to slashing your grocery bill.** Tossing out a coupon for an item you buy often is like throwing away money. Join the ranks of shoppers who really know how to outsmart the manufacturers by clipping coupons and using them creatively.

"I love to watch the dollars get subtracted from my total grocery bill and know that I am helping my family by saving money," says busy mom MaryTara Wurmser, who leads the "Kids & Family" discussion at *www.Epinions.com.* She routinely buys more than $300 in groceries for less than $100 — just by using coupons carefully. Here's how to save the most.

+ Stack the deck. "Find out when stores are doing double or triple coupon for the biggest savings," Wurmser says. "The rest of the time the biggest savings come from combining the store special and stacking a coupon on top of it — sometimes getting your item for pennies or even for free."

+ Widen your net. "Coupons are all over the place — not just in the Sunday paper," Wurmser says. "Check in magazines and the Internet. Go to manufacturers' Web sites, and sign up for their mailing lists."

+ Get help. Start a coupon-swapping group so you'll have coupons on items you use. It's a great way to meet other savings-minded folks and share tips.

✦ Be a good egg. Have your coupons organized when you get to the checkout line. Turning all coupons in the same direction will get them scanned more quickly. If you have a coupon for a free item, know the price so the cashier can write it down.

**Custom coupons at your fingertips.** There's no need to shuffle through the newspaper once a week to find the coupons you need. Look online for coupon Web sites that help you locate the items you want, then print the coupons at home. Some sites require you to register, but that usually doesn't take long. These are some of the most popular.

✦ *www.smartsource.com*

✦ *www.customcoupon.com*

✦ *www.coolsavings.com*

✦ *www.coupons.com*

✦ *www.couponsurfer.com*

**Get sorting for simpler savings.** You can't use your coupons if you can't find them. Try arranging them by expiration month, alphabetically by brand, or by aisle of the grocery store. Pick one of these tools to keep them organized.

✦ Binder with clear plastic sleeves for each category or month.

✦ Nested clear baggies, in which you place smaller categories, like yogurt, inside of larger categories, like dairy products.

✦ Accordion folder or large recipe box with dividers for categories or dates.

Keep your coupons in your car or your purse so you'll have them next time you drop by the store.

## When to find the cheapest produce

With the high cost of fuel, shipping out-of-season fruits and vegetables from afar is even more expensive. Get better taste and lower prices by buying produce at its peak season.

| Month | Best bets |
|---|---|
| January | oranges and other citrus fruits, cabbages, broccoli, cauliflower |
| February | oranges and other citrus fruits, papayas, broccoli, cauliflower |
| March | pineapples, mangoes, broccoli, lettuce |
| April | pineapples, mangoes, zucchini, rhubarb, asparagus, artichokes |
| May | cherries, apricots, okra, zucchini, asparagus, artichokes |
| June | watermelon, cantaloupe, strawberries and other berries, peaches, apricots |
| July | watermelon, cantaloupe, strawberries and other berries, tomatoes, summer squash, corn, green beans |
| August | watermelon, cantaloupe, strawberries and other berries, apricots, plums, cucumbers, corn, tomatoes |
| September | grapes, pomegranates, eggplant, pumpkin, tomatoes, spinach |
| October | grapes, cranberries, apples, pomegranates, sweet potatoes, pumpkins, winter squash |
| November | cranberries, oranges, tangerines, pomegranates, sweet potatoes, pumpkins, winter squash |
| December | pears, oranges and other citrus fruits, pomegranates, sweet potatoes, mushrooms, broccoli, cauliflower |

## Are coupons worth the trouble?

You bet! Using coupons to save just $20 each week adds up to $1,000 saved in a year. Redeem dollar–off coupons on double–coupon days, and it's not hard to reach that $20 in savings. One careful shopper reports paying $240 for $900 worth of groceries by using coupons, cashing in on her store's preferred–customer card, and watching the specials.

**4 ways to choose a cheaper package.** Even if you don't like to buy food in bulk, make these package picks to save money.

+ Buy frozen vegetables in bags rather than boxes. You can then pour out a serving or two of vegetables and reseal the bag for another meal.

+ Stay away from prepared single-serving juice, pudding, and gelatin. Your grandkids will like what you mix up just as well.

+ Instead of buying tea in bags, buy it loose and use a tea strainer or infuser ball. You'll save money and be able to brew up a wide variety of flavors.

+ Skip the single-serving packets of instant oatmeal. You'll save more than half the cost by buying quick oats in a can.

**Learn the truth about supermarket myths.** When *Consumer Reports* did a study of grocery store prices, selection, and customer satisfaction, they found some eye-opening results. Their findings toppled many common beliefs about where you get the best deals.

*Myth:* Items on endcap displays are on sale.

*Fact:* Sometimes stores use these high-traffic areas to grab attention for products nearing the end of their shelf life. Compare prices as you normally would, and check expiration dates.

*Myth:* Store brands are poor quality.

*Fact:* You get both good quality and low prices with store brands, which meet higher standards than in the past.

*Myth:* Products advertised in store circulars are on sale.

*Fact:* The store may use prepaid advertising space simply to draw attention to an item.

### Frozen fruit always in season

Find another excuse to skip your daily fruit. Even if your favorites are out of season, frozen versions are ripe for the pickin'. You'll find blueberries, strawberries, raspberries, peaches, even cherries and pineapple chunks, either sweetened or unsweetened. Enjoy them in smoothies, on cereal, in pies, or right out of the bag. They're picked and frozen while at their peak, so you get a bite of summer goodness in the middle of winter. Look for Dole, Europe's Best, and ShopRite frozen fruits priced at around 20 to 30 cents an ounce.

**Beef up savings on meat.** Good quality meat can strain your grocery bill, but there are ways to save. One super-shopper claims she fills her freezer for less than $100 by using these strategies.

+ Skip the full-price meats. Clip coupons, check sales fliers, and use your discount card. Some people use these money-saving strategies on other groceries yet pay full price in the meat department. That's where high prices make them most important.

+ Time it right. If you know your store's schedule of sales, you may be able to combine a special price with a discount card or coupon and get the best selection.

✦ Go light on package size. If a recipe calls for a pound of ground beef, check the labels for one that's right at a pound or maybe a little less. Package weights vary, so you don't need to pay 25 percent more to make the same meal. Nobody will notice the difference.

✦ Get help from the experts. Ask your butcher to wrap up smaller cuts of meat for you or discount a package near its sell-by date.

## A+ way to choose organic

Some types of produce have especially high levels of pesticides inside that can't be washed off. Here's a list to help you choose where to spend your money.

| Highest in pesticides | Lowest in pesticides |
|---|---|
| apples | bananas |
| cherries | blueberries |
| imported grapes | grapefruit |
| nectarines | kiwifruit |
| peaches | mangoes |
| pears | papayas |
| raspberries | pineapples |
| strawberries | plantains |
| bell peppers | plums |
| celery | watermelons |
| hot peppers | asparagus |
| potatoes | avocados |
| spinach | broccoli |

**Melt-in-your-mouth meat — for less.** Seek out bargain cuts like roast, ribs, even cheap stew meat. With a little TLC at home, you can turn them into the centerpiece of your dinner plate. Just spend some time marinating them in citrus juice or soy sauce, or add a tablespoon of vinegar to the cooking water. Cooking slowly in a crockpot also tenderizes tough cuts.

**Smart way to save time and money.** It may be cheaper to buy a prepackaged or frozen version of your family's favorite dish than to make it from scratch. A lot depends on what you can buy on sale and how much your family is in love with Aunt Gertrude's recipe.

For example, a family-size Stouffer's frozen lasagna feeds seven and costs about $13.50. That sounds like a lot. But if you add up the ingredients — lasagna noodles, sauce, ricotta and mozzarella cheese, ground beef, spices — you can spend more than $15.50. Add to that your time spent shopping for the ingredients and cooking the meal from scratch, and you may come out ahead taking the easy way.

**Savvy guide to bulk buying.** Stocking up and buying groceries in bulk may seem like the keys to saving money. Not always, says savings expert Cynthia Yates, author of *Living Well as a Single Mom: A Practical Guide to Managing Your Money, Your Kids, and Your Personal Life* and other books. Yates sees the value of buying staples like flour, nuts, and spices in larger containers when they're a good deal. But she says stockpiling is a waste.

"Buying anything to merely tote home to take space is not wise," she says. "What sense is buying a side of beef if you stash it in that cosmic black hole called the freezer, never to be seen again?"

How about those huge warehouse club stores that offer savings on large quantities of cereal, cooking oil, or just about anything else you might need around the kitchen? Yates says you can save money there despite the annual membership fees, which you will likely earn back with frequent shopping. But she cautions against buying large sizes of items you don't use a lot.

"If you need one can of anchovies for a special recipe, spring for the grocery store price instead of buying a half dozen shrink-wrapped at the warehouse store," Yates says. Otherwise, the extra five cans may end up as a wasteful expense.

"Buy only what you eat and eat what you buy," she advises.

## Free $ with Upromise account

Help send your favorite grandchild to college just by buying groceries. Get started by opening a free Upromise account at *www.upromise.com.* Then register your store's preferred-customer card, and you'll earn 1 to 5 percent when you buy certain participating brands. We're talking favorites like Nestle, Lysol, and Tylenol. The money goes into your Upromise account, then you can deposit it into your grandchild's 529 college savings account.

**Win the grocery game of high-low.** You can save by buying the loss leaders, or the items stores put on sale to lure you in. They hope you'll stay and do all your shopping — including purchasing products with prices that have been raised so the store doesn't lose money. Don't fall for it. Shop around to find the best deals on everything you need. Or better yet — buy only what you came for, then leave.

**Save at the supermarket with a price book.** As supermarkets lean toward offering everyday low prices instead of weekly specials, it's even more important to know where to find the good deals. You can do that with a price book — a notebook that records how much certain products cost at various stores. Keep track of the items you buy most often.

Find a small, inexpensive spiral notebook with lots of pages. Divide your price book into categories, like dairy, meat, and cereals. Then assign a page for each purchase of an item. Include the date, store, brand, size, price, and unit price — like price per ounce — for that purchase.

Start by entering items from the latest sale flier, then add information from your most recent shopping receipt. Every time you shop, add that new information. The best data comes from shopping at more than one store in the same month. You'll see patterns and know where and when to get the best deals on things you buy most. When you see a bargain, stock up.

**Don't be fooled by product placement.** Supermarkets are counting on catching your eye with items that earn them the most money. Favorite brands placed at eye level on the shelf are typically the higher-priced choices. Look to the top and bottom shelves for better deals. And don't assume that items in the sale bin are always the best bargain. Compare unit prices to be sure.

**Find good bread on the cheap.** You can buy the staff of life — even a popular brand — for nearly half its regular price at bakery thrift stores. Check packages, since items are probably nearing their expiration dates. But if you do it carefully to avoid crushing, you can freeze your bargain bread, rolls, buns, and tortillas to use later.

## Snoop out fake whole grains

If your digestion is less than regular, maybe you're missing out on roughage. Dr. John Johanson, a gastroenterologist in Beloit, Wisconsin, says not getting enough fiber is the biggest cause of poor digestive health. Most people get less than half the recommended amount.

Whole-grain bread should have at least 2 grams of fiber per serving, but labels can be misleading. Words like "multigrain," "7-grain," and "wheat flour" don't mean a bread is truly whole grain. Instead, look for whole wheat, whole rye, oatmeal, barley, or graham flour as the first ingredient listed.

# Be a kitchen magician

**Condiments and crumbs — good to the last drop.**
Don't waste the last bit of food in the container. Try these frugal ideas for making the most of what you buy.

- Add some oil and vinegar to that nearly empty mustard jar, sprinkle in salt and pepper, and shake. You just invented a tasty salad dressing.

- Sweet crumbs at the bottom of a box of cookies or dry cereal make a great topping for an ice cream sundae.

- Crusts of bread don't have to be for the birds. Use your food processor to turn them into crumbs, add some Italian spices, then freeze. Next time you need crumbs for breading or to top a casserole, reach for your homemade supply.

## Is it ripe? Check the label

Soon you may be able to tell which fruits and vegetables are ready to eat by looking at the color of a sticker. Engineers at the RediRipe company are working on these stickers, which will be stuck onto produce by growers and grocers. As produce gets ripe, it naturally emits ethylene gas. This gas is what makes the sticker change colors from white to blue. No more guessing about the sweetness of that melon or peach.

**5 cheers for the perfect cherry.** If your life isn't quite a bowl of cherries, grab a bag of this delicious fruit the next time you're in the supermarket. Not only will you enjoy all the health benefits cherries have to offer, but these sweet tidbits are just plain fun. Here are five must-know tips to bring out the cherry lover in you.

✦ June is the best and cheapest time of year to find sweet cherries in the United States.

✦ Cherries with stems attached last longer than those without stems.

✦ Pit fresh cherries with the pointed end of a vegetable peeler or clean, new needle-nose pliers.

✦ The Washington State Fruit Commission says you can freeze cherries whole, stems attached, by spreading them in a single layer on a baking sheet. Once frozen, pack them in freezer bags.

✦ Dried cherries are great in baked goods, salads, grain dishes, and trail mix. They're also a super source of nutrients and natural plant chemicals that fight cell damage and arthritis.

**Turn up the juice on lemons and limes.** A few simple tricks can prepare your lemon or lime for maximum juicing.

✦ Bring the fruit to room temperature.

✦ Roll it firmly between your hands or with pressure on a counter-top until soft.

✦ Microwave for about 15 seconds.

Of course, you can use a traditional juicer or citrus reamer, but there are other kitchen tools that will work as well. First, cut your fruit in half, then pick one of the following methods.

✦ Position one half between the arms of tongs and squeeze.

✦ Place both halves in a potato ricer.

✦ Stick a fork into the cut half and twist.

## Can blueberries cut colon cancer?

Maybe. Researchers think a natural chemical in blueberries, pterostilbene, may help prevent the disease. They gave this powerful antioxidant to half of a group of rats who were susceptible to colon cancer. The other rats didn't get the blueberry antioxidant. At the end of the study, the rats who got the pterostilbene had 57 percent fewer precancerous spots than those who didn't. You can also get pterostilbene from grapes, but blueberries contain much more.

**Simple step to seeded tomatoes.** Chop your tomatoes, and drop them into the basket of your salad spinner. Spin until all the seeds are removed. You're left with perfectly seeded tomatoes.

**Best fruits to buy unripe.** You buy bananas when they're still green, knowing they'll ripen in a few days. The same goes with some other fruits, like apples, apricots, cantaloupes, mangoes, pears, and plums. That's because these are climacteric fruits, which ripen when they're exposed to ethylene gas. Place them in a paper bag — or just leave them alone — for a day or two, and they'll soon be at their best. But buy nonclimacteric fruits, like honeydew melons and watermelons, when they're at their peak of ripeness.

**Better baking with frozen berries.** Blueberries are an outstanding source of nutrients that help battle memory loss, high blood sugar, heart disease, and cancer. That means you'll want to add them to your menu at every opportunity. Buy a bag of frozen blueberries when the fresh berries are not in season. Then throw a handful into your muffin mix, pancake batter, and quick-bread dough. No need to thaw — they'll defrost and warm right up in the oven. But toss them in a bit of flour before you fold them into the batter to keep them from sinking to the bottom.

**Pop a soda to keep fruit fresh.** Slice an apple or pear, and the cut edges can turn brown and unappetizing before your eyes. This happens because an enzyme in the fruit reacts to the oxygen in the air, a process called oxidation. Most people know to pour some type of acidic liquid, like lemon or orange juice, over the fruit to reduce the pH levels and prevent oxidation. But a lemon-lime soda, such as Sprite or Seven-Up, works just as well and has a lighter, less tart flavor.

## Pick the right apple for the job

With about 80 calories and 5 grams of fiber, an apple makes an ideal snack. But you can do a lot more with an apple than just munch on it. Use this table to select the best apple for your needs.

| Variety | Best uses | Season |
|---|---|---|
| Fuji | salads, baking | October–August |
| Gala | salads, applesauce | September–May |
| Golden Delicious | salads, baking, pie, applesauce, freezing | year–round |
| Granny Smith | salads, baking, pie, applesauce, freezing | year–round |
| Pink Lady | salads, applesauce, pie | November–August |
| Red Delicious | salads | year–round |

**Prep strawberries for easy eating.** Don't let the trouble of preparing fresh strawberries keep you from enjoying these tasty tidbits. Try one of these options for removing the stems and leaves.

✦ Push a drinking straw through the berry, starting at the bottom and exiting the leafy top. The core and leaf slide into the straw, and you're left with a neatly hulled berry.

✦ Use the pointed end of a large star tip from a cake-decorating kit by pushing it into the stem end. Twist and pull out.

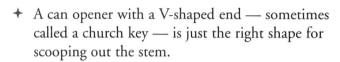

✦ A can opener with a V-shaped end — sometimes called a church key — is just the right shape for scooping out the stem.

### Vitamin C topples joint pain

That daily glass of orange juice may be just the ticket to slowing the damage of osteoarthritis. That's because one cup of OJ has nearly 100 milligrams of vitamin C. This sunshine vitamin helps your joints by building and repairing the cartilage that cushions bones. One study showed that people who got enough vitamin C every day — about 120 to 200 milligrams per day — saw their arthritis progress more slowly. So drink up, and help your joints.

**Squeeze out OJ savings.** Ready-to-serve orange juice in cartons and bottles saves time, but you pay for that speed. Frozen orange juice costs you nearly 25 percent less — and all you have to do is thaw it and mix with water. Mash the frozen mix with a potato masher or wire whisk for easier and quicker blending.

**Simple pomegranate peeling solution.** Don't fear this unusual fruit. Although it looks strange and tough to crack, it is worth the trouble of preparing it. Here's how. First, score the leathery rind in several places. Break open the pomegranate into a bowl of water. Your goal is to separate the many bright red seed sacs from the white pith. Scoop the sacs up from the water with your fingers. Inside the seed sacs you'll find the tangy juice and tiny, crunchy seeds — a good source of fiber.

You can buy good pomegranates at the lowest price from September through December.

**Kick up the benefits with raisin substitute.** The lowly prune got a facelift in 2001, when the prune industry renamed it the dried plum. But a prune by any other name still tastes sweet and is chock full of antioxidants. Sneak them into your family's favorite foods where raisins usually hide. Use your kitchen shears to snip a handful of prunes — dried plums, that is — into raisin-size pieces. Then stir them into the batter for healthful, delicious oatmeal cookies and quick breads.

**Try a perfect potato piercer.** You know you have to prick a potato's skin before cooking it in the microwave. If forks or knives give you trouble, try a corncob holder. It's the perfect tool for the job.

### Discover heart-healthy tropical fruit juice

Trade in your daily glass of orange juice for a serving of pomegranate juice. That's what volunteers in a heart study did for up to three years. By the end of the study, they had lower blood pressure and less thickening of the carotid artery walls. Researchers think the natural antioxidant flavonoids in pomegranate juice are what helped — no fancy formulas or secret ingredients.

## Fight Father Time with a humble dried fruit

Prunes are great for your digestion, and they may also help stave off the diseases of aging. Researchers tested various foods to see which have the most antioxidant power, or ability to fight damaging free radicals. Prunes scored nearly three times higher on the antioxidant scale as figs, raisins, and dates. That's good news, because experts think getting enough antioxidants in your diet may help battle changes to the brain that can sometimes come along with age, including Alzheimer's and Parkinson's disease.

**Beat beet stains with oil.** Keep fresh beets from staining your hands by rubbing one hand with a little vegetable oil first. Hold the beet in that hand and your knife in the other, dry hand. When you're through, a little soap and hot water washes away the oil.

**Season carrots to soften.** If you like your cooked carrots without the crunch, add a little salt to the water while cooking. They'll soften up in no time.

**Sweeten the deal on sweet corn.** There's nothing sweeter than summertime, and nothing says summer like corn on the cob. Give yours that touch of summer sunshine any time of year by adding a pinch of sugar to the pot before boiling.

Make it as healthy and tasty as possible by dropping the corn into already-boiling water rather than a pot of cold water. Chef Ursula Knaeusel of Ursula's Cooking School in Atlanta, Ga., cooks all vegetables this way to seal in flavor and vitamins.

"If you drink the vegetable, let's say you're going to make vegetable soup, then you can start with cold water," says Knaeusel. "But if you want to throw the water away, like for boiling potatoes or carrots or green beans, everything should go in boiling water." When corn hits the boiling water, the outside seals immediately.

**Roll through your romaine for easy chopping.** Spread your favorite lettuce out on a cutting board, and have at it with a wheeled pizza cutter. In no time you'll have a pile of shredded lettuce perfect for sandwiches, pitas, tacos, or even easy-to-eat salads.

**Trap juicy overflow.** Set your cutting board inside a larger cookie sheet whenever you chop juicy fruits or vegetables, like tomatoes, oranges, or watermelon. You'll keep the mess inside the cookie sheet and off your counters.

**5 ways to avoid onion tears.** You'll never shed another tear when preparing your famous homemade salsa if you understand the role science plays in the kitchen. Whenever you slice, crush, or cut an onion, it releases sulfur-containing compounds into the air. These mix with the fluid in your eyes, producing a mild form of sulfuric acid that irritates the nerve endings, producing tears. All you have to do is keep those potent fumes from reaching your eyes. Here are some things you can try.

+ Chill your onion for about 30 minutes before cutting.

+ Cut the onion under cool running water.

+ Chop near a fan, stove exhaust fan, or open window.

+ Wear goggles.

+ Cut the root end of the onion last.

**Bring droopy vegetables back to life.** Don't toss out celery or carrots that are looking a little limp. Revive them with a quick soak in cold sugar water. Sagging broccoli will snap back to attention, too, if you set the cut stalks upright in a chilly bath.

## Cancer protection from the produce aisle

Pick up a nice bunch of broccoli, and you may cut your risk of colon cancer. Experts think sulforaphane, a natural chemical in broccoli and other cruciferous vegetables, helps block enzymes that make tumors grow. Several studies show it may stop tumors in cancers of the colon, breast, lung, and prostate. So put your diet to work with a healthy bit of broccoli.

**Chop garlic with ease.** Place a few drops of cooking oil on the edge of your knife or on your garlic cloves before you start chopping, and the minced pieces won't stick to the knife.

**2 tricks to cut that fishy smell.** You're done cutting and preparing fish steaks or fillets, yet the smell lingers on your hands. Try these gentle remedies to get rid of the odor.

+ Scrub your hands with white fluoride toothpaste. Use it like soap, then rinse your hands completely.

+ Douse your fingers and hands with bottled lemon juice. Then wash your hands as usual.

**Sensational salmon from your own kitchen.** You can't beat salmon for good nutrition. It packs a wallop of healthy omega-3 fatty acids, which are great for your heart, eyes, and brain. Broil, grill, poach, fry, or roast salmon — it will taste great if you cook it right.

+ Leave the skin on while you cook salmon to hold in the oils. It will fall off easily once it's cooked.

+ Cook it enough — but no more. Salmon is done when it just begins to look opaque, change color, and become flaky. Cook it any longer, and it will lose some of its great flavor.

✦ Don't forget about finishing time. Salmon continues to cook even after you remove it from the heat, so take it out a minute or two before it's completely done.

**Pick the meat the pros eat.** Chefs and meat buyers really know their beef. Take their advice the next time you select a steak.

✦ Stick with beef labeled USDA prime for the best quality steak. That's especially important if you're cooking the meat on its own rather than adding it to a dish.

✦ Look for meat that has a rosy pink rather than dark purple color.

✦ Instead of taking pieces from the refrigerator case, ask the butcher to cut a fresh steak for you.

✦ Use cuts of meat that have the bone in for a richer flavor.

✦ Find a fairly thick steak, about 1½ to 2 inches. That thickness will let you sear it without overcooking the center.

But beef is not the only meat worth buying. Chef Ursula Knaeusel of Ursula's Cooking School, Inc., in Atlanta, Ga., likes a good pork tenderloin. She finds it to be the most tender cut of meats, and not nearly as expensive as beef tenderloin.

## Save your eyesight

Eating enough leafy greens is important, no matter your age. Nutrients in these garden-fresh goodies may help fend off age-related macular degeneration (AMD), a leading cause of blindness. That's what researchers found when they studied people's eating habits. Those who got more lutein and zeaxanthin, important carotenoids in spinach and collard greens, had a lower risk of AMD compared to people who ate less. Loading up on these fabulous foods reduced the risk of blindness by nearly half.

**Improve flavor with a little TLC.** You spent time selecting a great piece of meat — don't spoil it now. Take care in the cooking to prepare a meal like the pros make.

Chef Knaeusel has been teaching students to cook for 35 years. She says it's important to begin by searing a steak to seal in the juices.

"You should start with a hot frying pan or pot," she says. "I fry everything in a pot because of splattering. Sear it in really hot oil, then turn it over so it's seared again." Don't put salt on the meat before you begin, since that will draw water out of the meat.

Knaeusel prefers cooking meat in the kitchen rather than on a grill. "I think it has a much more delicate taste, a finer taste than when it's grilled," she says. Frying or poaching the meat are good bets.

Other chefs like to sear meat in a frying pan first, then finish it in the oven in a cast-iron skillet.

**4 great ideas for cooking ground beef.** Here are smart ways to make cooking with ground beef easy-breezy.

+ A potato masher mixes up your meatloaf ingredients in a snap. But according to the National Cattlemen's Beef Association, overmixing ground beef will make your meatloaf, burgers, or meatballs dry and dense. So whatever tool you use, stir sparingly for a lighter, moister texture.

+ Perfect patties are just a jar lid away. First, make balls out of your ground meat about the size of an ice cream scoop. Sandwich each between layers of waxed paper to make the burgers easier to handle and store. Press down on the ball through the paper with the lid from a gallon jar. Leaving the waxed paper in place, stack the perfectly shaped burgers in the refrigerator, or freeze them for later.

+ After you brown the ground beef, use a pastry blender to get rid of the large clumps.

✦ Transfer cooked ground meat to a colander, and rinse it with warm water. You'll wash away any extra fat clinging to the meat. What a healthy idea.

---

### Meal-planning help at your fingertips

What can you make for dinner without having to run to the store for that last ingredient? Find recipes for dishes to make with the items you already have in your pantry at *www.recipematcher.com*. You type in the ingredients you have on hand, and the free Web site locates recipes for dishes that use those items.

---

**A heavenly tip for deviled eggs.** Spoon all your ingredients for deviled egg filling into a resealable plastic bag. Zip it closed and squish the contents together from the outside. Once everything is thoroughly mixed, snip off a corner of the bag and squeeze the filling into your waiting halved egg whites. If you have a pastry bag, you can use that.

**Follow this "eggspert" advice.** According to the American Egg Board, here's the best way to boil and peel an egg.

✦ Start with eggs that aren't too fresh. Once they've been stored about seven to 10 days, they'll peel easily.

✦ Place eggs in a single layer in your pot, and add water to at least one inch above the eggs.

✦ Cover, bring just to a boil, and remove from heat. Boiling at too high a heat or for too long will make the white tough and rubbery, and turn the yolk hard and a gray-green color.

+ Keep the eggs covered, and let them stand in the hot water for 15 to 18 minutes.

+ Cool them immediately and thoroughly under cold water.

+ Tap each egg gently to break its shell, then roll it between your hands to crackle it all over.

+ Hold under running water and start peeling from the large end of the egg.

Some people claim adding a bit of salt or vinegar to the cooking water makes boiled eggs easier to peel.

## Whittle your waist with eggs

Eating eggs for breakfast may help you lose weight. Researchers tested this idea on a group of 30 women. Half the group ate a breakfast that included two eggs, while the other half ate a bagel breakfast. By lunch time, the women answered questions about how full they were. Women who enjoyed the egg breakfast were less hungry and ate fewer calories all day. Protein and fat in eggs may be key to keeping you satisfied longer.

**3 cheap DIY flavored coffees.** Fancy drinks at the coffeehouse can drain your beverage budget. Try making these favorites at home.

+ Vanilla latte light. Make a dry mix using one-half cup each instant coffee, low-fat powdered milk, and sugar. Use two teaspoons mix in a cup of hot water, and stir in a quarter teaspoon of vanilla.

+ Mock mocha cappuccino. In a large mug, mix an envelope of hot cocoa mix, a tablespoon of instant coffee, and hot water. Stir in a splash of milk.

✦ Fake frappuccino. Brew a strong pot of coffee, using twice the coffee you usually use. Add a 14-ounce can of sweetened condensed milk and refrigerate. Mix in a splash of vanilla, then blend in a blender with ice.

**"Perc" up your coffee-brewing skills.** Making coffee in a drip coffee maker is not rocket science. Just follow these tips from coffee expert Kenneth Davids, author of three books on coffee, and editor of the Web site *www.coffeereview.com.*

✦ Keep it fresh. The most common mistake people make is to let brewed coffee sit too long on a burner or in a thermos. "With the glass decanter and hot plate, if you don't drink the coffee immediately — within 15 minutes — the flavor is shot," Davids says. "A better strategy is to take it off the hot plate as soon as it's finished brewing, then heat it up in the microwave later."

✦ Start with good-quality coffee. Davids recommends looking for coffee that says "100% Colombian" on the label. "That's going to be much better than the standard brands, which are full of robusto coffee," he says. If you don't want to pay the high price of gourmet coffee — yet you enjoy a darker roast — try one labeled "para el gusto Latino," or "for the Latin taste." The Italian brand Medaglia d'Oro is a great inexpensive option, available at most grocery stores.

✦ Use as much coffee as you like rather than following the manufacturer's directions. After all, it's your pot of coffee — experiment for a few days to see what you like best.

✦ Take your time. "The best routine, if people can handle it, is to keep whole beans in a jar with the seal, take out as much as they're going to brew, grind it, and brew it," Davids says.

**Help your coffee hold its grounds.** A common problem with making coffee is using paper filters that don't do the job, says coffee expert Kenneth Davids.

"I've had people write to me with problems, and it turns out they're not putting the paper filter in firmly and smoothing it out around the sides of the receptacle," he says. "The filter folds over, and the water spills out over the back of the paper filter and diverts around the coffee. They get a kind of thin, listless coffee with some grounds in it." Use the right size and style of filter for your machine, and push it firmly into place.

You can also try wetting the coffee filter before you insert it into the brew basket of your coffee maker. It will stick to the sides without crumpling.

**Quicker coffee saves your morning.** If your morning routine means "gotta have coffee but don't have a lot of time," then you'll want to try this do-ahead tip. Set out a week's worth of coffee filters. Spoon the right amount of coffee grounds into each, then stack them. Place the filled filters into a round plastic container, seal, and store them in the fridge or freezer. Each morning, simply grab a filter off the stack and begin brewing. Coffee experts prefer to grind beans right before they brew up a pot, so decide whether speed or perfect taste is most important to you.

**Be a cheese whiz — shred your own.** Nothing says convenience like a package of shredded cheese — especially when you're throwing together a last-minute meal. But you really pay for the time savings. Get the best of both worlds by buying a big block of cheese and shredding it yourself. Freeze small portions in individual freezer bags, and they will be ready whenever you are. And don't shy away from soft cheeses like mozzarella and fontina, which usually make a mess on your grater or food processor. Simply stick these in the freezer for a few minutes before you shred.

**Perfect pancakes every time.**
Flapjacks. Hotcakes. Griddle cakes. No matter what you call them, when they are piping hot with a drizzle of syrup, they add up to a stack of morning heaven.

28

Make your next flipped-out breakfast a breeze with — of all things — a turkey baster. It squeezes out just the right amount of batter onto your griddle and shapes perfectly round pancakes without a drip.

**Fancy oils on the cheap.** Flavored oils give your cooking an extra kick and your bread a tasty dip. Making your own is easy and saves you from paying fancy prices. Make a garlic-flavored oil by combining a quarter cup of extra virgin olive oil with two cloves of crushed garlic and the zest of one lime. Let it stand for 15 minutes. For a spicy southwestern flavor, use two crushed chile peppers instead of the garlic cloves. Strain the flavored oil through cheesecloth. Store your oil in the refrigerator, and use it within a week.

**Smart way to save oil.** Convert your plastic bottle of cooking oil to a convenient dispenser that doesn't waste oil. Take a new bottle of oil and remove the plastic cap. Carefully punch a small hole in the bottle's safety seal using a paring knife or metal skewer. Replace the cap for storage. Now you can get oil drop by drop.

# Cooking made easy

**Get crowned king of the coals.** Good grilling doesn't always come naturally. Avoid the bad habits that can make outdoor cooking inedible. Your barbecue guests will be so impressed they'll beg for seconds.

+ Keep the grill cover on, especially for indirect cooking. Removing the cover lets heat escape and makes cooking take longer.

+ Don't hover and fuss. It's best not to turn over the meat more than once for direct cooking, like small steaks. If you're doing indirect cooking, you don't need to turn it at all.

+ Leave off barbecue sauces until the last 10 to 30 minutes of cooking. Put them on too early and the meat can get overly brown or even burned.

+ Dig out your long-handled tongs or spatula rather than grabbing a fork. You'll save your hands from getting burned and keep from losing juices when you prick the meat.

## Don't contaminate your cooking

After you take raw meat to the grill, don't use the same plate to take the cooked meat back in. Bacteria from raw meat can live on the platter, then be transferred to your cooked meal. Make sure you grab a fresh plate.

**Try out a versatile roast.** A beef tri-tip roast, also called a triangular roast, can take the heat — no matter how you cook it. The Texas Beef Council suggests you marinate the meat, then grill, broil, or roast it, either whole or cut into steaks. There's no need to tenderize this tasty boneless cut.

## Special ingredient makes meat safer

Pickled or salted buds of the caper plant, called capers, could be your secret ingredient for good health. When researchers added them to cooked ground meat and let the mixture digest in a test tube, antioxidants from the capers slowed the oxidation process. Oxidation happens naturally, but it may be linked to cancer in the long run. Include some capers in your meat dishes, and you'll add both flavor and antioxidants, which stop that harmful process.

**Take indoor cooking to the great outdoors.** Grills — they're not just for meat anymore. With a little thought, you can cook just about any food you usually prepare indoors outside on a grill.

Diane and Tom Dunn, frequent tailgaters and fans of the Atlanta Falcons, have seen it all as they follow their favorite football team to home and away games. From deer sausage and mayonnaise-basted grouper in Tampa to crab cakes and clam chowder in Baltimore, tailgaters like to show off local favorites.

"The best smell is in Kansas City, where you start smelling the barbecue before you even get to the stadium," Diane says. Other grill favorites include scallops wrapped in bacon, oysters Rockefeller, or just about any type of shellfish. She likes to prepare corn on the cob. "Leave it in the husks," Diane says. "Soak it thoroughly in water, then put it on the grill. Best corn you will ever taste. We recommend Silver Queen, Golden Queen, or Honey Select corn."

Get really creative by taking your home-baked pizza outside. Carefully place pizza crust on the grill, heat both sides for about three minutes each, then add toppings and finish cooking. Use a pizza stone if you're worried about dough seeping through the grill.

Don't forget dessert. Finish off the meal with some apples wrapped in foil or pineapple slices placed directly on the grill. You can even sauté banana slices in margarine in a skillet, add some brown sugar, then serve over ice cream for an outdoorsy bananas foster.

## Convert recipes for crockpot cooking

Prepare your favorite meals in the crockpot by extending the cooking time.

| Cooking time, conventional method | Cooking time, crockpot, low power | Cooking time, crockpot, high power |
|---|---|---|
| 15–30 minutes | 4–8 hours | 1½– 2½ hours |
| 30–60 minutes | 6–8 hours | 3–4 hours |
| 1–3 hours | 8–16 hours | 4–6 hours |

**3 tricks for fabulous crockpot cooking.** This slow-cooking method lets you fix old-fashioned meals with little preparation time or attention needed. Follow these hints so they come out great every time.

+ Don't fill the crockpot more than three-quarters with liquid. Any more and it may boil over.

+ Save time by putting ingredients in your crockpot the night before, stashing it in the refrigerator, then taking it out and turning it on in the morning. When you get home, dinner's ready.

✦ Even if you add seasonings at the start of cooking, taste your dish again when it's ready. Spices can lose flavor during the long cooking, so you may need to add more.

**Slow cooker saves the day.** No more last-minute chaos whipping potatoes with one hand while you stir gravy, bake rolls, and set the table with the other hand. Prepare your mashed potatoes ahead of time. Then keep them warm in your slow cooker set on low until dinnertime.

**Master the art of cake-making.** Cake recipes are everywhere. Good advice on the nitpicky details that make them turn out great, however, is hard to find. For that, check out *The Cake Bible* by Rose Levy Beranbaum.

This beautiful volume is more than a cookbook, although it does contain some 150 recipes for cakes, frostings, and fillings. It's also a treasure trove of information on how and why to mix and bake for best results. Here are a few nuggets of great advice from Beranbaum.

✦ Don't make stiff royal icing or meringue on a humid day. Sugar soaks up water, so your results will end up soft and sticky, and they won't set well.

✦ Weighing cake ingredients is faster and more exact than measuring them. But if you're careful, you can get good results by measuring. Recipes in the book include both weights (ounces or grams) and measurements (tablespoons or cups). You can buy a simple kitchen scale for less than $15.

✦ The best cake pans are made from materials that conduct heat well, like dull aluminum. "Stainless steel pans, with their shiny, heat-reflective finish, are poor heat conductors and should not be used for baking cakes," Beranbaum writes. "They make pretty planters if you already happen to have them."

*The Cake Bible* was named cookbook of the year by the International Association of Culinary Professionals in 1988.

## Roll out crusts evenly, every time.

Keep your pie crust or cookie dough a uniform thickness with a little help. Place a wooden dowel at each side of the dough mound, then roll the pin across the dowels. You'll need to pick dowels the same thickness you want the dough to turn out.

**Try a neater way to make cookies crumble.** Don't spend money on packaged cookie crumbs for pie crusts, cookies, and toppings. It's cheaper to make your own, plus you get fresher ingredients. Toss your graham crackers or other cookies into a self-sealing plastic bag. Remove the air, and have a go at them with your rolling pin. You'll get a bagful of fresh crumbs with no mess.

### Help your dough rise to the occasion

Bread dough rises best in warm, humid conditions — but that doesn't always describe your kitchen. Create the perfect environment with your dishwasher. Don't use any soap, turn the dishwasher on just long enough for hot water to fill the bottom, then turn it off. Cover your dough, place it on the bottom rack of the dishwasher, and close the door.

**Create perfectly patterned cookies.** The cross-hatched side of a meat mallet will flatten your cookie dough and leave a textured imprint worthy of a professional baker.

### 3 steps to stop diabetes

You don't need drugs or starvation diets to fight off type 2 diabetes. Here are three easy ways to keep the disease at bay.

* Replace refined carbohydrates with tasty whole grains. More fiber in your diet will help balance blood sugar.

* Stay away from the wrong fats. Instead of the saturated fats in meat and dairy foods, go for monounsaturated fats in olive oil, avocados, and nuts. This change may help lower your blood sugar and "bad" LDL cholesterol levels.

* Make some simple lifestyle changes, like exercising, losing some weight, and quitting smoking.

**Easy way to check oven temperature.** Good baking requires an oven you can rely on. Try this method from *Cook's Illustrated* magazine to see how your oven's temperature runs.

Place an oven rack in the middle position, and heat your oven to 350 degrees Fahrenheit for 30 minutes. Put one cup of water in a two-cup glass measure. Use an instant-read thermometer to be sure the water is exactly 70 degrees. Adjust by adding hot or cold water. Place the cup of water in the center of the oven for 15 minutes, door closed. Remove the cup and read the water's temperature with the instant-read thermometer. Swirl the water to even out hot spots.

If your oven is correctly calibrated, the water should be within 2 degrees of 150 degrees Fahrenheit. If not, have it adjusted to get the best results from cakes and cookies.

**Correct top causes of cake catastrophes.** Even the best cook can suffer the occasional flop. When your favorite cake recipe fails to perform, see if you've committed one of these four culinary crimes.

✦ If you overmix the batter, your cake can fall or become tough and dry. Set a timer instead of guessing.

✦ If your oven is too hot, the crust browns before your cake finishes rising. The top peaks and cracks through the dark crust, and large holes or tunnels develop inside the cake. Check the setting with an oven thermometer.

✦ If you underbake, your cake can fall, come out soggy, or have a sticky crust. Try raising the oven setting by 25 degrees.

✦ If your baking powder is old or if you don't measure it precisely, your cake can either sink in the center or overflow your pan. Always measure carefully and check the expiration date on your container. If you're close, see if it is still fresh by stirring one-half teaspoon into one cup of tap water. Fizzing is a good sign. In addition, store baking powder somewhere cool and dry — not in the fridge.

## Avoid the #1 cause of big bellies

It's not beer or tempting desserts, and it's probably on your table at least once a day. Trim your waistline by switching from white bread to whole grains. A study of nearly 500 people and their eating habits found those who ate the most white bread had the greatest gain in waist circumference, or belly size, over time. People who favored white bread had even more growth around their middles than those who enjoyed meat and potatoes. Skip the white bread, and try tastier and slimmer alternatives like whole–wheat, oatmeal, and whole–rye bread.

**Boost health without lowering flavor.** Whole-grain flour adds fiber, vitamins, and minerals to your baking, but it also changes the way things taste. Add a little and your bread or cookies become hearty — add a lot and they're tough. Solve this problem by replacing only some of the traditional all-purpose white flour with whole-wheat pastry flour, oat flour, or buckwheat flour. You may also need to add a smidgen more liquid to the recipe to keep the texture enticing.

## Time-to-boil test

Check your microwave's power so you'll know how long to cook packaged foods. Use the minimum suggested cooking time for high-wattage ovens.

Fill a two-cup glass measure with water and ice cubes and stir until ice melts. Pour out water to the one-cup mark. Heat it in the microwave on high for four minutes, watching through the window to see how long it takes to boil.

* Less than two minutes — high-wattage oven, 1,000 or more watts.

* Two and one-half minutes — medium wattage, about 800 watts.

* Three minutes — low wattage, 650 to 700 watts.

* More than three minutes — very low wattage, 300 to 500 watts.

**Bypass these 2 microwave blunders.** Microwave cooking is so easy — even your grandkids can do it. But that doesn't mean there's no way to mess things up. Hone your skills and avoid these common mistakes.

✦ Using the wrong cookware. Ceramic or glass containers are good choices, but skip containers made of Styrofoam, straw, wicker, and wood. Some metals can be used, but only those approved by the manufacturer for use in a microwave. Also check the manufacturer's directions for containers made of china, pottery, earthenware, and melamine.

✦ Not cooking food long enough to kill bacteria. Uneven heating can be a problem because it allows bacteria to survive in the cool spots.

Follow package directions on microwavable foods, and know the wattage of your microwave. Try the time-to-boil test to figure it out. *(See box.)* You should also stir food to even out cooking, and let your cooked dish stand for a minute or two before you serve it.

**Quick and easy "baked" pumpkin.** When the weather is hot and you don't want to turn on the oven, use your microwave to cook a pumpkin.

Cut the pumpkin in half and remove its stem. Place cut sides down in a glass or ceramic baking dish, and microwave on high power. Begin with five minutes per pound, rotating halfway so the pumpkin cooks evenly. Continue cooking until the pumpkin feels soft. Scrape out seeds, remove the skin, and your baked pumpkin is ready to puree or mash. You can also use this method to cook acorn or butternut squash.

**Keep fish flaky and moist — in the microwave.** First, drizzle a little olive oil and sprinkle your favorite spices on the fish for extra flavor and moistness. Cook fish at 70 percent power. Measure how thick your fish portions are. For fish a half-inch thick, cook for two and one-half minutes on one side, then turn over and repeat. Same goes for thicker fillets, but they'll need more cooking time. Start with about three minutes on each side for one-inch pieces. When it flakes easily, it's done.

## 4 big reasons to go fish

This nutrient-packed delight brings a lot more than just great taste to the table. Fish is also high in omega-3 fatty acids, which may help ward off several ailments that often come along with aging. A 14-year study of nurses found those who ate more fish — about two to four meals per week — cut their risk of stroke by nearly 50 percent. Eating fish may also help fight arthritis, Alzheimer's disease, and cataracts. So catch some salmon or trout for a healthy dinner plate.

# Food storage do's and don'ts

**Avoid waste with first in, first out.** Even if you freeze it, food doesn't last forever. Do like the grocers do and rotate your stock. Place new purchases at the back of the freezer, and move older items to the front. You'll be more likely to see and use them.

You can also use this trick in your pantry, placing new boxes of pasta behind old boxes. If you hit the sale jackpot on cereals or canned fruits, mark each package with the date so you'll know when it's time to toss.

**Smart way to save on milk.** Don't be afraid to stock up on milk when it's on sale. You can freeze it safely for up to a month.

+ Pick jugs of milk with an expiration date as far in the future as possible.

+ First thing when you get home, open the milk, pour out a glass to enjoy, then reseal the milk. If you don't remove some milk, the container will expand and explode.

+ Freeze it.

+ When it's time to thaw some milk, put the frozen container in a sink of water overnight. Shake it up in the morning, and it's ready to use.

**Shred before you freeze for later ease.** You can make cheese last longer by freezing it, but it will be crumbly and hard to slice after it thaws. Shred it before you put it into the freezer to avoid that problem. While you're at it, slip the cheese's label into the plastic bag so you'll remember what kind it is.

**Meet your vow to avoid veggie waste.** Plan ahead and you'll never again toss out fruits or vegetables that are old enough to make your stomach turn. It's all about buying and storing them right.

+ Purchase produce in more economical large packages, then split your bounty with a friend.

+ Keep around those staples that stay fresh the longest, like carrots, celery, onions, apples, and oranges. If you must have bananas or pears, buy only what you'll eat in a few days.

+ Choose frozen vegetables in bags rather than boxes. You can open the bag, pour out what you need for a meal, then reseal the bag and pop it back in the freezer for later.

**Savor the flavor of fresh herbs.** Fresh herbs like basil and oregano make your Italian cooking taste marvelous. Too bad you can grow them only a few months out of the year — and have you seen the price of fresh herbs in the supermarket?

This summer, freeze a bumper crop of basil for your winter pesto. Strip the basil leaves from the stems, then rinse them. After they're dry, chop them to the size you like to use. Freeze in small batches in freezer bags, and be sure to label each bag. Your basil will be good for up to six months.

**Bypass food-freezing blunders.** A bad experience with freezing and thawing food could mean you didn't do it right. Follow these simple rules, and you won't be left out in the cold next time you want to save food for later.

+ Banish freezer burn. Air can dry out the surface of your food, causing gray ice crystals to form. That means a bad taste. Squeeze out all the air from around the food when you seal it into bags.

+ Keep it small. Divide food into small portions so it freezes more quickly. The faster food freezes, the fresher it will taste later. Also, you're more likely to find a use for small portions of frozen foods than for large ones.

✦ Bag it right. Freezer bags may cost more than other plastic bags or wrap, but they're worth it. Containers meant for the freezer are durable enough to keep your goodies safe.

## Keep food fresh and safe

"Check the temperature of your refrigerator and freezer with an appliance thermometer," says Katherine Bernard, acting manager of the USDA Meat and Poultry Hotline. The refrigerator should be 40 degrees Fahrenheit or below, and the freezer should be 0 degrees or below. That way food will stay fresh until you're ready to eat it. Use this information to decide where to store your groceries.

| Food | Refrigerator lifespan | Freezer lifespan |
|---|---|---|
| Ground meat | 1–2 days | 3–4 months |
| Steaks, roasts | 3–5 days | 6–12 months |
| Pork chops, pork roast | 3–5 days | 4–6 months |
| Whole chicken | 1–2 days | 12 months |
| Lean fish (flounder, cod) | 1–2 days | up to 6 months |
| Fatty fish (salmon, perch) | 1–2 days | 2–3 months |
| Luncheon meats | 3–5 days | 1–2 months |
| Milk | 5 days | 1 month |
| Cheese | 3–4 weeks | 4–6 months |
| Ice cream | – – | 2–4 months |

**Rice in a flash — from your freezer.** Cooking rice takes time, especially when you choose healthy brown rice. Get a head start on your next casserole or stir fry by cooking a large batch of rice, then storing the leftovers. It keeps in an airtight container for up to six months in the freezer. Thaw it on the stove with a little water added.

**Extend the life of ground beef.** It's a shame to buy costly meat, then have to throw it out when it's not eaten. When ground beef has been hiding in the back of your freezer for three or four months, it's time to take it out and cook it. If you're still not ready to eat it, refreeze the meat in one-pound portions in zipper freezer bags. Now it has a new lease on life, and you can use it later for casseroles or chili.

### On-the-spot nutrition info

Packaged foods carry nutrition information on the back of the box, but that can be hard to decipher when you're grabbing breakfast in a hurry. Kellogg cereals now contain important nutrition facts in large print on the front of the box. That includes Guideline Daily Amounts (GDAs), or facts about nutrients people want to eat more or less of, like calories, sugar, or vitamin C. Look for green tabs with GDA numbers near the top of the box.

**Simple way to prevent pantry pests.** Even the cleanest kitchen can be prone to a bug infestation. That's because insects that over-run food can get in while it's in the processing mill, at the store, or during transportation. They may spread from flour, cornmeal, or rice to noodles or cookies, making it all unfit to eat. Avoid the problem by freezing new bags of grain for at least four days. Then store in an airtight container.

**Get peak flavor from bulk herbs and spices.** Dried spices and herbs in little jars are not cheap, but there is another choice.

"Buying in bulk gives you the opportunity to buy top-quality spices for a third or less of what it would cost to buy them prepackaged," says Ellen Bouchard, bulk herbs and spices manager for Frontier Natural Products Co-op.

Bulk spices should keep as long as the prepackaged variety — as long as you store them correctly. "Store them in glass containers with tight-fitting lids," says Bouchard. "This will prevent oxidation, which deteriorates the flavor, color, and aroma." Keep air away from your spices by putting them in containers that are the right size, without too much extra air. And keep them in a cool, dry, dark place.

"A common mistake is to place the spice rack over the stove," says Bouchard. "While this is certainly convenient, being exposed to all the heat and humidity from cooking will cause the spice flavor and color to deteriorate quickly."

Whole spices and herbs should last about one to three years, while the ground varieties stay good about six months to one year. That varies depending on the type of spice. Peppercorns and others with little oil can last longer, while spices like ground cloves, which have more oils, lose their flavor quickly.

## Crack the code of spice freshness

If your pantry contains red and white rectangular tins of McCormick spices — except for black pepper — they're at least 15 years old. Glass jars of McCormick spices with "Baltimore, MD" on the label are also that old. It may be time to toss them. To check the freshness of your spices using the product code, go to *www.mccormick.com* and click on "All about spices" on the left-hand side, then on "Keep your spices fresh."

**Neat-as-a-pin produce pickup.** Tired of getting your fingers wet from bagging lettuce or broccoli in the produce aisle? Try this trick. Grab a plastic bag from the roll and put it on your hand like a glove. Use this hand to pick up the head of lettuce, then slip the bag inside out to cover the produce. Veggies are sacked, and your hands are still dry.

**Recycled bags keep leftovers fresh.** Stop fighting with plastic wrap that won't stick to your plastic or acrylic food containers. Save your plastic produce bags, and use them to cover those food bowls. Grab a twist tie or clothespin to seal the deal.

**Slice up fresher cake.** Extend the life of your tasty pound cake. Keep it moist and fresh by placing an apple slice inside the storage container.

**Perfect use for bamboo steamer.** Cool, dry, dark, yet with some air circulation. That describes the perfect place to store potatoes, onions, and garlic to keep them from sprouting or getting moldy. Place your unused bamboo steamer on the countertop to create the perfect storage environment, and fill it up.

# Food safety 101

**4 steps to a safer kitchen.** Even the most nutritious food may contain germs. "Bacteria are everywhere in our environment," says Katherine Bernard of the USDA Meat and Poultry Hotline. "Raw meat, poultry, seafood, and eggs are not sterile. Neither is fresh produce such as lettuce, tomatoes, sprouts, and melons. Any of these foods can harbor bacteria." You can't see or smell these dangerous critters. That's why you should follow some basic rules to avoid getting a food-borne illness.

+ Clean up. Wash your hands and countertops with hot, soapy water after you handle raw meat. Clean cutting boards and utensils in the dishwasher.

+ Separate foods. Use one cutting board for meat and poultry, and use another board for vegetables and breads. When you put raw meat or seafood in the refrigerator, keep it in a sealed container so juices don't spread to other foods.

+ Cook thoroughly. You can't always tell when meat is safe to eat by how it looks. Use a meat thermometer to be sure. When you reheat gravy or soup, bring it to a rolling boil.

+ Chill food promptly. "One of the most common problems with serving is to leave food at room temperature longer than two hours," Bernard says. Keep hot food hot, at 140 degrees Fahrenheit or warmer, and cold food cold, at 40 degrees or cooler.

**Uncover food-safety myths.** Just because your grandma told you something doesn't make it true. Separate safe-food fact from fiction.

*Myth:* Mayonnaise causes food poisoning.

*Fact:* Foods that contain raw eggs, like homemade mayonnaise, cookie dough, or eggnog, may contain *Salmonella* bacteria. Eating those foods — if they're not handled properly — may make you sick. But store-bought items, including mayonnaise, contain pasteurized eggs. They're safe to eat if you handle them correctly.

*Myth:* A coddled egg is safe to use in salad dressing.

*Fact:* Coddling an egg, or gently simmering it in the shell just long enough to coagulate the white, doesn't kill bacteria. Substitute pasteurized eggs or egg products, like Egg Beaters, in your caesar salad dressing.

*Myth:* Packaged food is good until its expiration date passes.

*Fact:* Some dates are "use-by" dates, while others are "sell-by" dates. They let you know when the product is at its best quality and freshness. But they don't tell you that a food is absolutely safe or unsafe. You still have to handle and store it properly.

**Tidy mixing is in the bag.** You like how meatballs and meatloaf turn out when you mix them by hand, but what a mess. Try this trick to keep raw hamburger off your hands and out from under your nails. First, put all the ingredients into a large bowl. Then grab two small plastic baggies, and put them on your hands like loose gloves. Your fingers stay clean while they're free to move and mix.

**Simple way to keep string clean.** Tie up raw turkey without contaminating the entire roll of string. Take a clean plastic cup, such as a yogurt or sour cream container with a lid. Cut a slit in the lid, put the roll of string inside, and thread the string through the slit. You can pull out as much string as you need without dragging the rest through raw meat juices.

**Avoid dining-out dangers.** Eating out should be fun, not risky. Take these precautions so you don't suffer unpleasant aftereffects from your next restaurant experience.

+ Use your eyes. If the restaurant doesn't look clean, don't eat there.

✦ Order food completely cooked. Just like when you dine at home, your meat, poultry, seafood, and eggs should be cooked thoroughly to kill germs. If your meal arrives cold or undercooked, send it back.

✦ Skip the citrus. A recent study of lemon slices placed on the edge of beverage glasses shows they may not be safe. Researchers tested the rind and flesh of lemon slices in 21 restaurants. Nearly 70 percent of the lemon slices were contaminated by either bacteria or yeast or both.

✦ Get your doggie bag into the refrigerator quickly. "I would recommend within two hours from the time that the food was prepared," says Mary J. Weaver, technical manager for NSF Retail Food Safety. "In warmer weather, I would recommend within one hour. Bacteria grow most rapidly between the temperatures of 40 degrees and 140 degrees Fahrenheit, so it is very important to keep foods out of this temperature range."

## High-tech help sniffs out spoiled food

There's help on the way to determine if food is still good — even if you can't tell by looking or smelling.

◆ The DaysAgo digital counter attaches to a container and counts the days leftover food has been in the refrigerator. Order two for $10 online at *www.howmanydaysago.com*.

◆ A SensorQ label is attached at the store inside packages of meat and poultry. It changes color when the bacteria count gets too high.

◆ The hand-held SensorFreshQ monitor tests the air over your recently opened package of meat or poultry. It lets you know if lots of bacteria are present — but not if they're harmful bacteria. It's about $90, available online at *www.fqsinternational.com*.

**Practice safe reheating.** Don't assume your restaurant takeout container can be used to reheat food in the microwave. It may not be safe. The Food and Drug Administration regulates materials used for containers that will touch food and those meant to be used in the microwave — but these are not always the same. Some plastics may melt at high temperatures. One possible culprit is polystyrene, the plastic used in Styrofoam.

"Styrofoam is not designed for reheating purposes," says Mary J. Weaver, technical manager for NSF Retail Food Safety. "I would recommend placing the food on a microwave-safe dish and using that to reheat the food."

It's best to use a glass dish for reheating, or pick a plastic container that says it's microwave safe. "If the container is labeled microwave safe, your best bet is to follow the manufacturer's instructions," Weaver says.

**4 bad habits worth breaking.** You don't need to pay top dollar for fancy matching storage containers for your leftovers, but be sure you cook and store safely. That means using kitchenware that's made to be used in the kitchen. Skip these bad habits.

✦ Storing food in film canisters. It's a bad idea to use any non–food-grade container or plastic bag to store food because it may contain chemicals.

✦ Baking in a brown paper bag. It's made to bring groceries home from the store, not to cook food in the oven. The U.S. Department of Agriculture warns paper bags can catch on fire, transfer germs to your food, or release toxic fumes. An oven roasting bag is worth its small price.

✦ Cooking in a trash can. Seems like a clever way to roast a turkey or cook up a big batch of something, but it's dangerous. Galvanized metal cans contain toxic materials that can seep into your food.

✦ Reusing single-use items. That means water bottles, disposable forks and spoons, and margarine tubs. They're made to be used once, and it's nearly impossible to clean them properly without damaging the materials.

## Know your food's foes

Here are some common bacteria that can contaminate food and make you sick. Take these steps to stay safe.

| Bacteria | Food it's common in | Ways to avoid it |
|---|---|---|
| E. coli | ground beef | Using meat thermometer, cook to internal temperature of 160 degrees Fahrenheit |
| Salmonella | ground chicken, beef, turkey, pork | Using meat thermometer, cook to internal temperature of 160 degrees Fahrenheit |
| | eggs | Cook thoroughly until yolks and whites are firm |
| | ice cream and fruit (when shipped with contaminated meat or eggs) | Separate raw meat and poultry from other foods in your grocery cart and refrigerator |
| Campylobacter | poultry | Using meat thermometer, cook to internal temperature of 165 degrees Fahrenheit |

### Check labels for allergy info

People who are allergic to certain foods, like shellfish, nuts, or eggs, used to have trouble picking safe foods. But a new law changes this. The Food Allergen Labeling and Consumer Protection Act (FALCPA) requires food labels to state clearly if the item contains one of the eight most common food allergens. Those are milk, eggs, fish, crustacean shellfish, peanuts, tree nuts, wheat, and soybeans. Check the label every time you buy a food in case the ingredients have changed.

**Smart tips for buying bagged produce.** After recent scares, when outbreaks of dangerous *E. coli* bacteria were traced to bagged produce, you may be afraid to buy these items. Don't be. You don't need to give up the convenience of buying salads, spinach, or baby carrots in bags. Follow these safety tips from the U.S. Food and Drug Administration to keep your healthy greens from causing harm.

✦ Keep all fruits and vegetables separate from meat and seafood when you bring them home from the store.

✦ Put bagged salads in the refrigerator within two hours of buying them, and keep the refrigerator at 40 degrees Fahrenheit or below.

✦ Read the label of precut, bagged salad or produce to see if it's been washed. If it has, you don't need to wash it again.

✦ If you buy loose produce or salad in open bags, wash it thoroughly under running water just before you eat it. Wash your hands well before and after you wash the veggies to avoid transferring bacteria to other foods.

**Wash food for better health.** Fresh fruits and vegetables look lovely at the store, but they're not clean enough to eat. Wash them first — even if they're labeled organic.

+ Rinse under running water. You may want to first sprinkle on a bit of baking soda, then scrub and rinse.

+ Use a brush to remove dirt and bacteria. This is especially important for apples, potatoes, carrots, and other produce with hard skins.

+ Cut away bruised or damaged parts of the fruit or vegetable.

+ Dry with paper towels.

### Safety hints for nonstick pans

Overheating pans with nonstick coatings may cause them to release a chemical called perfluoroctanoic acid (PFOA). It's unclear what PFOA does in your body, but some think it may cause cancer or harm your nervous system. PFOAs won't be used to make cookware after 2015. For now, you can safely use your nonstick pans if you follow these tips from DuPont, the maker of Teflon coating.

+ Use low or medium heat. That means no broiling, which requires a temperature of about 500 degrees Fahrenheit or higher.

+ Don't leave an empty pot or pan on a hot stove or in a hot oven.

+ Always follow the manufacturer's instructions.

**Wipe out top 5 germiest kitchen spots.** Get 'em where they live — dangerous bacteria, that is. Focus your cleaning efforts on these top five homes for bacteria, and you'll go a long way toward making your kitchen safer.

+ Kitchen sponge. Think this is too expensive to replace often? Then kill the bacteria by popping your sponge in the dishwasher. Put it in the silverware basket, and use the hottest cycle.

✦ Cutting board. First you cut raw chicken on it, then you slice fruit. Bad idea. Tiny cracks in the board let bacteria survive and then move to other foods. It's best to use a separate cutting board for foods like raw meat.

✦ Sink drain. It's hard to see down there, but a sink drain is a dark, moist place for bacteria to hide. Disinfect it regularly, just as you do the countertops.

✦ Handles of doors, appliances, and faucets. Everyone touches these, so they're great places to spread bacteria. Use a disinfectant spray or wipe on them every day.

✦ Hand towels. They're a nice decoration, but shared cloth towels also share germs. Dry your hands using paper towels instead.

**Simple step to a spotless drain.** Sanitize your kitchen sink, drain, garbage disposal, and connecting pipe to remove trapped food and the growth of bacteria that comes along with it. You can make a solution of a teaspoon of chorine bleach in a quart of water, then pour it all down the drain. Hot water and soap may remove what you can see, but they won't kill the bacteria.

**Cast your net for the safest seafood.** You've heard fish is good for you, and it's true. Healthy omega-3 fatty acids in fatty fish — like salmon, sardines, tuna, and trout — may help your heart, ward off some kinds of cancer, and protect your eyes and brain.

But don't go overboard. Some fish and other seafood may be contaminated by mercury, which can cause nerve damage and heart problems. It may also contain polychlorinated biphenyls (PCBs), thought to cause cancer at high levels. So be careful about what kinds of fish you eat and how often. You can enjoy the safest varieties, like salmon, flounder, tilapia, and shrimp, more than once a week. Other varieties, like tuna steaks, halibut, red snapper, and grouper, are more likely to be contaminated. Eat them once a month or less. Women who are pregnant or nursing — and children — should choose even more carefully to avoid dangers to developing bodies.

# Kitchenware essentials

**Cook like the pros.** Good cooking doesn't always come from pricey cookware, but some traits of high-end pots and pans may help bring success to your kitchen. Heavy-gauge materials spread and hold heat evenly so food cooks consistently. They also help pans keep their shape.

But Chef Ursula Knaeusel of Ursula's Cooking School, Inc., in Atlanta, Georgia believes you'll cook best using pots and pans that are comfortable for you. "Professional chefs often use pans from very heavy material, with the bottoms heavier than the sides," Knaeusel says. "The whole reason home cooks don't use them is they're so heavy and large. The average housewife cooks for four to six people, and she doesn't like to lift this heavy pot."

Other qualities to look for in your cookware include lids that are sturdy and can take the heat, and handles that are well attached and won't heat up with the pan.

**Never pay retail on kitchenware.** Pots, pans, knives, and everything else you need in the kitchen go on seasonal discount — just like clothes and shoes. You can often find items on special around the time they're most in demand. That means sales on cutlery around Easter and Thanksgiving, and specials on picnic and cookout gear during the summer months. Watch store ads for special deals on certain top brands of cookware. You'll find fancy pots and pans offered as loss leaders with prices you can't beat.

**Top picks in kitchen knives.** Good knives are expensive. If you can afford only one or two, stick with these versatile styles.

+ Chef's knife. You can chop, mince, and slice with this all-purpose choice. Look for an eight- to 12-inch chef's knife for less than $50.

+ Paring knife. The smaller size allows for more control as you peel or pare.

+ Serrated knife. It's great for slicing bread or biscuits using a sawing motion.

Try wrapping a rubber band around your knife's handle for a better grip.

## Outwit arthritis in the kitchen

Are your hands a bit weak from arthritis? Are jar lids hard to open? Is arthritis pain keeping you out of the kitchen? Take back control with these changes.

◆ Wrap a large rubber band around a jar lid to get a better grip. Or put on your rubber dishwashing gloves and give a twist.

◆ Instead of closing plastic bags with twist ties, use clothespins or plastic clips. Opening the bags will be much quicker.

◆ Change your drawer pulls to large, easy-to-hold handles. You'll thank yourself every time you open a drawer without pain.

**Rediscover the benefits of cast iron.** It's simple, cheap, and cooks like a dream. Your grandma's cast-iron cookware heats food evenly and maintains a natural nonstick finish. Follow these basic rules to keep your cast iron pans in good condition.

+ Wash with care. "Never wash cast iron in a dishwasher," says Mark Kelly, Marketing Communications Manager of Lodge Cast Iron Cookware company. Instead, use hot water and a stiff brush, and avoid scouring.

+ The first few times you use a new pan, cook foods with little water content and low acidity. Don't trap steam with a lid, since it may remove the protective coating.

✦ If your food tastes like metal or takes on a brownish color, rust may be rubbing off from the cast iron. Wash your pan and season it again.

✦ Store pans with lids off so they dry completely. You can place a paper towel inside to soak up water and avoid rust.

**Season pans for nonstick finish.** You can buy new cast-iron cookware pre-seasoned, but traditional pans and griddles need a little help. Season your pans before you use them to create a natural nonstick coating.

Some cooks are picky about the fat used for seasoning, but that's a personal preference. "It all depends on your tastes and heritage," says Mark Kelly of Lodge Cast Iron Cookware company. "For example, Italians in New York and the Northeast use olive oil. Some people like duck fat. Others like bacon grease." Crisco also works.

Wipe some shortening or animal fat inside the pan, then place it upside down on a cookie sheet in the oven. Bake it for about an hour at 300 to 500 degrees Fahrenheit. Sprinkle on salt, wipe out the pan, and repeat the process.

### Cast out RLS with cast iron

People who suffer from restless legs syndrome (RLS) have trouble staying still. They feel an urge — over and over — to more their legs, and they may have itching and pain. They also tend to have low levels of iron stored in their bodies.

Experts say cooking with cast-iron skillets can help get more iron into your food. That may help relieve RLS symptoms and let you put your feet up — without feeling restless.

**Secrets to making copper glow.** The lovely shine of copper cookware may be in danger if you use the wrong cleanser or too much elbow grease. Don't use abrasive cleaners or scrubbing pads, and stay away from caustic products like baking soda, liquid bleach, or floor cleaners. Get your copper spotless yet still shiny by trying one of these methods.

+ Scrub the inside with a lemon wedge sprinkled with salt.

+ Mix salt, white vinegar, and cornmeal in equal parts, rub on the pan's inside, then rinse it off.

+ Dip a cloth in ketchup and rub the inside or outside surface.

+ For the outside of the pan, polish with a paste made from a quarter cup white vinegar and two tablespoons of salt.

+ Cleaners made just for copper, like Calphalon Radiance and Twinkle Copper Cleaner, are also safe choices.

**Keep nonstick coatings clean and safe.** Avoid icky buildup on nonstick pans. That can happen when you spray them with cooking spray over and over. Instead, spray the food, then put it in the pan. Your cookware will stay clean and smooth.

**Put flaky pan worries to rest.** Inexpensive pans with non-stick coatings may lose their smoothness over time. Repeated scratching can put ruts in the nonstick finish and make you worry about where those bits of coating have gone. But you don't have to throw the pan out. The Food and Drug Administration has determined that these particles don't pose a health hazard. The coating is nontoxic, so even if it sneaks into your food it won't make you sick. Unless you find it affects your cooking, save yourself the cost of a new pan.

**3 slick tricks for spotless enamel.** One great thing about enamel cookware is how pretty it looks — until it gets stained. Try these all-natural cleaning methods.

✦ Rub on a paste of baking soda and water and leave it for an hour. Add more water to the paste, mix to dissolve it, and boil for 20 minutes.

✦ Boil up a batch of water and citrus peel in your enamel pot for 20 minutes. Wash as usual.

✦ Fill the pot with water and a handful of salt, and let it soak all night. Then boil the saltwater for 20 minutes.

**Lighten up tough tea stains.** Black tea makes a great fabric dye, and it also stains your ceramic cups. Get them back to their pearly whiteness with these tricks.

✦ Treat them like your dentures. Fill the stained teacup with water, then drop in a denture-cleansing tablet. It will do the job in about three hours.

✦ Rinse away the dark stain with a couple tablespoons of white vinegar.

✦ Scour your teacup with a sprinkling of baking soda and a damp sponge.

**Clean burnt pans in minutes.** Scrubbing stainless-steel pots shouldn't be your muscle-building workout. Sprinkle some dishwasher detergent on the burned food, fill the pot halfway with water, then put it on the stove to heat with the lid on. When the pot boils, turn down the heat to let it simmer for a few minutes. Brush out the burned mess, and you're done.

**Bring your glassware out of the fog.** A good soak in vinegar can keep your crystal glasses from looking cloudy. Mix a cup or two of vinegar in a gallon of hot water, and let glasses go for a dip. Leave them for several hours.

**Get a grip on dining with chopsticks.** Sure, you can always ask for a fork when you eat at a Chinese restaurant. But chopsticks work best to pick up and dip sushi or other Japanese tidbits. Here's how to get your fill at the table using these traditional Asian utensils.

Place one chopstick in the crook of your thumb, narrow end down and about two-thirds from the point. Hold the other side with your ring finger. Your middle finger should be resting on top. This chopstick stays still while you eat. Hold the other chopstick like a pencil, between your index finger and the tip of your thumb. This chopstick moves, opening and closing your chopstick grabber to pick up food. Keep the tips of the two chopsticks even.

---

### Make your own pastry slab

Create a pastry-rolling surface that dough won't stick to. You can buy a 12-inch square marble floor tile for a couple of dollars at a home-improvement store. Stay away from tile with a rough or textured surface. Wash and dry the tile, then add adhesive grips to the back so it won't slide on your countertop. You're ready to roll.

---

**3 unique uses for coffee filters.** You love your new drip coffee pot, but it uses a different paper filter than your old one. What can you do with the leftover filters?

+ Brew loose tea leaves in a cone-shaped filter. Fill it half full, fold and staple it shut, then drop it into your pot of hot water.

+ Prevent splatters and save on paper towels by using a ruffled filter to cover food in the microwave.

+ Keep scratches off your good china by stacking them with ruffled filters in between.

# Clever cleaning solutions

**The 5 cleaning products you should never be without.** You don't have to spend a fortune on cleaning products to keep your house spotless. The only five you need cost less than $10 for the lot of 'em. They'll help you repair, clean, shine, and protect everything in your home for pennies. Even better, you probably have everything you need in your house right now.

+ Baking soda, also known as bicarbonate of soda or sodium bicarbonate, is made up of fine particles. That means if you mix it with a bit of water to form a paste, you can scour pots, pans, sinks, bathtubs, and ovens. And because it's absorbent, it's famous for soaking up odors.

+ White vinegar is often called a household wonder cleaner. It's inexpensive, nontoxic, and useful for dozens of chores. It's the acid in vinegar that cuts through grease and germs and inhibits bacteria and mold.

+ Bleach is simply a chemical mixture of chlorine gas, sodium hydroxide, and water. It's the chlorine that makes bleach such a great disinfectant. This one inexpensive household product kills disease-causing bacteria and viruses in your bathroom and kitchen, gets rid of mildew, and makes your laundry whites whiter. Why bleach is a great stain remover is a little more complicated, but it has a lot to do with a chemical reaction that removes color.

+ Ammónia can be a tricky product to use because of the important safety measures you must take. The vapors can irritate or even burn your skin, eyes, or lungs, so you always want to work in a well-ventilated area. And never use ammonia with bleach. This mixture produces a dangerous gas.

+ Liquid hand dishwashing detergent contains surfactants — organic chemicals that actually change the properties of water. They help quickly wet the surface of whatever you want to clean, make dirt easier to loosen and remove, and trap oils so they can't settle back on the surface and are easily rinsed away. Most hand dishwashing detergents cut grease and are biodegradable.

| *7 ways to clean with baking soda* | |
| --- | --- |
| sour sink drains | Freshen smelly sink and tub drains by sprinkling two tablespoons baking soda down drain. Run warm water for a minute afterward. |
| grout | Make a paste of baking soda and water, apply to grout, and scrub with an old toothbrush. Do not rinse. |
| tub and tile | Combine half-cup water, half-cup liquid dish soap, and 1 2/3 cup baking soda. Then add two tablespoons vinegar and apply mixture immediately to tub or tile. Wipe and rinse. |
| carpet odors | Add 10 drops of essential oil, like lavender, to two cups baking soda. Stir well, pour into shaker jar, and let it sit for two days to dry so it doesn't stain your carpet. Then sprinkle on carpet, wait 30 minutes, and vacuum. |
| microwave | Make a paste of four tablespoons baking soda mixed with water, apply with a sponge, scrub, and rinse well. |
| brass, copper, bronze, and aluminum | Sprinkle baking soda on a slice of lemon and rub on metal to remove tarnish. |
| sterling silver | Line glass or plastic bowl with aluminum foil, sprinkle on salt and baking soda, and fill with warm water. Soak silver to remove tarnish, then rinse, dry, and buff. |

**Shaker-top jars make cleaning easy.** Any kind of container with a shaker top is well worth saving and reusing. Pour baking soda into a large one and use to sprinkle in toilets, sinks, and bathtubs while cleaning.

## 10 ways to clean with vinegar

| | |
|---|---|
| windows and mirrors | Mix one part white vinegar and three parts water, spray on windows, and dry with newspaper. |
| toilets | Pour one cup undiluted white vinegar into bowl, let stand five minutes, and flush. This white vinegar formula makes any toilet automatically spic and span. |
| dishwasher | Place a cup containing white vinegar on bottom rack of dishwasher and run through full cycle to remove soap buildup in your machine. |
| tile mildew | Spray on equal parts white vinegar and water, wipe with a sponge. |
| bathtub film | Wipe down with white vinegar and rinse with water. |
| stainless steel, ceramic sinks, chrome, and appliances | Dip sponge or cloth in white vinegar and wipe clean. Polish to a shine with soft, damp cloth. |
| clogged shower heads | Fill a watertight plastic bag halfway with white vinegar, place over shower head so head is submerged in vinegar, and secure with a rubber band. Leave on overnight, then rinse with hot water. |
| vinyl floors | Pour half a cup white vinegar into one gallon warm water and grab a mop. |
| white rings on wood furniture | Rub with equal parts olive oil and white vinegar. |
| foul odors | Boil one tablespoon white vinegar in one cup water to banish bad smells. Set a cup of white vinegar in a room to absorb the smell of stale smoke. |

**Add pizzazz to your cleaning routine with citrus peels.** Save your citrus rinds and make your own fresh-smelling cleaning solution. Put rinds from oranges, lemons, limes, or grapefruits in a jar of white vinegar and seal. Let brew four weeks, then strain the liquid. You can use this brew to clean your home just like regular vinegar.

## 4 ways to clean with bleach

| | |
|---|---|
| mildew | Mix 8 to 12 ounces bleach and 2 ounces liquid dish soap in one gallon of water. Wipe down mildewed areas. |
| tile and grout stains | Pour one part bleach and 10 parts water into a spray bottle, squirt on stubborn tile and grout stains. Let soak for 10 minutes, then scrub with a toothbrush and rinse. Wear rubber gloves and eye protection. |
| porcelain sink stains | Fill sink with warm, not hot, water. Add a few ounces of bleach, and let stand for one hour. For stubborn stains, dampen paper towels in bleach and lay on stains before you go to bed. Remove in the morning and rinse well. |
| toilet bowls | Pour one-quarter cup of bleach in the bowl and let sit one hour, then flush. Stains may need a little scrubbing. Avoid bleach if you use a tank-held cleaner, as the two chemicals could react. |

**No-sweat secret to cleaning your shower curtain.** Dread cleaning the bathroom? Scour your tub and shower curtain overnight, without scrubbing. Lay the shower curtain in your bathtub and fill the tub with cold water and bleach. Weigh the curtain down if it tries to float. Let it soak overnight, then rinse and rehang. You'll have a clean shower curtain and a clean bathtub.

If you'd rather not get your hands dirty, put it through the washer with laundry detergent and half a cup of baking soda. Add one cup of white vinegar at the start of the rinse cycle. Toss in a few towels for extra scrubbing power.

## 6 ways to clean with ammonia

| | |
|---|---|
| windows | Mix together seven pints cold water, a half cup of soapy ammonia, and one pint rubbing alcohol. Tint with two drops blue food coloring, mix well, and pour into a spray bottle. |
| general household | Combine two tablespoons ammonia, one teaspoon liquid dish soap, and one pint rubbing alcohol in a gallon jug. Finish filling jug with hot water. Cap and pour into spray bottles as needed. |
| walls and showers | Pour half cup ammonia, quarter cup vinegar, and quarter cup baking soda into bucket with one gallon warm water. |
| bathtub rings | Wipe off with a sponge and undiluted ammonia. Wear rubber gloves. |
| drip pans | Soak overnight in a large tub full of hot water and four cups of ammonia. Scrub clean the next day while wearing rubber gloves. |
| crayon on walls | Rub with a cloth soaked in ammonia. |

**The 3 biggest no-nos when cleaning jewelry.** According to Gerald Golech, instructor for the Gemological Institute of America, "Using harsh chemicals or abrasives that could damage certain gemstones or scratch the metal" is the biggest mistake people make when cleaning their jewelry. "Diamonds are very durable, but you have to be very careful with other gemstones, like emeralds or pearls," he cautions. His three biggest no-nos:

+ Think twice about lemon juice. "I've heard people say, 'clean pearls with lemon juice.' That's the opposite of what you want to do." Lemon juice is highly acidic. "It can actually dissolve the material pearls are made of."

+ Avoid chlorine bleach at all costs. "It can actually damage some of the metals and more fragile gemstones."

✦ Don't use ammonia, also found in jewelry cleaners, on porous organic gems like pearls or turquoise.

What should you do? A mild soap, like dishwashing liquid, and a soft-bristled toothbrush will often do the job. "Use a new toothbrush, because toothpaste often has abrasives in it that could scratch the metals," Golech advises. Commercial jewelry cleaners sometimes contain metal brighteners that can shine-up dulled metals.

Don't clean your jewelry over the sink without plugging the drain. "That's a common problem. People accidentally drop their pieces down the drain." And have a professional inspect pieces you wear about once a year to find loose stones and thin prongs before they become a problem.

## 6 ways to clean with liquid dish detergent

| | |
|---|---|
| floors | Add dish detergent and a cup of lemon juice to a bucket of hot water, then mop your floors. |
| windows | Mix two tablespoons white vinegar and a tiny squirt of dish detergent into one quart of water. Pour into spray bottle to clean windows. |
| sinks and countertops | Stir together dish detergent and small amount of baking soda in bowl until they form a paste. Use as a nonabrasive cleanser for scrubbing. |
| shower doors | Combine dish detergent and warm water to dissolve soap scum on shower doors. |
| tools | Soak greasy tools in dish detergent and warm water before putting them away. The soap will cut right through grime. |
| driveways | Scrub off grease and gasoline stains with dish detergent and warm water. |

**Say "so long" to scuff marks.** Scuff marks don't have to stain your floors forever. Here are three ways to rub them out.

+ For vinyl or linoleum floors, poke a hole in a tennis ball, insert a dowel or old broom handle, and rub the scuff mark with the ball.

+ Erase scuffs on tile with a clean pencil eraser.

+ Remove them from tile or vinyl with a damp cloth and a little white toothpaste or baking soda.

## Simple strategies to keep you safe

Never combine chlorine bleach with acidic products, including vinegar, toilet bowl cleaners, and rust removers — or with ammonia cleaners, such as window cleaners and some hand dishwashing soaps. Don't reuse empty commercial cleaner bottles to hold homemade brews. The new cleaner could interact with the old. Plus, you might forget what's really in the bottle. Whether you're using commercial cleaners or making your own, wear proper gloves and eye protection and have good ventilation.

**First line of defense during cold and flu season.** One person with the flu can contaminate 60 percent of household surfaces with the virus. That makes cleaning during cold and flu season a major priority. Experts recommend these simple steps as your first line of defense.

+ Sing happy birthday twice while washing your hands in warm water. You need to lather up for about 20 seconds to kill cold and flu viruses.

+ Turn to alcohol-based wipes and hand sanitizers when you can't wash with soap. Rub your hands together until the gel sanitizer dries.

✦ Clean with disinfectant wipes or sprays regularly. The flu virus can survive on surfaces for two to eight hours. Wipe down doorknobs, faucets, toilet flushers, TV remotes, house keys, refrigerator door handles, cabinet knobs, countertops, light switches, computer keyboard and mouse, and other commonly touched surfaces.

✦ Cough and sneeze into tissues or your upper sleeve, not your hands. Remember, viruses can survive for hours, so don't leave tissues lying around. Throw tissues away as soon as you use them.

**Whip up your own wipes.** Why buy expensive cleaning wipes when you can make your own for pennies apiece? First, get a roll of good, strong paper towels. Cut the sheets in half, and fold to fit in a plastic storage container. For general cleaning, pour in one part white vinegar and one part water. For disinfecting, make a solution using your favorite liquid cleaner. Check the directions on the bottle. Gently pour over your towels, seal the container, and let sit overnight.

**Smart moves prevent common injuries.** Spring cleaning can easily lead to spring visits to the doctor, with thrown-out backs from too much lifting or accidents with cleaning chemicals. Get your house spic and span without hurting yourself.

✦ Keep a basic set of cleaning tools and products on each floor of your home.

✦ Slip furniture coasters under the feet of heavy pieces. They're made with super-slick bottoms so furniture slides easily across carpet or hard floors.

✦ Lift the right way. Stand with your feet shoulder-width apart, bend your knees, tighten your stomach muscles, and lift with your legs.

✦ Don't overdo it. Instead of trying to clean the whole house in one weekend, plan to clean a room a day. You'll feel less stressed, not to mention less sore.

✦ Follow the directions on cleaners and wear protective gear, such as rubber gloves and eye protection, when necessary.

---

### 3-minute task saves you $1,000 a year

School kids aren't the only ones who brown bag their lunch. Lots of adults do, too. Packing your lunch the night before, if you work or plan to leave the house for the day, can save you both time and money. Eating lunch out can easily cost you $5 a day, but you can make your own at home for about $1. Add it up, and this three–minute task can save you more than $1,000 a year. That's like getting paid $54 an hour for your time.

---

**Insider secrets to removing carpet stains.** The biggest mistake you make when cleaning your carpet is probably overwetting it, says David Tassa, a Certified Master Cleaner and owner of Diversified Cleaning Systems.

Do-it-yourself carpet cleaning machines use hot water extraction, the method most carpet manufacturers recommend. But overzealous home-owners end up soaking their carpets in too much water. "Overwetting actually breaks down the glue between the two backings and causes what's called delamination," he explains.

Another problem — using too much soap. You end up with soap left in the carpet, which attracts more dirt. "The carpet gets dirty faster, so they clean it again, and again, getting it too wet every time. In two years' time, the carpet is shot."

Instead of cleaning the whole carpet regularly, spot treat messes as soon as they strike. You don't have to buy expensive stain removers, either. Tassa says, "Patience will remove more spots than anything."

"Remove as much of the spill as you can. Scoop up excess amounts, blot off as much as possible, then apply some water." He suggests wetting the spot and agitating — but not scrubbing — it with your finger or a damp rag. "Throw the rag on it, let it sit for 15 minutes, then come back and blot it." You'll be amazed at how many stains you can remove with water alone, he says. And if that doesn't do it, "Put a couple of drops — not squirts, just drops — of dishwashing detergent in a cup of warm water," then wet and blot with that.

**5 steps help you face the day.** Wake up ready to face the day and all set to go when you do these 5 little things the night before. You won't believe how much better you'll feel in the morning.

+ Load dirty dishes in the dishwasher and clean the sink.

+ Prepare your morning coffee. Measure out the coffee grounds and pour water in the holding tank. Come morning, all you'll have to do is flip the "on" switch.

+ Pack your lunch for tomorrow.

+ Walk around with a basket and pick up all the out-of-place items. While you're in each room, put back the items that belong there.

+ Sort the mail into bill, junk, and other piles, then file in the appropriate places.

**6 secrets to faster kitchen cleanup.** Minimize kitchen messes with a few simple tips.

+ Leave your dishwasher open and the racks pulled out while cooking. Drop in each dirty dish and utensil as soon as you finish using it.

+ Measure out dry ingredients first, then wet ones so you only need one measuring cup.

+ Marinate meats in sealable, disposable, plastic bags.

+ Measure over wax paper to keep spills off your counter. Pour the dry ingredients that spill back into their containers.

+ Line your produce drawer with paper towels, so juices are easier to clean up.

+ Tear open produce bags but leave the produce in them. If food goes bad, it's less messy to toss.

### Little-known allergy from a helpful bug

Ladybugs may be good for your garden, but — if you're allergic to them — they won't do your body any favors. New research shows ladybug allergies are as common as cat and cockroach allergies, but less well-known. You can seal these critters out of your home by repairing window screens, making sure doors and windows close tightly, and caulking cracks. Vacuum up dead ladybugs and empty your vacuum outside.

**Ban bats from your belfry.** Brown bats earn their keep in the world, eating as many as 10 mosquitoes a minute. While you might want them in your yard, you probably don't want them in your house. Luckily, you can send bats packing with things right in your kitchen. Try these safe, proven, homemade remedies.

If you already have bats in your belfry, figure out where they're roosting. After they leave for the evening, seal up all openings to the outside more than 2 inches wide. Duct tape offers a temporary fix. For a more permanent solution, plug with silicone caulk or steel wool, or staple fine plastic netting over holes. Unlike squirrels, bats won't try to chew their way in.

If your main concern is discouraging them in the first place, try these clever tricks.

+ Hang strips of aluminum foil 2 inches wide and at least 7 inches long in the areas they like to roost, such as attics, cellars, and porches. Hanging Mylar balloons will deter them, too.

+ Put a bright light in the attic or roosting spot and turn it on in the evening.

+ Spray aerosol dog or cat repellant on their nighttime hangouts, but do it during the day while they are gone. These sprays can drive them away for months at a time.

**The top 3 mouse-catching myths.** Show your mouse guests the door by avoiding these three common mistakes.

+ Thinking your cat will catch it. Most house-raised felines are too well-fed and slow-moving to catch a mouse in motion. What's more, their pet food is likely to attract rodents.

+ Buying sonic devices. Sudden noises may scare mice, but they quickly become used to regular, repeated sounds like those emitted by electronic and ultrasonic devices. Plus, the noise from these gadgets doesn't penetrate walls and other objects.

+ Setting too few traps. Use plenty, and set them no more than 10 feet apart in places where mice are active. Mice love peanut butter, chocolate, dried fruit, and small bits of bacon. Bait the trap but don't set it the first time. Once they take the bait, re-bait and set the trap.

You can keep them out for good by sealing up cracks leading to the outside. Stuff steel wool into any hole bigger around than a pencil, seal it with caulk, and smooth.

**Chase away ants with peppermint.** Ban ants from your home and let them know they're not welcome. Brew up a strong batch of peppermint tea, pour into a squirt bottle, and spray the areas they like to hang out, like inside cabinets, on countertops, and floors. If you're worried about tea staining these surfaces, simply add some peppermint extract to water and spray.

According to folk remedy, you can chase away ants with the popular Christmas candy version, too. Just drop crushed peppermint sticks on an anthill or sprinkle near the entrance to your home.

**Banish bothersome bugs with lemons.** It's easy to wipe out fleas and have a spotless, fresh-smelling house when you finish. Here's how — add the juice from four lemons to a half-gallon of hot water and mop your floors. Or make a homemade spray to chase fleas out of fabric. Put 10 drops of lavender, rosemary, or eucalyptus essential oil in a spray bottle with water, and lightly mist pet beds, upholstered furniture, and carpets after vacuuming.

## 11 minutes to better mood, sleep, memory

Eleven minutes in the morning and evening are all you need for better sleep, more energy, improved mood, and sharper memory.

Start with a full minute of deep breathing, which can slow your heart rate, lower blood pressure, and help regulate your blood sugar. Then get moving. Spend the next 10 minutes stretching, walking, lifting light weights, or whatever physical activity you enjoy.

The point is to be in motion. Exercise gives you a natural energy boost that chases away fatigue, releases chemicals in your brain that improve your mood, and helps you fall asleep faster and sleep better at the end of the day. Plus, better quality sleep can lead to a better memory.

**Stop allergies cold with a houseplant.** Are you breathing in mold, or something even worse? Chuck the air purifiers and pot some English ivy instead. When researchers put ivy a sealed container with mold and dog feces, this beautiful plant removed 78 percent of airborne mold and 94 percent of dog fecal particles in the air. And that was after just 12 hours. Make English ivy is your houseplant of choice, and you could cut back on allergies and keep the air in your home fresh for free. It's a simple, natural trick to keeping allergens to a minimum. Remember to keep the plant away from small children and pets because it's toxic if eaten.

**Amazing ways to use dryer sheets.** Clean window blinds, TVs, and computer screens, add a fresh scent to luggage and closets, and even shine your shoes — all with a dryer sheet. You would normally throw it away after using it just once, but fabric softener sheets have many lives.

+ Dust window blinds and TV and computer screens with dryer sheets. They grab dust easily and help repel future dirt.

+ Clean caked-on food by placing a sheet in a dirty pan, filling with water, and soaking overnight.

+ Place a new fabric softener sheet in the vacuum cleaner bag to freshen a room while you sweep. Change the sheet every few weeks or when the scent starts to fade.

+ Keep thread from tangling by pulling a threaded needle through a dryer sheet before sewing.

+ Stick them in stored luggage to ward off musty odors.

+ Tuck a sheet in a smelly shoe to banish bad odors, then use it later to buff that boot or pump to a nice shine.

+ Replace old scented sachets with a dryer sheet in dresser drawers, closets, and stored, out-of-season clothing.

**Breathe better air at home.** You try to keep your home clean and smelling fresh, but you may be doing more harm than good. Air fresheners, candles, cleaning products, disinfectants, aerosol sprays, paint, and dry-cleaned clothing can release toxic chemicals called volatile organic compounds into your home — compounds linked to cancer, as well as heart, liver, nervous system, and breathing problems. You can improve the air in your home with five simple steps.

+ Keep the humidity level between 40 and 50 percent during very cold weather and between 40 and 60 percent the rest of the year to minimize pollutants.

+ Always use commercial cleaners and disinfectants, aerosol sprays, and air fresheners with lots of ventilation. Open windows or run exhaust fans that vent outdoors.

+ Switch to more natural cleaners. Baking soda, vinegar, liquid dish soap, and plain old water are safer, less toxic, cheaper, and just as effective as most commercial cleaners.

+ Avoid imported candles. They are more likely to have lead wicks, and burning them can cause unsafe lead levels in your home. Scented candles, on the other hand, are more likely to produce potentially harmful soot particles.

+ Leave windows open to let in fresh air when burning incense. Incense can release large amounts of pollutants, including compounds linked to contact dermatitis, asthma, and cancer.

**Make stuffed animals good as new.** To freshen up musty-smelling stuffed toys, toss them in the dryer on "low" with a sheet of fabric softener. If they're dingy enough to need washing, simply drop each in a pillow case, tie shut, and wash in cold water on the gentle cycle. Tumble dry on low.

**How to care for fine feather pillows.** Pacific Coast Feather Company, a leading maker of feather pillows, offers these tips to make yours last for years to come.

+ Check to make sure your pillow is machine washable. If it is, wash with a mild detergent in warm water on the gentle setting. Washing two pillows instead of one can help balance the load.

✦ Put pillows through two rinse cycles, then two back-to-back spin cycles to remove as much water as possible.

✦ Dry on low heat. Keep drying until you don't feel lumps. These mean the pillow is still wet inside, even if it feels dry to touch. Fluff the pillows by hand between cycles.

In between washings, fluff up flattened down pillows by popping them in the dryer on air-dry with a couple of clean tennis balls and a dryer sheet. Be warned — the tennis balls will make quite a racket.

## Feathered relief from allergies

If you're hounded by allergies, consider switching to feather pillows. Studies show synthetic pillows can harbor more dust mites, as well as seven- to eight-times more pet allergens than feather pillows.

**Quick way to wipe wicker clean.** Wicker may be beautiful, but it can be a bear to clean. Take the roar out of this chore by spraying a clean paintbrush with furniture polish or a dusting spray and sweeping it across the wicker. You'll get between the weaves and into all the crevices.

# Cut clutter chaos

**End unwanted junk mail.** Get rid of junk mail quickly and easily with one easy step. Write to the Direct Marketing Association and ask to be removed from all mailing lists. The DMA will put your name and address on a "do-not-mail" list. Companies that are members of the DMA must then remove your name from their mailing lists. Send a postcard or letter with your name, home address, and signature to:

Mail Preference Service
Direct Marketing Association
P.O. Box 643
Carmel, NY 10512

The amount of unwanted mail you get should start dropping about three months later. If you still receive unwanted solicitations, contact those companies directly and ask them to remove your name from their in-house mailing list.

**Cut catalog clutter for good.** Mailbox clogged by unwanted catalogs? Stay off their mailing lists for good. Cancel catalogs you don't want by calling the toll-free customer service phone number on the catalog and asking them to take you off their list. Also, let them know you don't want your name sold or rented to other businesses.

Next, write to the Abacus Alliance to have your name removed from the catalog industry's main mailing lists at Abacus, Inc., P.O. Box 1478, Broomfield, CO 80038. You can also e-mail your name and address to Abacus at *optout@abacus-us.com*.

**Foolproof plan prevents mail pileups.** Go through your mail as soon as you carry it inside. Decide right then what to keep and what to toss, then take action. Write that check, file that letter, or pitch that catalog. Do it now, and you'll take a load off your mind — and your kitchen counter.

## How long to hold onto papers

Are you holding on to papers from 20 years ago? Afraid to trash "important" documents? This handy guide will help you know how long you should keep certain documents — and when it's okay to toss them. Remember, laws and IRS rules tend to change, so check with an attorney or accountant before shredding legal or financial documents.

| Documents | For how long? |
| --- | --- |
| 401K records | quarterly statements until you check them against the annual summary; annual summaries until you retire or close the account |
| IRA records | forever, if you made nondeductible contributions |
| pay stubs | until you check them against your annual W–2 form |
| bills | for most bills, until you receive the cancelled check or the next bill showing you paid |
| receipts | for big-ticket items, for as long as you own the item; for items under warranty, until the warranty expires; for credit card purchases, until you check them against your monthly statement |
| ATM receipts | until you check them against your monthly bank statement |
| tax-related documents | any bills (including medical bills), receipts, checks, or other records you used to calculate your taxes, for seven years |
| tax returns and payments | preferably forever but at least seven years |
| home-selling and home-improvement expenses | for six years after selling your home (includes records of legal fees, agent's commissions, remodeling expenses, and documents proving the original purchase price) |
| car records | until you no longer own the car |

**Get unruly cords and Christmas lights under control.**
You can use a cardboard tube to easily store those pesky electrical cords
and holiday lights. Just wrap lights around empty paper towel or wrapping
paper tubes, then stow away with Christmas decorations.

Another use — keep cords in order around the house with empty toilet
paper tubes. Fold up cords on hair dryers and appliances, then stuff the
excess inside the tube. Leave enough length to reach the outlet. Slide
extra cords into empty tubes to maintain order in your junk drawer, too.

**Tangle-free tip for hanging Christmas lights.** If you
love to light up your house for the holidays, an old garden hose reel will
make decorating a snap. Wind your Christmas lights around a stand-
alone reel with a handle when you take them down. Cover with a plastic
garbage bag to keep the dust off during storage. They'll unwind with
ease and go up twice as fast the next year.

**Instant storage behind every door.** Hanging shoe bags hold
more than shoes. They're even better at organizing bathrooms, pantries,
hobby rooms, or anywhere else you have a door. Tack them up and use
the pockets to hold shampoos in the bathroom; pliers, screwdrivers, and
batteries in your tool room; spices and powdered mixes in your pantry; or
crochet hooks, knitting notions, and buttons in your craft room.

**Cheap storage for every room.** Inexpensive melamine shoe
cubbies make terrific storage for almost any room in the house. Stack
them on a shelf, set them on the floor, or attach them to a wall. Use
them to hold:

+ scarves, gloves, hats, and galoshes in your hall closet.

+ yarn, rolled-up fabric, and sewing notions in a craft room.

+ paired socks, sweats, stockings, or pajamas in your bedroom closet.

+ toys and stuffed animals in a child's room.

+ washcloths, hand towels, and pretty bottles of bath salts in your bathroom.

+ bills, catalogs, and incoming and outgoing mail in your home office.

**Get your garage in order with a filing cabinet.** Stick that old, rusty, piece of office equipment in your garage. Separate sandpaper grades, different-size saw blades, sewing patterns, and tool instruction manuals in hanging folders with labels. Use leftover drawer space for drills, wound-up cords, spray cans, jars of stain, extra light bulbs, or anything else that fits.

**Give your clutter to a good cause.** When you de-clutter or remodel your home, you are bound to end up with a garage full of stuff you no longer want. You can't lose by donating it to Habitat for Humanity.

This nonprofit organization accepts donated appliances, furniture, rugs, plumbing and electrical fixtures, and more through its ReStore. Your gift will either go into a family's Habitat home or help raise money to build a home, says Sharon Hazel, Manager of the Newnan-Coweta Habitat for Humanity ReStore in Georgia. "Any donated item we're not able to use directly in building a Habitat home, we resell to generate money to purchase the building materials and services to build Habitat homes."

Everything you donate should work and be in good condition. "When it comes to upholstered furniture, we'd prefer there be no tears, snags, animal hairs, smells, or stains." Slight scratches are fine, she says, if they can be painted over. "Appliances must be less than 10 years old and in 100 percent working order." Even used toilets, sinks, showers, and tubs are welcome, says Hazel, "as long as the porcelain is not cracked and someone can reuse it."

Call your local Habitat for Humanity and ask if they have a ReStore. Find out which items they accept and if they pick up. Some offer free pickup, others ask for a small, tax-deductible donation to pay for gasoline. When you donate, you'll get a receipt for the tax-deductible amount of your gift.

**Free, fast drawer dividers.** Make your own free drawer dividers out of cardboard boxes. Simply cut the box into strips to fit in your drawer. Notch the ends so the pieces fit together and interlock. Arrange different-size strips in your drawers to make custom compartments.

**Old tie racks help organize your kitchen.** Hang scrub brushes and towels from a small tie rack on the inside of your kitchen sink cabinet. Mount another on a wall near the stove for cooking utensils.

**Cut the clutter in your cleaning closet.** Mount a thin towel rack on the inside of the door and hang spray bottles from it by their triggers.

### Divide and conquer kitchen clutter

Look at your kitchen. No doubt you do different things in different areas — wash dishes in one part, prepare food in another, and make toast or coffee in another area. These are your zones. Divide your kitchen into zones, and organize your cabinets and drawers based on what you use most in each. Cookbooks go in the meal prep area, while mugs go in the coffee-making zone. Baking pans and nonstick sprays should be in your baking area.

**Refill station saves you money.** Set up a refill station in your utility room and buy soaps, dishwashing and laundry detergents, cleaners, and personal products in refillable containers. Then save money at the store buying bulk refills and pouring into the smaller bottles at home. Store the extra in your utility room, and keep the smaller containers around the house wherever you need them.

**Expert advice for fixing closet disasters.** Diana Auspurger knows closets. President of both the Association of Closet and Storage Professionals and her own custom closet company, Creative Storage, she's seen almost every type of mistake. Here's her guide for getting it right.

+ Size your shelves. "Shelves in the closet don't really need to exceed 16 inches deep unless it's a linen closet." Make them too deep, she says, "and you end up with a jumbled mess." Measure the folded garments or objects you plan to store, and size your shelves accordingly.

+ Hang at the right height. "If your dress is 60 inches long, you want your rod at 65 inches. If you allow too much space for long hanging, you've cheated yourself out of extra shelf space."

+ Let it go. People keep clothing they never wear, often out of guilt. "So often, people hang on to clothes because they can't forgive themselves for buying something that didn't suit well. Forgive yourself for making a bad buy," advises Auspurger, "and let it go."

+ Get real. Along the same lines, be realistic when buying new clothes. "People gravitate to wearing ultra-comfortable things," she points out. If it doesn't feel good when you try it on in the store, "don't buy it, because you probably won't wear it."

+ Match, don't mix. "Using the same item in a closet over and over again — the same hanger or shoe box, for instance — creates a sense of uniformity. And uniformity renders a sense of organization." Create an instant aura of order simply by storing items in similar containers.

**Foolproof storage for tight closet spaces.** Closets were made for clothes, but not necessarily shoes. Create well-heeled shoe space instantly with these three ideas.

+ Got plenty of rod space but no shoe space? Shop for shoe cubbies that hang from your closet rod.

+ Invest in a shoe rack that mounts to the inside of your closet door. These are sturdy, solid racks made just for shoes.

✦ Leave them in their boxes. Tape a photograph of each pair on the outside of the box and stack them on shelves, or buy clear plastic shoe boxes to see at a glance what's inside.

**Handy trick for hanging handbags.** Get purses off closet floors and shelves with this nifty trick. Clip an extra shower ring around the closet rod and loop purse straps through the ring's opening. Do the same with belt buckles and scarves. To save even more space, attach all your belts or handbags to one hanger by clipping several rings onto a plastic hanger.

## Safer storage for Rx

Straightening your medicine cabinet is as much a matter of safety as neatness. Follow these guidelines for storing prescription and over-the-counter drugs.

* Clean out your medicine cabinet every six months and remove medications that are expired, dried out, discolored, or crumbling.

* Check eye and ear drops, too. Once these expire they may start breeding bacteria and fungus.

* Remove the cotton in pill bottles. Cotton absorbs moisture, which can affect medicine.

* Store drugs in a cool, dry place — not in your bathroom or near the kitchen stove. Most bathrooms are too humid, and areas by the stove get too warm.

* Keep your medicines on a different shelf or in a different cabinet from your spouse's so you don't accidentally take the wrong ones.

**Create space for hanging accessories.** Pegboards don't belong only in the garage. Cut one to fit on your closet door, then paint it and hang. Insert tool hooks to hold scarves, jewelry, ties, and other accessories.

**Instant bathroom storage secrets for tiny spaces.** Tiny bathrooms hold tons of storage space. You just need to think creatively. Try these ideas on for size.

- ✦ Horizontal towel bars waste space. Go vertical with towel hooks, one for each person who uses the bathroom.

- ✦ Screw a sturdy cup hook into the side of the vanity, and hang your hair dryer, curling iron, or hand towels.

- ✦ Glue long magnetic strips to the inside of your medicine cabinet doors. Use them to hang small, metal grooming tools, like tweezers, scissors, and eyelash curlers.

- ✦ Screw smaller cup hooks on the inside of vanity doors to hang brushes.

- ✦ Lift reading materials off the top of the toilet tank. Place a stand-alone magazine caddy by the toilet or mount a hanging one on the vanity or wall.

- ✦ Stand a coat rack in the corner for bathrobes if more than one person uses the bathroom.

**Impose order on sample-size chaos.** Bring order to the jumble of free shampoo samples and travel-size toothpastes. Instead of cramming them in your medicine cabinet, divvy them up into sealable plastic bags. Pack them in your suitcases so they're ready to go when you are.

**Sure-fire way to stay organized.** You can organize your whole house just by taking it in small bites. Pick a manageable project you can tackle in 30-minutes, and do a new project every day — 30 minutes a day, every day. Break bigger projects, like organizing the hall closet, into smaller bites. Take on your home one drawer, door, and floor at a time. Once you're organized, keep it that way by spending 10 minutes straightening up before bed every day.

**4 chores you can do while watching TV.** Catch up on your favorite TV shows and get your house clean at the same time. No more guilt! Here are just a few household chores you can do while watching TV.

+ Clip coupons, magazine articles, and newspaper stories you want to keep. File them away while sitting on the sofa.

+ Load and unload the dishwasher during commercials.

+ Surround yourself with dirty laundry and stain remover. Pre-treat laundry while your show is on, and put it on to wash and dry during commercials.

+ Dust, sweep, and do other light, quiet chores while the television is on.

**Foolproof plan for doing nagging tasks.** If you are retired, you may feel like you have all the time in the world to accomplish special organizing or cleaning tasks. Yet, you never seem to find just the right moment to balance your checkbook, purge your files, or organize your recipes. And if you work outside the home, it's easy to let things slip.

The solution is simple — schedule appointments for everything. Buy a calendar with plenty of room to write in daily appointments, and set up dates and times for everything on your to-do list. Space things out, giving yourself plenty of time to accomplish special tasks in addition to your other daily commitments.

# Frugal fixes for the home

**Free home repair for seniors.** No matter what your income, services like legal assistance, home repair, even housekeeping chores can be yours at no cost through your local Area Agency on Aging. Over 35 years ago, Congress passed the Older Americans Act, which created a network of support services to help seniors with:

+ household chores, such as laundry, grocery shopping, cleaning, and meal preparation

+ transportation for doctor appointments, errands, and shopping

+ in-home healthcare for seniors who do not need 24-hour care

+ hot meals, delivered

+ friendly telephone calls or in-home visits for homebound adults or those living alone

+ legal assistance, including advice, counseling, and representation in civil matters

+ Medicare benefits counseling

+ utility and heating assistance for low-income seniors

+ home repair, including roof patches, plumbing repair, and insulation

+ pension counseling

Anyone 60 years or older is eligible for these benefits, although some programs give priority to seniors most in need. For more information, or to sign up for services, call the Eldercare Locator at 800-677-1116 or go online to *www.eldercare.gov.*

**Spot sham chimney sweeps.** Regular chimney cleanings keep dangerous chemicals from building up inside your chimney and make certain all the parts are working properly. But don't get taken for a ride. Interview chimney sweeps before hiring them, and ask for a Level 1 chimney inspection and sweeping. If the sweep doesn't know what that means, find one who does.

## Improvements that add the most value

Nationally, adding a deck, replacing siding and windows, and doing minor kitchen and bathroom makeovers earn the most bang for your buck when you sell your house. However, experts warn of a downward trend in the dollar–for–dollar return on remodeling projects.

If you are remodeling to meet your own needs, this may not matter to you. But if you are remodeling in order to sell your home, think twice before sinking lots of money into a major project. Ask a local real estate agent to tour your home and offer advice on which upgrades are worth making.

**5 biggest mistakes when hiring a contractor.** Even the simplest home improvements can go awry if the wrong person is doing them. That's why hiring a good, honest contractor should be your first priority.

✦ Interview more than one. Get estimates from at least three contractors. Don't hire the first one who calls you back, or the guy who solicits you off the street.

✦ Check their references. Along with an estimate, get a list of references. Call them and ask if the contractor finished on time and within budget and if they were happy with the work.

+ Look for experience. Ask each contractor how long he's been in business — the longer, the better. In particular, look for a contractor who has experience with your type of project.

+ Check their insurance. Make them show you written proof of insurance — either a card or certificate — that covers them and their workers. Otherwise, you are liable for on-the-job mishaps.

+ Get it in writing. Insist on a contract that details the start date, scope of the job, and estimated cost. A handshake won't protect you if you have to sue a contractor over shoddy or unfinished work.

**Room design made easy.** Choose the look you want for your room with a "decorating diary." Fill the pages of a notebook with ideas you find — paint card samples, pictures clipped from magazines or furniture ads, scraps of fabric, and your own notes and measurements. As you collect images, colors, and textures you love, you'll discover a common theme that becomes the room's "look."

**Clever tips take the pain out of painting.** Does the thought of painting make your blood pressure rise? Try these four solutions to the most common problems.

+ Protect carpet while painting baseboards. Tear off strips of 1-1/2 inch painter's or masking tape, lay them on the carpet against the bottom of the baseboard, and use a plastic putty knife to push the edge of the tape under the baseboard.

+ Stop the bleeding. Run a credit card or plastic putty knife along the edge of painter's tape to create a tight seal between the tape and the wall. Paint won't leak under the tape, giving you a clean line.

+ Always remove tape once the surrounding paint is tacky — no longer wet, but not quite dry.

+ Reuse old plastic shower curtains as free drop cloths to protect floors.

**No-mess way to pour paint.** Invest a couple of bucks in a plastic spout that snaps onto the rim of one-gallon paint cans. It will give you a clean pour plus an edge on the inside to scrape excess paint off your brush. Best of all, it's plastic so it cleans up easily with water.

**Don't let stairs trip up paint job.** When you paint stairs, paint every other step the first day. Do the rest a day or two later, once the first batch has dried, so you can still get up and down the stairs.

### Buy exactly the right amount of paint

Take the guesswork out of paint shopping. Three handy Web sites will calculate in an instant how much paint you need for almost any project. Now if only choosing the colors were that easy.

- www.kilz.com/calculator
- www.behr.com (click on "Expert Advice")
- www.benjaminmoore.com/paintcalculator

**Minimize carpet wear and tear.** According to David Tassa, a second-generation cleaner and owner of Diversified Cleaning Systems, vacuuming regularly is the best way to lengthen your carpet's life. "The old adage is every grain of sand has nine cutting edges," explains Tassa. "People get little grains in their carpet, mush them around, and don't vacuum."

These gritty bits of dirt "literally cut the carpet fibers. As it gets shorter and spreads out, each carpet tuft blossoms like a flower." This effect makes carpet look worn, gray, and dingy. Vacuuming, wiping shoes on welcome mats, and removing your shoes while at home will keep your carpet looking beautiful, longer.

## Peel off stuck-on wallpaper with ease

Gently score wallpaper with a scoring tool from your local hardware store, and apply one of these easy, homemade stripping solutions. Let the solution soak in for 10 minutes, then scrape off wallpaper with a plastic scraper. Apply more as needed.

| Ingredient | Directions |
| --- | --- |
| fabric softener | Mix one part fabric softener to two parts very hot water. Spray or roll on with a paint roller. |
| vinegar | Spray on equal parts white vinegar and hot water. Thoroughly wet wallpaper and begin scraping once it bubbles up. |
| liquid dish soap | Add 1-ounce dishwashing liquid that contains a degreaser to two cups hot water. Spray on wallpaper. |

**Fluff up dented carpet.** Steam the area with an upholstery steamer, or lay a towel over the dent and use a steam iron. Let steam penetrate the carpet fibers, then fluff them with a fork as if you're fluffing steamed rice. Keep steaming and fluffing until the dent is gone.

**Silence squeaky floors for good.** These four tricks work like magic to quiet almost any creaky floor.

+ Generously dust talcum powder between the noisy boards of hardwood floors. Lay down a towel and step on it to work the powder into nooks and crannies. If you still hear a squeak, apply more talcum powder.

+ Work liquid wax between the boards of waxed wood floors. Don't try this on floors with a varnish or urethane coating.

+ Squeeze a long bead of construction adhesive along the crack where the floor boards meet the joists, for floors where the joists are exposed. Do this from the underside of the floor.

+ Buy an inexpensive tool called the Squeeeeek No More to fix carpeted floors when you can't get to the joists. It guides a screw through the carpet into the underlying floor joist. Then it snaps off the screw head so it's totally hidden by carpet. Check your local hardware store for this product or buy it online at *www.squeaknomore.com*.

**Find the right mattress for your body.** Few things are more crucial to a good night's rest than a good mattress, but finding one isn't always easy. Roger Herr, a physical therapist and member of the American Physical Therapy Association, offers these guidelines to help.

+ Higher bed sets may be easier to climb in and out of, says Herr. Look for an 18 inch-tall mattress set, and invest in a higher bed frame, if necessary.

+ "Are you thin and bony or larger-framed and longer?" Herr says your body type helps determine what kind of mattress you need. A heavier, bigger-boned person may need the extra support of a firm mattress with large inner coils. Petite or bony people do better with a less-firm mattress and higher coil density (smaller, tightly packed coils).

+ Foam mattresses constantly adapt to your body, making them a good match for frail, thin, bony people or those in a lot of pain, says Herr. Keep in mind, the denser the foam, the firmer the mattress.

+ Avoid foam mattresses if you sweat a lot or get hot easily. The rubber retains body heat, a boon for some sleepers but a bust for those who like the breathability of traditional coil mattresses. Plus, the foam stops sweat from evaporating.

Remember — don't buy a sales pitch. Buy a mattress that feels good. "People get caught up in the bells and whistles, and they just don't listen to their bodies," warns Herr. "No book, no Web site, no salesperson can know how your body sleeps best."

## Don't let the bedbugs bite

Bedbugs are coming back with a vengeance. These blood-suckers hide in mattresses and upholstered furniture, emerging at night to feed on their hosts. They're hard to stamp out once inside your home, so your best bet is to prevent infestation in the first place. One new product, the AllerZip by Protect-A-Bed, may help. It encases the mattress or box spring and zips closed around it, sealing out bedbugs, dust mites, and allergens. Call Protect-A-Bed at 866-297-8836 to find a dealer near you or visit *www.protectabed.com.*

**Pick the perfect pillow.** Pillows help keep your neck and spine in alignment by supporting the curve in your neck. Roger Herr, a Seattle-based physical therapist, recommends picking a pillow based on your favorite sleeping position.

+ Back sleepers "want a medium-supportive pillow," says Herr. Too low, and it won't support the curve in your neck. Too high, and it kinks your neck, making breathing difficult.

+ Side sleepers do best with "a thicker, medium to firm pillow to support the head and keep it in line with your neck and back." The broader your shoulders, the more pillow support you'll need as a side sleeper.

+ Belly sleepers, on the other hand, need a "low-profile, thinner pillow with less density and support."

Herr also recommends people with bony knees, arthritis in their legs, or who have had hip surgery sleep with a pillow between their knees to improve their spinal alignment. But in the end, he says, "You know what feels good to your body. You're fine as long as you sleep well and your pillow helps you wake up feeling better than when you went to sleep."

**Smooth sliding for stuck drawers.** Remove the drawer and lightly sand the runners with a scrap of sandpaper. Clean off the dust. Then rub a candle or bar of soap along the runners to "grease" them up. For a fresh smell, use scented soap or candles. For metal drawers, spray a little lubricating oil on a soft cloth and wipe along the runners.

**Free fixes for damaged furniture.** Before you kick those beat-up pieces to the curb, try some tender, loving care to give them new life.

+ Turn the tables. Fix a wobbly table just by turning it. Find the wobbly leg and the one diagonally across from it. Lift the table so that both legs are the same distance off the ground. Begin turning the table around its center until both legs are resting on the floor and — voila! — no more wobble. This trick only works on square or rectangular tables.

+ Flatten the warp. Wood tends to warp over time, and varnishing it only on one side speeds up the process. To flatten out table tops and other warped boards, remove the bent piece. Evenly wet the side that curves inward with a damp cloth. Wipe excess water from the other side. Clamp each end of the board or table between two long, flat pieces of wood. Tighten the clamp until the board is flat, and let dry a day or two. Repeat if necessary.

+ Mend upholstery. You can sew coarse fabric, but leather and finely woven upholstery will show the stitching. Go thread-free by cutting a piece of canvas or other thin fabric in a shape slightly larger than the tear. Peel back the torn upholstery and use a spoon handle to slide the scrap under the torn edges. Paint latex fabric glue on the meeting faces. Lay the torn flap flat and hold in place with upholsterer's pins until the glue sets.

**Keep tiny tools from getting lost.** Put Styrofoam scraps to use holding small tools like drill bits and mini-screwdrivers. Lay the foam flat and push the tool headfirst deep into the foam. Label each resulting hole with a magic marker so you know which tool or bit fits into which hole, and return them to the same spot when you finish using them.

**Slick tricks loosen stuck light bulbs.** Apply a thin film of petroleum jelly, WD-40, or another lubricant to the threads of a light bulb before you screw it in. It will go in easier and come out without a fight the next time you replace it.

If a glass bulb separates from its base when you unscrew it, try this handy tip. Turn off the power to the light fixture, peel a potato, shove the raw spud into the metal base, and turn. The potato will grip the bulb's threads from the inside as you unscrew.

## How to deal with asbestos

Many older homes contain asbestos, a mineral fiber once used in roofing and siding shingles, insulation, joint compound, vinyl floor tiles, pipe insulation, and other building materials. Unfortunately, inhaling these fibers can lead to lung disease, including cancer.

Household materials made with asbestos are most likely safe as long as they're in good condition and not crumbling. If they are damaged, however, don't try to remove them yourself. Call a certified asbestos professional to repair or remove them.

**Homemade clip keeps pencil handy.** Stop searching for your pencil in the middle of a project. Take one leg out of a regular clothespin, and insert your pencil instead. Then clip the gadget to your pocket or cuff.

**Keep tools in tiptop shape.** Prevent rust from forming by cleaning off dirt after each use, then wiping the metal parts with WD-40 before storing them. Keep them in a low-humidity environment to lengthen their working life. To remove light rust from tools, spray with WD-40, then scrub with a heavy-duty sponge. Wipe off the rust and excess lubricant before storing. Don't try to sand off rust. Sandpaper scratches the metal.

**Suck up oil spills.** Spring into action by spreading a thick layer of Kitty Litter on a fresh driveway or garage oil spill. Let sit for 12 hours, then sweep away. Next, sprinkle on a layer of dry cement and let sit for a day or two before sweeping off. The cement powder will suck up what's left of the oil and even bleach the driveway back to its original color. For old oil spots, spread on a little paint thinner before covering it in kitty litter.

**Quick patch for concrete cracks.** Hairline cracks in concrete can quickly widen. Fortunately, patching concrete is a cinch. Start by brushing out the loose concrete and dirt with a wire brush. For the patch to stick, the crack must be half an inch deep and wider at the bottom than the top. To deepen or widen it, insert a chisel into the crack and use a hammer to undercut the concrete and widen the base of the crack. Brush out the debris again and flush out with a hose. Sweep away standing water just before pouring in the concrete patch.

# Straight talk on home safety

**Critical tips for surviving a break-in.** Keep your cool, and follow this expert advice to increase your odds of surviving unharmed.

+ If someone breaks into your home while you are there, cooperate with them. They may relax and be less likely to hurt you.

+ If you think you hear someone breaking in at night, leave — if possible — without alerting them. Then call the police from a neighbor's house or your cell phone.

+ If you awake to someone in your bedroom, pretend you are still asleep. Wait until the coast is clear, then call the police.

+ Don't look an intruder in the eye. Intruders are more likely to hurt you if they think you can identify them to police.

+ Give a code word or phrase to a friend who calls you often. If they happen to call during a home invasion, you can tell the intruder your friend will be suspicious if you don't answer. Then you can alert your friend to dial 911 by saying the code word.

**Trip up thieves while on vacation.** Secure your automatic garage door when you leave on vacation by unplugging the auto-opener and bolting the door panels shut from the inside. Then leave the house through your front door.

**Best way to deter burglars.** Burglars decide how to break in based on which door looks easiest to open. Encourage burglars to look elsewhere by following this advice.

+ Choose exterior doors made of metal or solid hardwood at least 1-3/4 inches thick, with door frames made of equally tough material. Doors should hinge on the inside with hidden or nonremovable pins and close securely in their frames.

✦ Install extra-tough doors and locks leading from the garage into your home. Burglars love entering through garages because they have plenty of cover from prying eyes.

✦ Buy deadbolt locks with a bolt that extends at least 1 inch and hardened steel inserts to keep burglars from sawing through it.

✦ Make sure your deadbolt has a reinforced strike plate anchored in the door with extra-long screws for added security.

✦ Consider a double-cylinder deadbolt on doors that have glass within 40 inches of the lock. You need a key to unlock these from inside, too.

**Take steps before disaster strikes.** Plan two escape routes from every room, and let everyone in your home know where they are. Keep the routes easily accessible at all times and free of obstacles. Make sure you can find them by touch or feel, since you may not be able to see in the dark.

### Disaster help for people with disabilities

Handicapped people need special help reaching safety during natural catastrophes. If you're one of them, register with your local fire or police department or your local emergency management agency. Also, register with your electric company if you use critical medical equipment that relies on electricity.

**Store water safely for emergencies.** If you're on well water or untreated public water, add a small amount of household bleach before storing it as part of a disaster kit. Use only regular liquid bleach that contains 5.25 percent sodium hypochlorite, not scented or colorsafe bleach. Stir in 16 drops per gallon of water and let stand 30 minutes. Sniff the water carefully. You should smell a slight bleach odor. If not, stir in another 16 drops and let stand 15 minutes.

You don't need to add bleach to water before storing if the city treats your tap water with chlorine. Keep it in food-grade plastic bottles, such as 2-liter soda bottles, in a cool, dark place. Milk jugs don't seal tightly enough. Replace stored water every six months, whether it's self-treated or city treated.

**Key features make radio a lifesaver.** Crank radios couldn't be handier — just turn the handle on the side to charge it. No batteries or electrical outlet necessary. Look for one with AM, FM, and WX bands that accepts as many different power sources as possible — batteries, AC, and crank. You can listen to the government's weather broadcast from the National Oceanic and Atmospheric Administration using the WX band. Some crank radios even come with flashlights and a cell phone charger — other potential lifesavers.

**Protect your heart from lead contamination.** Lead threatens more than young children. In adults, even normal, or "safe," levels of lead in your blood boost your risk of dying, especially from heart attack and stroke. Worse, a whopping 38 percent of Americans fall within this deadly range.

The United States banned lead in many products years ago, but the danger persists as this country imports more of its goods. Here's your guide to the most common sources of home lead and how to protect yourself.

+ Watch for peeling paint. Homes built before 1978 likely house some lead-based paint. Experts say lead paint is only a problem when it begins to chip and flake, or during remodeling when sanding and scraping it release lead dust into the air. A lead abatement specialist can remove lead-based paint from your home.

+ Check canned goods. In 1995, the United States banned the use of lead solder in cans, but cans made in other countries may still contain it. Be on the lookout for wide can seams sealed with silver-gray solder. The lead can seep into the food inside, especially once the can is open. Acidic foods speed up this contamination process.

+ Don't buy these dishes. Lead-glazed dishes, ceramics, china, and pottery can leach lead into food, too, as can leaded crystal glassware. Most of these dishes are made in other countries.

+ Steer clear of cheap jewelry. Costume pieces for adults, as well as inexpensive, metal amulets, may contain lead.

+ Beware mini-blinds. Tests have found lead in nonglossy, vinyl mini-blinds made in other countries.

## Pass by home lead test kits

The U.S. Consumer Product Safety Commission (CPSC) warns not to trust the results of home lead test kits. In more than half of all cases the CPSC studied, these do-it-yourself kits showed a product contained no lead when, in fact, it did. Have an expert test paint and other items in your home, instead. Call the National Lead Information Center's Lead Hotline at 800–424–LEAD for help finding an expert.

**Cut air pollution inside your home.** "Indoor air pollutants are fairly commonplace in our homes," says Laura Spriggs, Communications Manager for GREENGUARD Environmental Institute. Furnishings, building materials, and cleaning products can all give off gases containing volatile organic compounds (VOCs). "Controlling VOCs at the source is the best way to limit exposure and protect the air you breathe."

One VOC, formaldehyde, is especially widespread in homes. It's often a part of laminated furniture, shelving, and wall coverings. "In many cases, the adhesives that bind wood together contain added urea formaldehyde." Start being choosy about the furniture you buy. "Avoid wood furniture products that contain higher levels of adhesives, such as particle board, medium density fiberboard (MDF), or plywood. Solid wood is a better option."

Unhealthy products give off fewer and fewer VOCs over time, so you don't necessarily need to kick old pieces to the curb. Instead, Spriggs suggests "taking steps to maintain and protect them using low-emitting materials." For instance, "formaldehyde also evaporates from paints, varnishes, and chemicals used for sealing and finishing walls," she warns. "When refurbishing or re-staining furniture use sealants and stains that are certified for low chemical content and emissions. And make sure to perform staining outdoors and with proper protective equipment, such as gloves and a respirator."

Whether you're stripping furniture, painting walls, or cleaning the kitchen, Spriggs says you can "avoid dangerous chemicals by selecting products that are certified for their levels of chemical emissions (GREENGUARD) and content (Green Seal)."

### Burn cleaner, healthier candles

Paraffin candles made from petroleum products can give off harmful compounds, including formaldehyde, while burning. Soy candles, made from hydrogenated soybean oil, burned cleaner than paraffin and about as clean as beeswax in lab studies. So think about trading in your petroleum-based candles for natural soy or beeswax.

**Age-proof your home.** Your body ages, but your house stays the same — the same steep stairs, hard-to-reach cabinets, and slippery bathtubs. Or does it?

Rebecca Stahr, a 50+ Housing Specialist and founder of aging-in-place consultants LifeSpring Environs, believes otherwise. "There are literally hundreds of ways safety concerns can be reduced and alleviated" around the home. "Choices do exist. Doing nothing, that's the wrong choice." Check out these simple changes she suggests you can do yourself.

+ install grab bars in the shower, by the toilet, and in other wet areas

+ lay rubber strips in bath tubs and showers to prevent slipping

+ replace stationary shower heads with hand-held, flexible ones

+ put a telephone in the bathroom, one you can reach from the floor

+ install roll-out drawers in cabinets for easier access to pots, pans, and other kitchenware

+ pull up rugs, hide electrical cords, and get rid of low-seated furniture

+ use more and higher-wattage light bulbs

+ paint surfaces in contrasting colors so you can see them better

## Natural remedy soothes sunburns

Soak a washcloth in milk or cream, seal it in a plastic bag, and cool in your refrigerator or freezer. Remove the washcloth and apply to the sunburn for quick relief.

**Douse the risk of house fire.** Space heaters are the main cause of house fires from December through February, according to the safety gurus at Underwriters Laboratories, Inc. (UL). In hopes of slashing that statistic, UL offers these basic tips on space heater safety.

+ Buy a heater with the UL seal, an automatic shut-off feature, and a guard around the heating element.

+ Check electric space heaters for frayed wires or insulation before you plug them in. Turn the unit off immediately if it seems to be overheating.

+ Keep anything that could catch fire at least 3 feet away from the heater.

+ Turn off liquid-fueled space heaters and let them cool completely before refueling them. Only use the type of fuel recommended by the manufacturer. Other kinds may burn too hot and start a fire.

# Trouble-free appliances

**Know when to fix and when to replace.** Don't wait until your refrigerator breaks to think about buying a new one. Every type of appliance has a life expectancy. If you have an appliance nearing the end of its golden years that needs repairs, consider replacing it rather than fixing it. Old appliances gobble up much more energy than newer, more efficient models. In fact, a new Energy Star-qualified appliance can pay for itself in utility savings alone within a few years.

**Unbeatable way to get the best deal.** Decide which brand and model you want before you go shopping. Call at least four appliance stores for a price on the exact model you've chosen, then ask if that's the lowest price they can give you.

The Internet may beat in-store deals. Two sites, *www.shopzilla.com* and *www.shopping.com*, will compare prices from many stores for you. Simply search these Web sites for the brand and model you've chosen.

**Shop the scratch-and-dent specials.** Major retailers, like Sears, have appliance outlet centers that sell damaged, almost-new appliances for a fraction of the cost of new ones. Rental stores, like Rent-A-Center, also sell scratch-and-dents. "If somebody has a washer delivered, and one side got banged up a little, that drops the price considerably and doesn't affect the washer," points out Rick Doble, editor of *Savvy Discounts* newsletter. "If you put the washer in the basement, who's even going to notice?"

Just make sure it still has all its original pieces, including an owner's manual, remote controls, hoses, cables, and any hardware you need to install it. These items are sold as-is, and most stores won't accept returns.

**4 questions to ask yourself before buying extended warranties.** They may sound like a good idea, and even a good deal. But before you splurge at the register, ask yourself these four questions to help you decide if it's worthwhile.

+ How long does the manufacturer's warranty last? Most products come with a free manufacturer's warranty that lasts from 90 days to a year. Some last longer, making an extended one a waste of money.

+ Will your credit card company extend the manufacturer's warranty? Some do by up to one year, making an extended warranty unnecessary. Call your credit card company and ask if they offer this perk. If so, you may want to buy the appliance with your credit card instead of paying cash. Just be sure to pay off your credit card bill when it arrives.

+ How much does the appliance cost? Spending $30 on a warranty for a $100 microwave doesn't make much sense. Chances are slim you'll need the coverage, and when the microwave does finally break, it will be almost as cheap to buy a new one. Don't buy a warranty that costs more than 20 percent of the product's price.

+ Does the extended warranty cover routine service? Some resemble service contracts where you can have a technician perform routine maintenance free for the life of the warranty. In that case, buying the extra coverage might be worth it, since regular maintenance can extend the life of your appliances.

### How long will your appliances last?

A new study conducted by the National Association of Home Builders sheds some light on how long you can expect your appliances to last. "Of the major appliances in a home, gas ranges have the longest life expectancy at 15 years. Dryers and refrigerators last about 13 years," say study authors. Smaller appliances, on the other hand, tend to have a shorter life. Most trash compactors last only six years, dishwashers and microwaves nine. Curious about linoleum, faucets, or granite countertops? You can read the whole report at *www.nahb.org.*

**Say goodbye to baked-on spills.** Want to hear an amazingly simple way to remove grime from a blackened oven? Sprinkle a thick layer of salt on spills while they're still hot and soft — and keep cooking. The food will burn to a crisp you can easily scrape off once the oven cools.

**Homemade cleaner wipes out microwave messes.** Clean your microwave easily with this fragrant, natural cleaner. Simply stir together water, lemon juice, lemon slices, and grated lemon peel in a microwaveable container. Then heat on high for several minutes, letting the concoction boil. Once it cools, wipe down the inside of your microwave with a damp cloth. Substitute white vinegar if you don't have lemons on hand.

**3 cheap ways to freshen your garbage disposal.** Don't waste money on fancy cleaners. You have all the power you need in your pantry.

+ Pour half a cup of baking soda down the disposal, followed by a cup of vinegar. Cover all the drains and let the mixture fizzle out. Remove the covers and rinse the disposal drain with hot water.

+ Cut a lemon, lime, or orange in half and drop it down the disposal with a handful of baking soda. Turn on the disposal and flush with cold water. If you skip the baking soda, flush with hot water instead.

+ Fill an ice cube tray with white vinegar. Freeze solid, then drop the vinegar ice cubes down your disposal and grind up under cold water.

If these clever cleaners don't get rid of the smell, try cleaning the rubber opening to your disposal with liquid dish soap and a toothbrush. Be sure to get the underside, too.

**6 secrets to spotless dishes.** Tired of wasting time and money rewashing dishes? Make your dishwasher do it right the first time with these can't-miss tips.

✦ Prerinse dishes only if your dishwasher is more than five years old. Newer machines can handle the grime.

✦ Lean glasses against the tines in the rack. Placing them over the tines can leave water marks.

✦ Load some silverware handle up and others handle down to keep the pieces from nesting.

✦ Resist the temptation to load plates and bowls facing in the same direction. Reverse direction when you reach the middle of the rack. Plates and bowls should face the center.

✦ Buy only as much detergent as you can use in two months, and throw it out if it gets old. The older the detergent, the worse it cleans. Store it in a cool, dry pantry — not under your kitchen sink.

✦ Load flat cookie sheets, pans, and platters along the sides, but not along the front. They could block the detergent tray from opening. Move your silverware basket to the middle of the rack if you need more side space.

## Give your body an energy boost with a fruit smoothie

In a blender, whip three-fourths cup of oats until powdery, then add a cup of low-fat milk, one peeled and chunked ripe banana, and a cup of low-fat flavored yogurt and blend until smooth. Or get exotic with strawberries, blueberries, mangoes, even kiwi. Add a teaspoon of honey for more natural sweetness.

**Whip blender into tip-top shape.** Cleaning your blender has never been easier. Add a few drops of dish soap and warm water, then blend on high speed for 15 to 30 seconds. Next, dump the water and take apart the blender. Buff stainless steel blades with glass cleaner. Gently clean plastic parts with baking soda and warm water. Rinse everything and let air dry. To keep your blender blades sharp, don't wash them in your dishwasher.

**Banish bad refrigerator odors fast.** Put a handful of charcoal briquets in a bowl in the refrigerator, and throw them away once the odors disappear. Just don't use briquets that have been treated with lighter fluid.

**7 steps to lengthen your refrigerator's life.** With just a little tender loving care, you can keep your refrigerator running smoothly and looking new.

+ Wash the rubber gaskets that seal the doors with warm water and mild detergent, never bleach. Rinse and let dry. You can use a toothbrush to get down in the grooves of the gasket.

+ Clean the compressor coils about once a month. You'll find the coils on the bottom of most newer models, while older models may have them on the back.

+ Remove and wash the defrost pan once a month. Look for it behind the toe plate or on the back of the refrigerator.

+ Clean behind and beneath the refrigerator regularly, and check to make sure it's level after you roll it back in place.

+ Wash the outside with a sponge and warm, soapy water, then rinse and dry.

+ Wash shelves and drawers by hand in warm, soapy water. Never use petroleum-based cleaners on any plastic parts.

+ Wax the outside of the refrigerator once a year with a good appliance wax or paste auto wax to guard against rust.

## 4 refrigerator problems you can fix in a jiffy.

Some problems you don't have to live with, like these common refrigerator complaints.

+ If the temperature in your refrigerator is too warm, clean the condenser coil and make sure air can circulate around it freely.

+ A noisy refrigerator could point to loose parts, but a simpler solution is to check that it's level and the floor beneath structurally sound.

+ Does your refrigerator sweat on the inside? See if the doors are aligned and if the gaskets seal properly when you close the doors.

+ If your refrigerator sweats on the outside, see if the energy-saver switch is turned "on."

### Give broken appliances a new lease on life

Finding a part for broken appliances is as easy as a Texas two-step. Start by checking the owner's manual. Manufacturers often include a parts list, order form, and phone number to order directly from them. Other stores specialize in selling replacement parts.

• RepairClinic.com at 800-269-2609 or online at www.repairclinic.com

• Partstore.com at 866-925-PART or www.partstore.com

• AppliancePartsPros.com at 877-477-7278 or www.appliancepartspros.com

**#1 strategy to maintain your washer.** Have you ever given your washing machine a birthday party? With this one ingenious, life-extending tip, you'll want to buy it candles and a cake. Periodically check the rubber fill hoses that carry water to your washer. Look for bulges, cracks, blisters, and bare spots, and consider replacing them every five years — their average life span.

**The most important do-it-yourself dryer maintenance.** Lint traps only catch some lint. The rest gets blown out through the tube that vents your dryer to the outside. Replace your white plastic vent tube with a rigid metal tube. Building codes no longer allow vinyl, or plastic, tubing because it can easily catch fire. Flexible foil or plastic vent tubes and those with ridges are much more likely to trap lint, creating another fire hazard. Rigid metal tubing is least likely to trap lint and can help contain a fire should one start.

No matter what type of vent tube you use, be sure to clean it regularly. Clean the entire length of the pipe, and make sure you remove the lint completely. Long, flexible brushes designed just for this chore make it a snap. Vacuum up lint behind and underneath the dryer, too, and clean the lint screen every time you use your dryer.

**10-second solution for faster drying.** Dryer sheets and lint can leave a residue on your dryer's moisture sensor that keeps it from telling when your clothes are dry. If you like to use your dryer's moisture-sensing cycle but your clothes still come out damp, try wiping the sensors with a cotton swab dipped in rubbing alcohol. Moisture sensors look like two thin, flat strips of metal inside the dryer's drum, usually located at the front or back where they will come into direct contact with clothing.

**Breathe easier in winter.** Humidifiers can be lifesavers for people with chapped lips, dry sinuses, or asthma attacks in winter. But a dirty humidifier does more harm than good. Change the water every day by emptying the tanks, drying all surfaces inside and out, and refilling with fresh — preferably distilled or demineralized — water.

Clean the unit every three days by descaling it with household vinegar then disinfecting it with bleach. Check the manufacturer's instructions. Generally, you'll pour 8 ounces of white vinegar into the base and let it soak for 30 minutes, swishing occasionally. With a toothbrush or other soft-bristled brush, gently scrub the interior to remove scale and mineral buildup. Dump out the vinegar, rinse the machine thoroughly, and allow to air dry.

Once dry, pour a mixture of one teaspoon bleach to one gallon of water into the base and let sit for another 30 minutes, swirling occasionally. Rinse out your humidifier with plenty of fresh water until you can no longer smell the bleach. Replace the filter once a year or as often as the manufacturer recommends — more often if it's dirty.

## Look to the sea for dry-eye relief

Artificial tears, especially those with preservatives, can disrupt the natural tears your body makes. Instead of reaching for medicine to wet your eyes, reach for your fork instead. Eating plenty of healthy omega-3 fats, particularly from tuna and other fatty fish, reduced women's risk of dry-eye syndrome up to 68 percent in one study. Omega-3, well-known for dampening inflammation, may also stimulate your eyes to produce more tears.

**Breathe easier without an air purifier.** An air purifier alone won't improve indoor air quality, according to a report from the American Lung Association (ALA). Some do-it-yourself steps are more effective. For instance, putting an impermeable cover over your mattress will do more to calm your dust mite allergy than running an air purifier by your bedside.

Still, people with severe allergies and asthma symptoms who have tried everything else may benefit from using an air purifier. Small, appliance-size models won't do much good, warns the ALA. Research shows only high-efficiency purifiers with larger filters trap enough particles to be useful. Look for one that produces less than 0.05 ppm of ozone, since ozone can be hazardous to your health.

If you do invest in a portable air purifier, place it near a specific source of pollution where it can trap the most particles. Keep all windows and doors in the room closed as much as possible, and leave enough room around the machine for air to circulate.

**Quick "once-over" keeps AC ticking.** Clean the air filters in room air conditioners every 225 to 360 hours of operation. That's roughly every one to two months for a unit that runs six hours daily. While you're at it, vacuum the discharge grill to keep it dust free. Twice a year, clean the evaporator and condenser coils, the evaporator and base pans, drain system, and the outside of the unit. Proper maintenance will help your AC last longer and cost less to run.

# High-tech-tips

**Secrets for opening difficult plastic packages.** Stop struggling. When you're buying an item you won't need to return, simply ask the salesperson or cashier to open it for you. If you'd rather do it yourself, nifty tools can make cutting things open a cinch. The Pyranna is specially designed to cut through hard plastic, or clamshell, packaging. You can buy it online at *www.pyranna.com*. OpenX, available at Walgreens, Target, Office Depot, Costco, and online at *www.myopenx.com*, makes short work of clamshell packs, as well as shipping envelopes, boxes, pill bottles, and other containers.

Then again, you don't need a fancy tool. You just need sturdy, sharp scissors and a little patience. With clamshell packages, start at the bottom or where the plastic is thinnest and cut carefully all the way around the edge.

## 6 strategies for saving money on electronics.

According to *Consumer Reports*, the key to getting the best deal on electronics lies in these six tips.

+ Avoid buying expensive extended warranties.

+ Be skeptical about low, low prices. The item may be refurbished, not new.

+ Haggle for a better deal. Bargaining can work just as well for electronics as it does for other items.

+ Check for online coupons to major electronics stores at coupon clearinghouses like *www.couponcabin.com*.

+ Use shopping bots, also known as Web robots, such as BizRate, DealTime, MySimon, Shopping.com, and Yahoo to compare prices when buying online.

✦ Buy it with your credit card. You'll get more protection if something goes wrong with the product. Some, like American Express, even extend the manufacturer's warranty for free.

**Wise way to protect valuables against theft.** Ask your local police department about borrowing their engraving pen, and use it to engrave your state and driver's license number on your valuable electronics, including televisions, cameras, computers, and cell phones. This will help authorities find you if the item gets stolen and later found. You can also include the words, "in case of loss" along with your phone number or e-mail address. Don't engrave your Social Security number or anything an identity thief could use.

**Make great home movies.** Making your own home movies sounds like fun, but get your first video camera and you may feel in over your head. Enter expert Joyce Bertolami, professional videographer with more than 25 years' experience and co-owner of the Joy of Video in Woburn, Mass. She offers these tips for capturing your best home-movie memories.

✦ Know what your camera can and can't do. According to Bertolami, understanding your equipment is an "overriding factor in producing a video worth watching." Learn how to use features like the manual controls to get consistently good shots in every situation.

✦ Invest in a camera stabilizer. "I have seen many videos shot free-hand that were painful to watch because of the erratic camera movement," she says. "Despite the fact that today's video cameras possess excellent image stabilization systems, the tripod remains a valuable tool."

Unfortunately, tripods are not very mobile. If you want to move around more but still get stable shots, invest in a monopod. "In our business of wedding and event video production, monopods allow us to be very creative while providing excellent camera stability."

✦ Learn to work with light. "Proper lighting is essential in producing a good video." For most home movies, the available light is enough. Bertolami's advice — "practice with your camera in different lighting conditions" to learn what works best and how to adjust your camera settings.

That said, leave heirloom events to the pros. "Creating a home movie can be an enjoyable hobby, but for the most important special events in your life — like weddings, anniversaries, and graduations — you should hire a videographer to create a professional production."

**Save money with hidden rebates.** Ask about available rebates any time you buy an electronic. Stores that offer instant rebates can save you the hassle of remembering to mail them. Manufacturers and retailers often offer rebates on their Web sites, too. Once you know what brand you want, go online before you buy and look for special offers and incentives. Can't find any on the manufacturer's site? Try typing the manufacturer's name, like Toshiba, and the word "rebate" into Google's search window at *www.google.com*. Rebate Web sites can also steer you toward bargains. Try *www.refundsweepers.com*, *www.rebateplace.com*, and *www.couponmountain.com*.

### *Maximize your rebate dollars*

Keep copies of receipts and rebate forms in a special file folder after you mail the originals so you remember to follow up if your rebate doesn't arrive on time.

**How to clean 3 common gadgets.** Getting the gunk off your favorite gadgets is not rocket science, say the experts at *Popular Mechanics*. You simply need a soft cloth, rubbing alcohol, and a light touch.

✦ Clean and kill germs on your cell phone by mixing together three parts water and two parts rubbing alcohol. Dip a cotton swab or soft cloth and gently wipe dirty areas.

+ The same water-alcohol mixture takes the smudges off video camera lenses. Run a special cleaning cassette through the video camera to clean tape heads and improve image quality.

+ To clean dust and ink buildup in inkjet printers, open the printer panel that covers the printer cartridges. With a dry cloth or small foam paintbrush, gently wipe away dust and dry ink. Close the printer and run the printer cleaning program to clear out the ink nozzle.

**4 ways to keep CDs and DVDs in tip-top shape.** The National Institute of Standards and Technology offers this advice on protecting and cleaning your CDs and DVDs.

+ Stand them upright in their cases like books. Don't store them flat for years at a time.

+ Keep discs in a cool, dry, dark place, away from heat, humidity, and direct sunlight.

+ Clean smudges and spills off discs by wiping them with a soft cotton cloth dipped in rubbing alcohol or special CD/DVD cleaning detergent. Never wipe in a circle around the disc. Always wipe from the center to the outer edge.

+ Don't write on discs with anything sharply pointed, like a pen, pencil, or fine-tipped marker.

If your disc starts skipping, check it for scratches. You can try filling the scratch with a furniture wax, like Pledge, or buffing it out with a very mild abrasive, like white — not gel — toothpaste. You can also buy repair kits.

**Plug in to protect against power surges.** A good surge protector will sacrifice itself during power surges and lightning strikes, saving your computer, television, printer, and other expensive electronics. However, not all surge protectors pass muster. Look for one with these features.

+ meets UL 1449 testing standards

+ protects all three electrical lines entering the outlet — Line to Ground (L-G), Line to Neutral (L-N), and Neutral to Ground (N-G)

+ has a clamping voltage rating no higher than 330V on all three lines

+ contains telephone and coax cable jacks, since power surges can travel up these lines, too

+ will turn off the power to plugged-in gadgets once it can no longer buffer against electrical surges

+ features a light that tells you whether the outlet it's plugged into is properly grounded

+ comes with a warranty that promises to replace any plugged-in devices if they are damaged by a power surge

### Easy way to recycle rechargeable batteries

You can safely throw away alkaline, lithium, lithium ion, nickel metal hydride, and zinc air batteries in the trash. Instead of throwing them away, however, consider recycling them. Recycling rechargeable batteries is as simple as a trip to the store. The battery industry banded together to create the non-profit Rechargeable Battery Recycling Corporation, which has recycling locations at Sears, RadioShack, The Home Depot, Lowe's, and many other stores. Call 877-2-RECYCLE to find a drop-off location near you.

They accept all types of rechargeable batteries — nickel cadmium (Ni-Cd), nickel metal hydride (NiMH), lithium ion (Li-ion), and small sealed lead (Pb). That includes regular rechargeables, as well as batteries in cordless power tools, cell phones, cordless home phones, laptop computers, and digital cameras, to name a few. Call2Recycle does not recycle alkaline or other nonrechargeable batteries, but your local waste management center might, so check with them.

**Best battery for electronics.** Batteries aren't just batteries any more. Now they're alkaline, lithium, or nickel metal hydride. The list goes on. These fancy formulations are more than a marketing gimmick. They make different batteries work better in different devices.

For instance, digital cameras need a lot of juice. They go through alkaline batteries quickly. Lithium and nickel oxyhydroxide batteries last longer in energy-hungry gadgets, making them a better choice for digital cameras. Rechargeable batteries are also good for powering thirsty devices. Alkaline batteries, on the other hand, are right for low-voltage devices, such as TV remotes and CD players.

**Give new life to old electronics.** Electronics and computers can contain lead, mercury, and other toxic chemicals that make them dangerous to toss in your trash when they break. Be smart — and safe — by recycling them.

- ✦ Go online. Visit E-Cycling Central's Web site *www.eiae.org* and click on your state to see a list of the electronics recycling locations near you.

- ✦ Swap it out. Best Buy will haul away old TVs when you have a new one delivered. The computer-maker Dell recycles all Dell products free. Buy a new Dell, and they'll recycle your old computer, no matter what brand, for free, too. Hewlett-Packard charges a small fee but gives you coupons in return. Apple offers a discount on new iPods when you recycle your broken one, with a similar deal on Mac computers.

- ✦ Drop it off. Bring used electronics, except televisions, to Staples for recycling. They charge $10 for large items to help cover shipping. Both Best Buy and Circuit City hold occasional recycling events in their parking lots where they accept old TVs.

- ✦ Give to a good cause. Charities like the National Cristina Foundation or Share the Technology give old electronics a second life and score you a valuable tax deduction. Visit *www.cristina.org* and *sharetechnology.org* to learn how to donate computers, digital cameras, printers, software, and more.

# Easy money management

**Save money with a better credit score.** Your credit score is a number between 300 and 850 that serves as a snapshot of your credit report at any given time. A higher credit score can help you save money in several ways.

+ Insurers may charge you a lower premium on your car or home-owners insurance.

+ Lenders may charge you lower interest rates, fewer fees, or smaller fees — and grant you higher credit limits.

+ Private mortgage insurance (PMI) may cost less.

+ Landlords will be more likely to accept your rent application. They may also charge you less for deposits and fees.

Here are some helpful tips for boosting your score to take advantage of these benefits.

+ Check your credit report to spot any major discrepancies that could be hurting your score. Correcting these errors can save you a lot of money.

+ Pay your bills on time.

+ Pay down your balances, especially on credit cards.

+ Take out credit only when you really need it. Too many open lines of credit can be a red flag.

**Boost your credit score quickly.** Missing a car payment can drop your credit score nearly 100 points, according to a recent study by Experian, one of the major credit reporting agencies. But Experian offers good news, too. Approximately 30 percent of American consumers raised their credit score 50 points in just six months. It's not as hard as it sounds because credit scorers give extra weight to what you've done most recently. Just make sure you don't miss any payments, and start paying down your balances. Your credit score could be quite a bit higher in less than a year.

## How to get your credit report

It's essential to know what's in your credit report. Here's how to contact each of the three major credit reporting agencies to order a copy:

- Equifax *www.equifax.com*
  800-685-1111
- Experian *www.experian.com*
  888-397-3742
- TransUnion *www.transunion.com*
  877-322-8228

**Avoid credit counseling rip-offs.** If you're struggling to pay your bills, credit counselors can help — but don't fall for the many scams out there. Beware of those that promise they can erase your poor credit history. They'll charge you hefty fees but won't be able to magically make any black marks disappear. A legitimate credit counseling service gets paid by creditors, so it should not charge you a fee. It shows you how to budget your money and may work with creditors to restructure lower payments, but it can't just eliminate your debt. To find a legitimate credit counselor, visit the National Foundation for Credit Counseling at *www.nfcc.org* or call 800-388-2227.

**Prepare for a long life by balancing investments.**
These days, people are living longer than ever. But they may not be adjusting their financial strategy to match. "I think at 50, a lot of financial

advisers advise their clients to take a short-term view on investing as opposed to a longer-term view on investing," says John Dillard, a certified public accountant from Duluth, Ga.

But Dillard warns about being too "squeamish" about investing. If you live to be 50, life expectancy tables indicate you may live another 30 to 35 years. If you're married, you also need to add your spouse's life expectancy. It could be decades before you'll need to use the money you're investing.

"I think in all of our investing and all of our issues, we need to keep things in balance," Dillard says. "I don't think we can save unduly for retirement, but I don't think we can live unduly for today. I think we have to look at things in balance and be realistic about our cash flow, our needs as well as our desires."

One of those desires may be starting a second career after you retire. "With the downsizing going on in corporate America, as well as people just desiring to do something different with the last 10 to 25 years of their working life, it's a great time to evaluate setting up a new business," Dillard says.

He recommends working with a business broker and taking advantage of the free resources provided by the Small Business Development Center, which has locations throughout the United States geared toward helping small business owners. Find one near you at *www.sbdcnet.org.* You can also get more financial tips from Dillard at *www.hiscpa.com.*

**Guard against loss with low-risk stocks.** You're considering a new stock or mutual fund, but experts say there's a recession coming. One way to protect yourself from losses is to look at the beta, which measures how a stock reacts to changes in the overall market. A higher beta comes with a higher risk. To play it safe in a down market, choose stocks with a low beta, such as 1 or less. Utility stocks are often a good option. Find a stock's beta on brokerage research reports and investment Web sites. Look for mutual fund betas on investment company's Web sites or in their prospectuses.

117

**4 questions to ask your financial planner.** Your financial planner will ask you a lot of questions about your spending habits, savings, and investments. Make sure to ask him a few questions, as well. In his book *Everybody Wants Your Money*, author David W. Latko suggests asking your prospective financial planner questions like these.

+ How long have you been a series 7-registered broker? Look for a minimum of five years.

+ What other types of financial licenses do you hold? Ask him to explain any cryptic letters attached to his name.

+ Are you covered by Securities Investor Protection Corporation (SIPC)? If the firm holding your securities goes broke, this insurance will pay you up to $500,000 per account.

+ How many clients have closed or moved their accounts with you over the past three years? You'll want to choose someone with five or fewer clients lost over any three-year period.

**Get financial advice for free.** Financial planners can help you manage your money — but they usually keep a nice chunk of it for themselves. Fortunately, you can find free financial advice if you know where to look.

Keep an eye open for free financial planning sessions in your area. These can be held at libraries, community halls, civic centers, or hotel ballrooms. It's a great opportunity to ask experts questions — without any high-pressure sales pitches. You can also get solid financial advice for free from the following organizations.

+ The Financial Planning Association at *www.fpanet.org*.

+ The Certified Financial Planner Board of Standards at *www.cfp.net*.

+ The National Association of Personal Financial Advisors at *www.napfa.org*.

✦ The National Endowment for Financial Education at
   *www.nefe.org*.

**Divide and conquer to outsmart your bank.** One-stop
banking may seem convenient, but you can make the most of your money
by splitting your checking account, savings account, and credit cards
among different banks. For example, use a low-minimum, no-fee checking
account to pay your bills. Link that account to a high-yield online savings
or money market account so your money earns interest between payments. Then find a credit card that gives cash back or other rewards, and
use that for your expenses. Just stay away from cards with annual fees.

**Get more cash back from your credit card.** When it
comes to rewards, bigger isn't always better. That 5-percent cash-back
credit card may actually pay you less than a 1-percent card. That's
because the fine print often hides restrictions that limit the amount of
cash you receive. Before you go for a flashy cash-back number, read the
card agreement to make sure you're really getting your money's worth.

---

### Find answers to your banking questions

Your bank teller may be friendly, but she may not know the
answers to all your questions. If you bank at a national bank,
go to *www.helpwithmybank.gov*, a Web site created by the
Office of the Comptroller of the Currency, a division of the
U.S. Department of the Treasury. This site has answers to
many frequently asked questions about credit cards, interest
rates, cashing checks, late payments, forgery and fraud,
mortgages, and more. You can even download forms from
the site to file complaints about your bank.

**Take advantage of banking perks for seniors.** Shop around for better bank deals. Some banks are courting people age 55 — or even 50 — and older with special banking deals and perks. These bonuses may include no monthly service fees, no minimum balance requirements, free or discounted checks, and free safe-deposit boxes and traveler's checks. Check the Web sites of the banks in your area, or ask a bank official about deals for seniors.

**Break free of debit card holds.** Your next rental car, hotel stay, or fill-up at a gas station may be costlier than you realize. If you use a debit card for these transactions, businesses may put a "hold" on your checking account for a much higher amount. That's to make sure you have enough money in your account to pay them.

Eventually, they'll charge you the correct amount and unfreeze the extra funds. But these holds can last up to three days, which means you could have less available money in your account than you realize — and you could end up bouncing checks or getting hit with overdraft fees. Play it smart and use a credit card for these transactions instead. Even if you plan to pay for your hotel stay with a debit card, give them a credit card when you check in.

## Quick and easy way to lose money

Stay away from the new no-swipe credit or debit cards. It may be convenient to simply wave your card in front of a little reader instead of swiping it, but research shows you're likely to spend 20 percent more at the checkout than if you use cash.

**5 simple ways to cut everyday costs.** Little things you take for granted can wreak havoc on your budget. Luckily, a few simple suggestions can make a big difference when it comes to cutting costs.

✦ Use your computer. Instead of making long-distance phone calls, send e-mails to your friends and family. Comparison shop for everything on the Web. You may be surprised how often you can beat in-store deals, especially if you can get free shipping and no sales tax.

✦ Trim the fat in your food budget. Pack your lunch instead of eating out. You can find new and exciting recipes on the Internet.

✦ Bundle up. If you have Internet, phone, and cable service, move all three accounts to one provider. You could save $20 or more per month.

✦ Shop smarter. By clipping coupons, you can save anywhere from 15 to 50 percent on groceries. Check out your supermarket's circular online. Do your Christmas shopping year-round so you can get items on sale.

✦ Entertain yourself. Find ways to spend less on entertainment. Rent movies instead of going to the theater, borrow books from the library instead of buying them, and go on a picnic instead of to a restaurant.

**Curb impulse buying at the supermarket.** They're rarely on your shopping list, but impulse purchases like magazines, gum, candy, and soda can pad your grocery bill at the last minute. Show some self-restraint by using the self-checkout lanes. A recent study found that only 12 percent of people who scan and bag their own groceries bought any items displayed at the checkout, compared to 17 percent in express lanes and 20 percent in regular lanes.

**Smart way to avoid late fees.** Being late with a credit card payment can cost you a fee of $30 or more. It can also have a negative impact on your credit score. Here's a trick to guarantee you never pay a late fee again.

Just set up a recurring payment through your bank's electronic bill pay service. Pick an amount that meets the largest minimum payment you would normally expect and does not exceed your monthly spending on that card. For instance, if you use a credit card for most of your charges and routinely charge more than $75 in a month, set up a recurring payment of $15 each month to the credit card company. If you routinely charge $200 a month, make it $35. When you get your bill, you can change the payment to match the correct amount for that month. But if you forget, your automatic payment will still meet the minimum payment required — and you'll avoid the late fee.

You can also set up automatic withdrawals from your checking account for other recurring expenses, such as utility bills or insurance premiums. You'll save on postage and won't have to worry about late fees. Just make sure to record those payments in your checkbook.

**Expect inconvenient fees from convenience checks.** Perhaps you've been tempted to use those "convenience checks" your credit card company sends through the mail. Before you do, read the fine print. Not only do these checks come with high minimum fees, they also charge the cash advance interest rate, which is much higher than the rate for purchases. It could reach 20 percent or more. Worse yet, interest starts accruing on the transaction date, so you don't get a grace period. Your best bet is to destroy these checks so no one else can use them.

**Drive away with a better car loan.** The Government Accountability Office recently found that credit union car loans boast average rates one to two percentage points lower than those of similar-size banks. You're also more likely to qualify for those low rates.

**Take action to avoid foreclosure.** Having trouble making your mortgage payments? Ignoring the problem won't make it go away. Contact your mortgage lender as soon as possible. Most mortgage companies are willing to work with customers they believe are acting in good faith and who call them early in the process. The longer you wait, the fewer options you have. Make it clear that you're serious about keeping your home and will take steps, such as reducing your spending or taking a second job. You can also sell assets, like a second car, to raise cash. Your lender may agree to reduce or suspend payments for a certain period of time or even restructure your mortgage to make it more manageable.

You should also seek free advice from a reputable housing counselor approved by the Department of Housing and Urban Development (HUD). Whatever you do, don't fall for scams where people promise to pay off your mortgage in return for signing the deed over to them. You'll end up still owing the money — and losing your house.

**7 ways to stop check fraud.** Con artists can use your own checks against you. They can wipe out your account or even steal your identity. Guard against check fraud by following these suggestions from the National Check Fraud Center.

+ Store your checks, deposit slips, bank statements, and canceled checks in a secure and locked location.

+ Destroy old canceled checks, deposit tickets, ATM receipts, and account statements unless you need them for tax purposes.

+ Make sure all your checks are there when you receive your check order. Alert your bank immediately if any are missing or if you don't receive your order.

+ See if any checks are missing if your home has been burglarized. Thieves may take only one or two checks from the middle or back of the checkbook.

+ Do not include your Social Security number or phone number on your check.

✦ Never make a check payable to cash. If it gets lost or stolen, anyone can cash it.

✦ Do not endorse a check until you are about to cash or deposit it.

**Get the scoop on overpayment scams.** More is not always better, as you will discover if you become the victim of an overpayment scam. Here's how it works. Scammers find you through online auctions or newspaper classified ads when you're selling something. You receive a check for more than the price of the item with instructions to wire the extra money elsewhere, perhaps to a third party. Excuses for this vary, but none of them are legitimate. Neither is the check, even if it clears initially.

By the time your bank realizes it's a fake, you're out the money you've wired and the item you provided. You are also responsible for the entire amount of the phony check and could even face criminal charges. Report any suspicious checks immediately. Better yet, never do business with anyone who insists you wire excess money elsewhere.

# Savvy shopper's survival guide

**Never ever pay full price for anything.** Find the lowest price on thousands of products. Here's the scoop.

✦ If you're savvy about computers and their prices and you know exactly what you want, browse the computer manufacturer's Web site. You may find specials that offer a lower price than retail stores.

✦ Get expensive jewelry for up to 50 percent off at a pawn shop. Bring an appraiser with you if you're worried about the value of an item.

✦ Buy children's clothes at consignment and resale stores. You may even find clothes for yourself.

✦ Shop at flea markets and thrift malls for collectibles, nostalgic goods, antiques, and much more.

And don't forget the Web. You can find deals on all sorts of items at *www.overstock.com*. Or try *www.shopping.com* and *www.shopzilla.com*. These price comparison sites not only give you plenty of options but also display the TRUSTe seal next to reputable merchants.

**"Stack" and save big at drugstores.** Go beyond coupons and you'll get incredible bargains at top drugstore chains like Rite Aid, CVS, and Walgreens. Shopping expert Stephanie Nelson discovered how anyone can do this — including you.

First, make a list of items you use frequently. Stock up on them anytime you can pay less than full price. Next, combine — or stack — the following strategies to get the lowest price possible. You might even get some items for free.

✦ Ask about the store credit program. This gives you cash back on your purchases, either at the register or during your next store visit.

✦ Don't just cut coupons from the newspaper. Cut them from store circulars, too. Nab circulars in the store or at the store's Web site. When you find a coupon for the same item in both the newspaper and the circular, you can use both coupons at the same time for extra savings.

✦ If coupons never appear in the store circular, join the store's loyalty card program to get coupon-like discounts.

✦ Keep an eye out for mail-in or in-store rebates.

✦ Ask about senior discounts

Remember, the trick to sizable savings is to stack several tactics together at the cash register. For example, you might combine coupons with store credit. If you'd like help, Stephanie Nelson's Web site lists the current opportunities for the best drugstore deals. Visit *www.couponmom.com* to learn more and save.

**Retailers' secret you need to know.** You can haggle with department stores, big box discounters, electronics sellers, and more. The trick is to know when to haggle, how to do it, and who to haggle with.

✦ People who sell big ticket goods often have a monthly sales quota to meet. Try haggling late in the month when they're more interested in making a deal.

✦ Haggle when the store isn't busy. Store employees are more likely to negotiate when they're not swamped with customers.

✦ Do research on prices before you haggle, so you'll know how deep a discount you can reasonably hope for. You can even bring in the store's newspaper ad, a competitor's ad, or a Web printout to help support your request.

✦ Be patient, considerate, and as nice as possible — even if you have to wait for approval or jump through a few hoops to get your deal. The savings will be worth it.

✦ Pick the right person to negotiate with. Only approach experienced and knowledgeable employees. The store may not allow newer hires to negotiate.

Once you get the hang of retail haggling, you may also find success at jewelry stores, banks, and hotels. You can even try to wring better rates out of your cable company, phone company, credit card company, and internet provider. Just call, tell them you're thinking about switching, and ask if you can get a better rate. You may be surprised at your own success.

## Cut costs of antiques, furnishings, and appliances.
Just because you won't pay full price doesn't mean you can only furnish your home with worn-out yard sale goods. Find attractive antiques, appliances, china, furniture, and accessories at estate sales and moving sales. Although these sales may be advertised right next to yard and garage sales, estate and moving sales usually feature items that are of higher quality and in better condition than their yard sale cousins. Just be sure you have a way to transport your new furniture or appliances home from these marvelous sales.

## Don't let your rebate check get away. "Rebates are becoming a rip-off," warns Harvey Rosenfield of the nonprofit Foundation for Taxpayer and Consumer Rights. "Requesting a rebate is like filling out a federal tax return, except that the private companies have an incentive to keep the customer's money." But you can still win at the rebate game and here's how.

✦ Don't throw out anything that comes with a product — including the packaging — until after you've mailed in the rebate. You may need all sorts of odd things from the packaging and package contents just to fulfill the rebate instructions.

✦ Read all the instructions and fine print carefully to make sure you qualify for the rebate. If possible, do so before you purchase the product.

✦ Make copies of everything including store receipts, bar codes, forms, product containers, serial numbers, and even the mailing envelope. Mail the originals with the rebate form.

✦ Answer every single question on the form including those that don't apply to you. If the form asks for a cell phone number and you don't have a cell phone, write "no cell phone" in the space.

✦ Never use your post office box as an address on the rebate form.

✦ Send in every last item the rebate form demands and staple it all together.

✦ Mail in your rebate right away. You may have as little as seven days before the rebate deadline.

✦ Use certified mail and ask for a receipt.

✦ Mark your calendar so you'll know when to call and start asking questions if your rebate check doesn't arrive on time.

**Stop getting burned by restocking fees.** Watch out. The next time you return an item to a store, you may not get all your money back unless the item is defective. That's because some retailers now charge a "restocking fee" for up to 50 percent of the original price. Take these steps to avoid such fees.

✦ Restocking fees may be more likely for items like appliances, computers, and electronics. Before you buy these products, look for a copy of the store's restocking fee policy. The store is required to display it where you can easily see it.

✦ Check for restocking fee notices at online vendor sites. Online vendors may be even more likely to charge these fees than regular stores.

✦ Notice which online and local shops don't charge restocking fees. Shop at these stores for happier returns.

✦ Always be ready to provide your receipt when returning an item.

## The savvy shopper's calendar of steals and deals

Everyone knows about annual closeouts for cars and Christmas decorations, but that's just the tip of the iceberg. You may be surprised at other pre-season bargains, end-of-season sales, semi-annual closeouts, and scheduled deals at the same times every year. Use this calendar to help you catch the fabulous sales you've been missing.

| Month | Sales |
|---|---|
| January | appliances, clothing, household linens, furniture, toys, luggage, and sleepwear |
| February | computers, air conditioners, exercise equipment, mattresses, lamps, furniture, and jewelry |
| March | winter coats, air conditioners, clothes washers and dryers, gardening and landscaping equipment and supplies, and winter sports equipment |
| April | paint, outdoor furniture, and gardening and landscaping equipment and supplies |
| May | televisions, jewelry, handbags, luggage, and outdoor furniture |
| June | summer sporting goods, sportswear, men's and boys' clothes, and sleepwear |
| July | swimsuits, electronics, major appliances, summer clothes, and air conditioners |
| August | summer clothes, coats, furniture, and shoes |
| September | children's clothing, air conditioners, paint, camping goods, fans, patio and pool items, and tires. |
| October | children's clothes, coats, fall and winter clothes, major appliances, school supplies, bicycles, fishing gear, and women's coats |
| November | boys clothes, blankets, water heaters, ranges, household linens, used cars, and jewelry |
| December | microwave ovens, jewelry, and Christmas merchandise |

✦ If you buy from a store that charges restocking fees, be careful when opening the item. Avoid damaging the packaging and don't throw anything away. Marred packaging or missing items can trigger a restocking fee.

**Best time to return merchandise.** Avoid weekend afternoons. Instead, show up during the first hour after the store opens. This is a great way to skip the long lines and endless waits. What's more, experienced employees usually prefer to work the day shift, so there's less chance you'll be the victim of a trainee's mistake.

**Know when buying more saves less.** Don't let a warehouse club leach money from your wallet. Get the savings your membership pays for with these clever ideas.

✦ Dare to compare. Some warehouse club items are true bargains while others cost you extra. To tell the winners from the losers, compare the per-unit price to what you'll pay at other stores. Limit your warehouse store shopping list to items that are cheaper there than anywhere else.

✦ Do the math. Your bargains should save you more than your membership fee costs. Use your per-unit price comparisons to determine how much you're saving and then estimate how much that savings will add up in a year. If it's less than your membership fee, don't renew your membership. But if your savings outweighs that fee, you're a savvy shopper who should keep your membership. Just remember to compare prices every year to make sure you're still saving money.

**Save more than before at warehouse clubs.** You'd love to take advantage of deals on perishables at your warehouse club, but you'll never finish that triple, extra-large package before the food spoils. So take a divide-and-conquer approach. Talk to friends about splitting the cost — and contents — of large packages of perishables.

You may even wish to shop as a group for the most convenience. Bring pencils, paper, and a small calculator to help divide costs accurately and keep track of how the items should be divided up. If you comparison shop on price, this clever method may boost your club savings well above the cost of your membership.

**Insider tips for a money-making garage sale.** Get ready to have your most successful yard sale ever. Expert Chris Heiska, the creator of *www.yardsalequeen.com*, tells you how.

✦ Advertise in the newspaper, but don't pass up opportunities for free ads. Put up flyers on local bulletin boards at the grocery store or your church. "Also, if you're computer savvy, go to *www.craigslist.org* and advertise your yard sale there for free," suggests Heiska.

✦ Put up signs but make sure they're large and easy to read. Check whether your neighborhood has restrictions on signs before you make them or buy them.

✦ Plan to hold your yard sale with a friend or other family members. "Having a yard sale is a lot of work so having friends or family with you helps the time go by faster, and it's a lot more fun and enjoyable," says Heiska. If you can't get enough family members or friends to help you, consider participating in a community based yard sale. For example, some churches may allow you to rent a table as part of their sale. "That way you're with a group of people. It's a safer environment than having people come to your house," Heiska explains.

✦ "When you have a yard sale, think of it as running a store for a day," Heiska advises. "You want to provide good customer service and be friendly."

"Be prepared and have a lot of small bills and change ahead of time. Keep your money secure. I always tell people to wear a fanny pack or carpenters apron," Heiska suggests "You've got to think of safety. Keep your money on you."

✦ Have newspapers ready to wrap breakables and provide bags to help take newly bought bargains home. Heiska even suggests having extra boxes handy so people can fill them with potential purchases.

---

### The World's Longest Yard Sale

Imagine more than 450 miles of yard sales to choose from. Starting the first Thursday in August every year, you'll find hundreds of four-day yard sales along U.S. Highway 127. They start as far north as the Ohio–Michigan border and range all the way down to Gadsden, Ala. Visit *www.127sale.com* to learn more.

---

**Save big with flea market do's and don'ts.** You can get terrific deals on plenty at flea markets if you just know how to shop. Remember these tips.

✦ Don't buy used items at a flea market if they'll quickly become outdated. For example, a year-old HD DVD player may be cheap, but finding DVDs to play in it may be tough. Be wary of buying used electronics, computers, and other items that may have short life spans.

✦ Arrive when the flea market opens to catch the best finds. Snatch up anything you really want because it may not be available in an hour.

✦ If you plan to shop for a specific product, check its retail price before shopping the flea market.

✦ Check back late in the day for the biggest bargains. Sellers are more likely to make a deal on items they don't want to tote home.

✦ Flea markets don't take returns so carefully check items for flaws before you buy.

✦ Flea market vendors almost never deliver. Don't buy anything large unless you can transport it home yourself.

✦ Be ready to pay in cash. Flea market vendors rarely take checks and credit cards.

✦ Bring a backpack, rolling backpack, or tote bag to hold your purchases.

**Get the best secondhand clothes.** You'd like to buy some snazzy secondhand clothes, but you've been sorely disappointed by the selection in the stores. Try shopping in early spring or early fall. Many people clean out their closets around that time, so that's when second-hand shops often have their widest array of styles, colors, and sizes.

**3 costly "bargains" to be wary of.** These often-touted bargains may not be bargains after all. Here's what you need to know.

✦ Online shopping. You can find fabulous discounts online, but sales tax and high shipping costs can wipe out your savings. Check shipping rates before you shop. If you're lucky, you may find information about sales tax on the same page. If not, check the "store locator" or "find a store" link to see if the seller has a location in your state. Expect to pay sales tax if they do. Sometimes you won't find this information because the site simply doesn't charge sales tax. But if you're surprised by a sales tax charge near the end of your purchase process, just shut down your browser before clicking the button that finalizes your order. Another vendor may sell the same product at a lower total cost.

✦ Television-shopping networks. Shipping can also wipe out the savings of "bargains" bought from television-shopping networks, especially if the product is big or heavy. Besides, if you're not careful, the ease of buying from these networks may tempt you to spend more than you planned.

✦ Outlet stores. These stores are supposedly filled with overstocks at discounted prices. But many retailers just send their lesser-quality clothing to the outlet stores. Instead of quality goods at bargain prices, you're just getting cheaper goods. Seek better bargains elsewhere.

**Get cash back when prices drop.** Oh, no! The item you bought from Amazon two weeks ago now sells for a lower price. Fortunately, if you contact Amazon, they'll credit your account for the difference. In fact, they'll do this anytime the price of an item drops shortly after you buy. But you don't have to constantly check prices. Just visit *www.refundplease.com* and type in basic information about your purchase.

When a price drop happens, they'll notify you right away. If you shop online at other stores, such as Target, Costco, or Circuit City, visit *www.priceprotectr.com* instead. This site performs a similar service but covers 14 other online merchants in addition to Amazon.

### Secret path to free shipping

You can't find what you're looking for in the store, but you don't want to pay the shipping fees from ordering online. No problem. Many retail stores offer in-store delivery if you buy from their Web site. That means your Web site order will be delivered to a location near you at no charge. Sears and Walmart are just two of the retailers who offer this convenient service. Check your favorite store's Web site to see if they offer this, too.

**How to find hidden discounts online.** Get even better prices from your favorite online stores. Before you shop a particular store, check *www.couponcabin.com*. You may find a coupon for free shipping or a product discount. Just find the name of the store and click the link. You'll either find a coupon code you can type in when you buy or link you can click on to take advantage of the coupon. If you don't find your store, don't give up hope. Instead, try *www.ecoupons.com*, *www.retailmenot.com*, or *www.keycodecoupons.com*.

# Trim your tax bill

**Save hundreds on your tax bill.** A 2002 study found that more than 1 million people could have paid $500 less in taxes if they had itemized instead of taking the standard deduction. In fact, you may be missing out on little-known deductions like these that you could be taking every day.

+ If your medical expenses are higher than 7.5 percent of your adjusted gross income, you can deduct the portion of your medical expenses that exceeds 7.5 percent. And you may be surprised at what sort of medical expenses are included. "A lot of people don't know that they can count their mileage when they go to pick up medicine or go to the doctor," says Mary Lynn Bolado, Area Manager at Jackson Hewitt Tax Service in Newnan, Ga.

  She recommends keeping a log book that includes the date, where you went, and the mileage — just in case the IRS asks questions. In addition to mileage, you can also take deductions for dental expenses, eye appointments, contacts, glasses, prescriptions, co-pays, insurance, and more. For details, see IRS Publication 502 available from *www.irs.gov*.

+ "Some people don't know that they can take their ad valorem tax on their car," Bolado says. Just be careful to only take the deduction for the ad valorem portion and not for all your car-related taxes.

+ Other deduction possibilities include deductions for state and local taxes, mortgage interest, real estate taxes, and charitable donations. Use tax software, your tax preparer, or visit *www.irs.gov* to determine which ones are most likely to apply to you.

## Get the charitable tax deductions you deserve.

People who don't know the new IRS rules for charitable deductions may lose those deductions on a technicality. Don't let this happen to you. Check out these valuable tips.

✦ Give to deductible charities. Your charitable contribution isn't tax deductible unless the IRS has already qualified your charity as a tax-deductible organization. The United Way, American Red Cross, and Salvation Army are just a few of the qualified organizations. To find out whether your charity qualifies, call the IRS toll-free at 877-829-5500 or visit *www.irs.gov* and search for Publication 78.

✦ The IRS now requires donations of used clothing and household items to be in "good used condition or better." This law even applies to furniture, appliances, towels, sheets, and electronics. Keep a list of what you donate and take pictures of each item in case you are required to prove the quality of its condition.

✦ Be careful with the value you claim for each household item or piece of clothing. To get an example of valid figures, try the free Salvation Army guide at *www.satruck.com/ValueGuide.aspx*. Some tax software can help you estimate the value of used items.

✦ You cannot deduct money donations unless you can show a written receipt from the charity, a canceled check, or a credit card statement. If you use a charity receipt, it must include the amount you contributed, the charity's name, and the date.

✦ If you donated a car, boat, or any item over $500, talk to your tax preparer. The IRS has special rules for donations of these items.

### Avoid backing your car into an audit

Donating your car to charity can trigger an audit — unless you follow the new tax deduction rules very closely. Visit *www.irs.gov* for a copy of IRS Publication 4303, "A Donor's Guide to Car Donations."

## Turn your hobby into a business for tax deductions.

In his book, *Lower Your Taxes Big Time*, CPA and attorney Sandy Botkin points out that the IRS doesn't just allow tax deductions for businesses that make profits. "If you don't have a profit three out of five years, you still could be deemed to be a business if you meet a bunch of facts and circumstances," he says. "This is what I call the 'facts and circumstances' test."

+ Develop yearly business plans showing five years of projected income and expenses, as well as yearly financial statements.

+ Be careful what you say. For example, if your business is network marketing and you say, "I'm only in this to buy my products at wholesale," the IRS may claim that as evidence your business isn't legitimate.

+ "Conduct your activity in a businesslike manner that is similar to other businesses," says Botkin. For example, have a separate bank account for your business.

+ Find out what similar profitable businesses are doing and do the same things.

+ Consider your prior business experience. If you're selling travel but have no travel experience, IRS may be suspicious.

+ Do advanced research into any business you consider going into and document that research, recommends Botkin. That helps establish business intent.

+ Devote time to the business regularly and frequently.

+ Review the history of income and losses and the measures you took to improve profits. The longer the losses, the more IRS is going to say you weren't in business to make a profit, Botkin warns. Take your financial statements to your accountant and see where you can cut back to improve your bottom line. "Hobbies don't do that," he says. "Business people — if they're not making money — they try and turn it around."

✦ Recognize that your income from other sources helps determine whether you're in a business or in a hobby. If you're a wealthy person with no farming background and you buy a farm that starts generating losses, the IRS may get suspicious.

✦ Be extra careful if your business relates to activities like antique collecting, stamp collecting, travel business, raising show horses, training and showing dogs, auto racing, or network marketing. The IRS is more likely to question these.

## Reduce your estate tax burden

You'd like your children to receive a nice inheritance, but you worry that estate taxes will steal a big chunk away from them. What's more, estate tax laws are expected to change soon, so you don't know how much of your money will be exempt from tax or how much your children stand to lose. Although financial and tax professionals offer products to help protect your estate, many of them are complex and confusing.

So take the simple approach. Give some of your money to your heirs now. You can give up to $12,000 to each child or grandchild annually without paying gift taxes. Offer the money as cash or use it to pay medical bills or tuition. It's all legal and IRS-approved. Even better, this simple technique ensures that more of your money goes to your heirs instead of the government.

**Survive a tax audit.** Don't panic if you receive notice that the IRS is auditing you. Prepare instead. Here's how to start.

✦ Visit *www.irs.gov* or call 800-829-3676 for a copy of IRS Publication 556, "Examination of Returns, Appeal Rights and Claims for Refund."

✦ If you used a tax preparer or accountant, notify her of the audit. Ask what she can do to limit the scope of the audit.

✦ Pay close attention to any audit-related deadlines and make sure you meet them.

✦ If you're having trouble getting or finding all the records you need, ask to postpone the audit.

✦ Get everything in writing. Take notes during all meetings or phone conversations with IRS personnel. Send a follow-up letter to the IRS that clearly covers what was said.

✦ If you must meet an IRS agent, arrive early. Answer any questions you are asked but limit your answers to "Yes," "No," and "I don't know" whenever possible. Avoid wearing status symbols, such as expensive jewelry and watches.

✦ Keep every document the IRS sends you.

**Stop overpaying property taxes.** You may be paying more property taxes than you owe. According to the National Taxpayers Union, up to 60 percent of taxable properties have been wrongly assessed for too high a value. Since your property taxes are based on that value, you could be overpaying your taxes right now.

To find out, visit your local assessor's office or Web site and request your home's assessment information. When you see it, inspect all the facts and numbers for mistakes. For example, check the accuracy of the square footage, the number of bedrooms, the number of bathrooms, the age of your home, and any descriptions of its features.

If you find errors, gather evidence, such as photos or a floor plan of your home, to prove that mistakes were made. Then contact your assessor's office and ask how to get the information and your future taxes corrected. You may be pleasantly surprised by how much money you can save.

## Watch out for audit-triggering tax mistakes

Tax laws change every year, so some tax laws may have changed since this book was published. To make sure these tips are still valid, talk to your tax professional, visit *www.irs.gov*, or call the IRS tax assistance line toll-free at 800-829-1040.

**Never pay property taxes again.** Seniors throughout nearly half the nation are eligible for this benefit, and you might be, too. Approximately 24 states and the District of Columbia offer property tax deferral programs to older adults. Homeowners who participate in these programs pay no property taxes until one of these happens.

✦ They sell their home.

✦ The homeowner dies.

✦ They permanently move out of the home for reasons other than health.

✦ The home gets a new owner.

Even if your property taxes skyrocket, you'll never be forced out of your home by a huge property tax bill. Just be aware that you must meet age, income, home ownership, and other requirements to qualify for this benefit. You should also know that interest may be charged on deferred property taxes. But don't worry. You won't be paying this interest every month. The combination of interest and owed taxes simply comes out of the proceeds when your home sells.

If you'd like to defer your property taxes, call your county tax assessor or state Department of Revenue. They can tell you whether a tax deferral program is available, how it works, and how to apply.

# Insurance know-how

**"Standard" insurance you don't really need.** Reliable insurance coverage is a godsend when you need it, but there are some policies you'll probably never use. Here are eight insurance plans experts say you don't need.

+ Life insurance if you're single. Life insurance provides money to live on if the breadwinner dies. If you have no dependents, your death won't create a financial hardship. The same is true if both spouses have ample individual income or an adequate retirement plan. Here's a rule of thumb — if your income won't be needed, don't buy life insurance.

+ Air travel insurance. If you die suddenly, it doesn't matter if it's from an airplane crash or a heart attack. Your family will still need financial support, so get regular life insurance with full coverage. Besides, most credit cards offer free coverage if you charge the tickets.

+ Mortgage-life insurance. These policies protect your lender if you die, since proceeds can only be used to pay off your loan. A better — and cheaper — choice is straight term insurance, which can be used for anything.

+ Private mortgage insurance. PMI is a special case because you usually have to get it when you buy a home with less than a 20-percent down payment. The cost of PMI simply becomes part of your loan payment. However, once you owe less than 80 percent of the value of your home, you can, and should, ask to cancel it.

+ Credit-life insurance. These are policies attached to bank and credit card loans. They pay off your loan if you die, or make your payment if you are sick, hurt, or out of work. It is very expensive insurance and sometimes you don't even know you're getting it. Buy term life insurance instead and forget about disability or unemployment policies because their payouts are so low.

✦ Life insurance on children. The death of a child is an emotional catastrophe, not an economic one. When no one depends on them financially, life insurance is little consolation.

✦ Cancer insurance. Unless you're pretty sure you're going to get hit by a particular disease, spend your money on more comprehensive health coverage. In any case, read the fine print closely. Many of these, and other one-disease policies, are cheap because they don't cover a lot.

✦ Rental car insurance. This really isn't even insurance. Rental car companies call it a "collision damage waiver." It's very expensive, and your own car insurance or your credit card company probably covers you. Check to be sure, especially if you'll be renting a car in a foreign country.

**Nab the best long-term care.** If you need to spend time in a nursing home or assisted living facility, you'll need help paying for it. Just one year in a nursing home can easily cost more than $50,000. Don't get caught off guard. You may be surprised to find out that Medicare doesn't cover long-term care, including help with activities of daily living like dressing, bathing, or using the bathroom. That's where long-term care insurance comes in. When considering long-term care plans, America's Health Insurance Plans — an association of nearly 1,300 insurers — says to keep these questions in mind.

✦ What services will be covered? Options include nursing home care, home health care, assisted living facility, adult daycare, alternate care, and respite care.

✦ How much does the policy pay per day for the above services?

✦ Does the policy have a maximum lifetime benefit? If so, what is it for each type of long-term care?

✦ Does the policy have a cap on length of coverage for each period of confinement?

✦ What is the waiting period before a pre-existing condition is covered?

✦ How many days must you wait before your benefits are available?

✦ Does the policy require assessments of daily living activities or cognitive impairments? Is a doctor's certification of need required? Does the policy require a hospital stay before coverage is allowed?

✦ Is the policy guaranteed renewable?

✦ Does it offer inflation adjustment?

Of course, you should also ask how much the policy costs. Prices vary and depend on your age, the level of benefits, and how long you are willing to wait until benefits begin. Most policies also come with a 30-day "free look" period. If it does not meet your needs, you can return the policy and get your money back during that time.

## List sheds light on nursing homes

Like Santa Claus, the Centers for Medicare & Medicaid Services are making a list — and you should check it twice before choosing a nursing home. This national list includes facilities that consistently provide poor quality of care. Called special focus facilities, these nursing homes receive twice the usual number of inspections. They are also fined until they either improve or are terminated from Medicare and Medicaid. You can find the list at *www.cms.hhs.gov/CertificationandComplianc/Downloads/SFFList.pdf*.

**Super ways to save on car insurance.** When shopping for a car, you probably consider price, gas mileage, and reliability. But you should also look into how much it will cost to insure. You'll pay much more for collision and comprehensive coverage for certain types of cars, such as those that cost a lot to repair or those that are frequently stolen. Among top-selling vehicles, the Dodge Ram pickup, the Chevy Silverado, and the Toyota Prius rank as the most expensive to insure, according to Insure.com. Several insurance Web sites have tools that let you compare insurance costs of various vehicles. Besides choosing a car that costs less to insure, here are some other ways to save on car insurance.

+ Shop around. Get at least three quotes, either online or by calling the company. Look for quality coverage, as well as a low price.

+ Maintain a good credit record. Insurers often take your credit score into account when pricing auto insurance.

+ Buy your homeowners and auto insurance from the same insurer. This can often result in big discounts. You may save 10 to 15 percent on your premiums.

+ Raise your deductible for collision and comprehensive coverage to at least $500 or drop it altogether for older cars. You will save hundreds of dollars on premiums.

+ Ask about discounts for being a safe driver or longtime customer, having anti-theft devices or safety features like air bags or anti-lock brakes, taking defensive driving courses, or driving a lower than average number of miles per year.

**Ask your agent about discounts.** You may qualify for auto insurance discounts. Just don't count on your insurance company to let you know about them. The Florida Office of Insurance Regulation recently called one insurance company on the carpet because it failed to notify customers with recently improved driving records that they could get insurance for lower premiums. Experts recommend that you periodically check with your auto insurance agent to learn whether you can qualify for new discounts or discounts that you haven't qualified for in the past.

## *Wise way to steer clear of skin cancer*

Driving comes with plenty of risks, including accidents, breakdowns, and flat tires. Now you can add skin cancer to the list. New research suggests frequent drivers are more likely to develop skin cancer on the left side in areas typically exposed to the sun from a driver's side window, such as the head, neck, arm, and hand.

That's because side and rear automobile windows are usually made of glass that filters the sun's cancer-causing UVB rays, but not the equally dangerous UVA rays. Windshield glass filters both. Tinting your windows or using UV filters on them can reduce the amount of UVA that gets through the glass. You can also shield yourself by applying sunscreen with an SPF of 15 or higher on sun-exposed areas and wearing protective clothing.

**Find the best deal on homeowners insurance.** Your home is your castle, but without a drawbridge and moat, you need protection from homeowners insurance. Here are some tips for saving money on this essential insurance.

✦ Shop around. Spend some time searching, and you should find a good deal. Ask friends, consult consumer guides, call insurance agents, or look online to compare prices and service. The National Association of Insurance Commissioners provides helpful information at *www.naic.org*. Narrow your choices down to three and get price quotes.

✦ Consider complaints. Don't just look at the price. Check each company's complaint records. A lower premium isn't worth much if you have to fight for each claim.

✦ Stay loyal. If you've kept your coverage with a company for several years, you may receive a special discount for being a long-term policyholder. You may save as much as 10 percent on your premium.

✦ Ask about other discounts. You may pay lower premiums if your home has safety features, like dead-bolt locks, smoke detectors, an alarm system, storm shutters, or fire-retardant roofing material. If you're at least 55 and retired, you may also qualify for a discount.

**Raise deductible to boost your coverage.** Small claims can lead to big headaches, including being dropped by your insurer. In her book, *The Insurance Maze*, Kimberly Lankford explains how to make the most of your homeowners insurance. Her advice — if you fear being dropped for submitting small claims, do not pay for coverage you won't use. Just by increasing your deductible from $250 to $1,000, you can lower your premium by as much as 25 percent. With the money you save on the premium, you can buy an extra $50,000 in total coverage. It's a simple way to save money and boost your coverage at the same time. Because many people are underinsured, the extra coverage could come in handy.

### Protect possessions with renters insurance

The average two-bedroom apartment contains more than $20,000 in possessions. Yet, a recent study found that two-thirds of Americans who rent do not have renters insurance. That's too bad because renters insurance covers not only your losses but also liability in case of injury or damage. You can get a policy that provides $20,000 of property coverage and $500,000 of liability coverage for about $20.

**Spend less for homeowners insurance.** Subtract the value of the land under your house when deciding how much homeowners insurance to buy. Otherwise, you'll pay more than you should. After a disaster, you may have to rebuild your house — but the land will still be there.

## Wave goodbye to bad flood insurance

When shopping for flood insurance, call your state insurance department to find out which companies in your area have cut back on coverage or steeply raised rates in the last few years. Once you eliminate those companies, you'll be far more likely to get reasonable rates and coverage you can count on.

**Tips to track down a missing policy.** One of your relatives has passed away, and you may be the beneficiary of his life insurance policy — but you can't find it. Try these suggestions from the American Council of Life Insurers.

+ Look through your relative's papers and address book for policies or the names of insurance companies or agents.

+ Check bank books and canceled checks for those made out to insurance companies.

+ Check the mail for a year. Premium bills and policy-status notices are usually sent annually.

+ Examine your relative's income tax returns for the past two years. Look for interest income from policies or expenses paid to life insurance companies.

+ Get in touch with your relative's former employers, who might know about a group life insurance policy.

+ Ask someone who may know about your relative's finances, such as his lawyer, banker, or accountant.

+ Try your state's unclaimed property office. Insurers who can't find the rightful owner turn the money over to the state after a few years.

+ Call every insurance agency licensed to do business in your state to see if your relative had a policy with them.

+ Contact the Medical Information Bureau, which offers a policy locator service for a $75 fee.

**Insider tip about variable life insurance.** Choose variable life insurance, and you may lose everything. With variable life insurance, the part of your premium that doesn't pay for insurance is invested in accounts similar to mutual funds. The higher your premium, the more money gets invested. This can boost your account when the stock market thrives. But if your account loses too much money, you may have to increase your premiums just to keep your policy from lapsing.

**Best ways to file claims.** Need advice about filing an insurance claim? United Policyholders, a nonprofit organization dedicated to educating the public on insurance issues and consumer rights, can help. Just go to *www.unitedpolicyholders.org* and click on "Claim Tips." Then read about the best ways to file claims for property damage — including fire, flood, earthquake, or mold — as well as tips for auto, health, long-term care, disability, and other types of insurance.

**3 tips for handling an insurance claim.** Insurers don't want to pay you. They'll look for any reason to deny or skimp on your claim. These steps can help you get the money you deserve.

+ Don't just accept an insurer's damage estimate. If your house is damaged, get bids from three qualified local contractors and have them spell out exactly what repairs are needed and what they will cost. If your insurer's estimate comes in much lower, you'll have solid evidence to argue for a higher payout.

✦ Stay civil. Losing your cool and yelling at an insurance representative will not help your case. In fact, it may hurt it. Get the name and telephone extension of anyone helping with your claim and work with them.

✦ Be persistent. If you're turned down for a higher payout or your claim is denied, appeal. Few policyholders challenge these decisions, but those who do are successful about half the time.

**Go up the ladder to speed up your claim.** Feel like your adjuster is stalling or delaying your claim? Write a letter to the claims manager who oversees the adjuster and ask him to speed things up. If that doesn't work, try the regional claims manager and, if necessary, the executive in charge of the claims department. You'll get results.

**Smart idea for pet owners.** You love your pet, but don't spend big bucks to insure it. Consumer Reports does not recommend pet insurance, especially for younger dogs and cats who are healthy. Just factor checkups into your budget instead. If you have a dog — particularly an older one — who is likely to need treatments from a vet, look for an accident-and-illness policy that costs less than $450. If you have a cat with similar needs, look for a policy that costs less than $360. If you can't find policies that cheap, set money aside for veterinary needs but keep it in an interest bearing account.

# Safeguarding your family's future

**Avoid common estate-planning blunders.** Build your family's future on shifting sands, and things probably won't go as you hope. Build it on the solid rock of good planning, and your wishes may come true. Here's a start.

+ Look to the future. "Put your goal out there first," says Edwin M. Saginar, an estate attorney in Alpharetta, Ga. "Then think in terms of — at what age do you want to retire, what would you like to do when you retire, and realistically what are you capable of earning?" This may seem backward, but knowing your final goal lets you see what you need to do to reach it.

+ Don't leave a large amount of money to a young person. "Instead of using it for something in the future, they'll buy a car" or otherwise splurge, says Saginar, "and not have the use of it later on." Instead, put the money into a testamentary trust and let the beneficiary have the profits every month or quarter. Saginar suggests you let the young person have half the principal at age 25 and the other half at 30 years of age.

+ It's best not to name a child as a joint owner of large assets. Doing so may seem like a good idea, since the assets can pass directly to that child when you die without going through probate. However, other children or beneficiaries are frozen out of the assets. Instead, name a child joint owner of a small account only.

**3 smart reasons to update your will.** Life is full of changes, and your will needs to keep up. It's worth spending several hundred dollars to update your will when these situations occur.

+ When there's a major change in your family, like marriage, divorce, or birth of a new grandchild.

✦ If your bank is the executor of your estate and the bank is bought out. Find out who your new executor is and be sure you trust him. Also, see if the fees to carry out your will have changed.

✦ If the federal estate-tax exemption changes, as it has done every few years lately. A higher exemption means you can leave more money to your heirs without paying taxes.

---

### Maintain control of your estate with an executor

A will ensures your property goes to the people you want to have it after you die. But that's not all. Without a will and a designated executor, the court will assign an administrator to distribute your property. Your estate must pay for an administrative bond to be sure the administrator doesn't run off with the funds. That's about $100 a year for each $100,000 in your estate, which means less money for your heirs.

---

**Save money with a DIY will.** You can spend about $40 on computer software that will let you create your own basic will. Or you can shell out $250 or more to have a lawyer handle the job. How do you know what you need?

If you're younger than 50 years old, in good health, and you don't expect to owe estate taxes when you die, you can probably get by with a simple will. But it may be worth your while to hire a lawyer if one of the following applies to you.

✦ You or your spouse expect to owe estate tax when you die.

✦ Your family is complex. You have a disabled child, adopted children, or children from a previous marriage.

✦ You have a business, partnership stakes, or real estate in more than one state.

151

✦ You wish to leave money to many beneficiaries and charities.

✦ You expect someone to contest your will, claiming fraud or your mental incompetence.

## Don't fall prey to common executor mistakes.

If a loved one dies and you're the executor of the estate, don't let your emotions rule. That could cost you money. Avoid these common errors.

✦ Don't think you're a trustee, or one who must watch over the estate in the long term. "The position of an executor is to essentially collect what is owed to the estate and then to disperse it after all bills are paid," says estate attorney Edwin M. Saginar of Alpharetta, Ga.

✦ Don't pay estate expenses out of your own pocket.

✦ Don't mingle your own money with estate money. Open a separate bank account for the estate, and use it to pay estate expenses.

✦ Don't forget to pay yourself. Executors are entitled to about 2 1/2 percent of money collected and dispersed, depending on the state.

✦ Don't rush to hire a lawyer to help. You may be able to settle a personal estate without one. Find out if your probate court prints instructions for an executor.

## Divide personal possessions and keep the peace.

Losing a parent or grandparent creates much sorrow. Don't make the pain worse by arguing over the inheritance. If your parent didn't give details about which child should have what, follow these guidelines to avoid bad feelings.

✦ Plan before you divide, and be sure everyone agrees. Perhaps each person will choose one item of similar value, then you'll all have another turn, and so on. Find a way to let everyone pick in a random order, then change the order for the next round.

✦ Select your favorites. Let each person write down the one belonging he most treasures. It may be nobody wants the same thing, so there won't be any arguments.

✦ Be fair. Don't sneak away with anything — even if you think it's rightfully yours.

### Share your living will to safeguard your wishes

Your living will lets family members know what kind of life-saving measures you want, like life support or other extreme care. But they won't know if they can't find the paper. Place a copy in several places, such as your wallet or a safe-deposit box. Even better, give a copy to your primary-care doctor so it's included in your medical records.

**Avoid probate — even without a will.** Let your heirs skip the hassle, time, and expense of probating your estate, yet still get what you want them to have. Probate, a state court process, decides who gets what of your individual property. It can take nine months or so to divvy up property through probate. A quicker option may be putting your assets into a living trust.

"A living trust not only avoids probate on your death, it also avoids probate if you should become incompetent while you're alive," says attorney Alexander Bove. "It maintains privacy and an orderly transition of your assets."

But a trust can have drawbacks. Privacy means the trustee, or person responsible for distributing property, can act beyond the watchful eyes of the court. Your other survivors may wonder if the process is fair and aboveboard. It can also be expensive, costing between $750 and $2,000 to set up.

## Estate planning for a blended family

A QTIP trust, or qualified terminable interest property trust, lets you provide for both your current spouse and your children from a previous marriage. You decide how much of your estate should go into a QTIP trust after your death. These assets give your spouse income for life. After your spouse dies, the principal goes to your children.

**Keep half your estate out of the government's hands.**
You'll need a simple AB trust, also called a bypass or credit shelter trust. It lets couples avoid some estate taxes. Here's how it works. Both spouses put their property into an AB trust. When one spouse, let's say the husband, dies, his half of the property goes to the beneficiary named in the trust, often grown children. A condition is that the wife can use that property for life, including any income it creates. When she dies, that part of the property goes directly to the children without being taxed in her estate. That means the wife's taxable estate is half of what it would have been if she had inherited directly from her husband.

**Don't get fleeced on a funeral.** You're a careful consumer when you buy other services, so why not in matters of death? Get smart and follow this advice.

+ Plan ahead, and write down what you want. Then your loved ones won't pay for expensive services you didn't really care about.

+ Shop around. The Funeral Rule is a federal law that requires funeral homes to give you a written list of all options, including prices. That way, you're not pressured into buying the most expensive items.

+ Get help from a memorial society or a group like the Funeral Consumers Alliance. They can give you information about inexpensive options in your area.

**The top 4 funeral myths.** Suffering the death of a family member or friend is painful enough without also being taken to the cleaners by a funeral home. Here are some things you need to know.

*Myth:* Embalming is required by law.

*Fact:* Embalming is not legally required or even needed if the body will be buried or cremated soon after death. Skip embalming and you can save hundreds of dollars. But some funeral homes require embalming before a viewing or visitation.

*Myth:* Some expensive caskets can protect the body.

*Fact:* "Nothing you buy, whether a vault or a casket, will preserve the body for an indefinite period of time," says Josh Slocum of the nonprofit Funeral Consumers Alliance.

*Myth:* An average funeral costs around $6,000.

*Fact:* That's the cost of a "traditional" or "full-service" funeral, including a casket and vault. Slocum says that price includes needless expenses. "Fewer and fewer people are choosing to do that," he says.

*Myth:* Prepaying your funeral takes the burden off your loved ones.

*Fact:* Family members will still grieve. And many prepaid plans are scams, with little state regulation of where your money goes and how you can make changes.

# Retirement: living the good life

**3 ways to make your money last a lifetime.** You've pinched pennies for years so you can enjoy your retirement. Don't overspend now. Financial experts Jonathan and David Murray, authors of *Two for the Money: The Sensible Plan for Making it All Work*, offer ideas on cutting costs while still living comfortably.

+ Ditch your life insurance if you're not working.

+ Move to a cheaper house, possibly in a less-expensive town, and drive a cheaper car.

+ Consider an annuity or reverse mortgage for guaranteed income. For more information about reverse mortgages, see page 319.

**Come out ahead — even if you don't start there.** You don't have to start out wealthy to end up quite comfortable. That's the message in Richard Paul Evans' book *The Five Lessons a Millionaire Taught Me about Life and Wealth*. He lists a few small changes that can make a big difference in building wealth, like taking responsibility for your money and sticking to a budget. Here's how Evans suggests you help your nest egg grow faster:

+ Save at least 10 percent of your salary and 90 to 100 percent of extra income.

+ If you get a raise, put the money into savings.

+ Use an automatic-withdrawal plan so you don't have to think about saving.

+ After you finish paying off a debt, put that extra money straight into savings.

## Get a quick glimpse of your net worth

This simple worksheet will tell you where you stand when it comes to money for retirement.

### Current assets

| | |
|---|---|
| Cash and savings accounts | + |
| Stocks and bonds | + |
| Retirement plans (IRA, 401(k), other) | + |
| Home, market value | + |
| Cars, market value | + |
| Other real estate | + |
| Life insurance (cash value) | + |
| Personal property | + |
| Business interests (partnerships) | + |
| Other | + |
| Total assets | = |

### Current liabilities

| | |
|---|---|
| Mortgage (principal only) | + |
| Car loan | + |
| Credit cards | + |
| Home improvement loan | + |
| Taxes owed | + |
| Other loans | + |
| Total liabilities | = |

Total assets – Total liabilities = Net worth

**4 steps to take at age 59-1/2.** Age 59-1/2 is a milestone when it comes to getting ready for retirement. You're old enough to spend the money you've been saving in retirement accounts, yet young enough to leave it alone if you need to. Be sure you're financially ready for the rest of your life by taking these steps.

+ Call former employers and ask if you have retirement benefits coming. They'll need your new contact information and beneficiary names.

+ Ask your current employer to help you figure out what pension, company stock, or insurance you'll get when you retire.

+ Check your standing with the Social Security Administration. Benefits are based on your highest 35 years of salary. If you worked fewer than 35 years, you may want to keep your nose to the grindstone a bit longer.

+ Get a financial adviser to help you determine how much money you'll need for a comfortable retirement. This will probably involve deciding how much you can expect from pensions and other sources as well as what taxes you'll have to pay. You can get started by using an online help tool, such as the retirement calculator at *www.bankrate.com.*

**Key factors in planning for retirement.** Most experts say you'll need between 70 and 100 percent of your current salary after you retire. The exact figure depends on several factors, including:

+ Inflation, which can vary between 3 and 14 percent.

+ Health care costs. Most retirees don't get insurance from their former employers, and long-term care can get expensive if you need it.

+ Taxes. You'll probably be in a lower tax bracket, depending on what type investments you own.

+ Spending. If you can cut the costs of daily living, you'll be on the right track.

+ Longevity. Of course, planning for 10 years of retirement is a different beast than planning for 30 years. Some experts say you should make financial plans as if you'll live to 95 years.

## Control your money and calm your fears

Money worries that keep you awake at night can damage more than just your beauty rest. Chronic stress can also raise your blood pressure, put you at risk for heart disease, and lower your immunity so you're more prone to illness.

The more control you have, the less you'll worry about money. You can control how much debt you take on, whether you stick to your budget, and how much money you save for a rainy day. Your body and your pocketbook will thank you.

**Top 3 retirement-planning blunders.** Smooth sailing into retirement requires a carefully drawn map. But some people get blown off course because they make these common mistakes about the best years of their lives.

+ Thinking Social Security, Medicare, and Medicaid will cover your financial and medical needs. "Many people assume they'll be able to work forever," says Cheri Meyer, program director of the American Savings Education Council (ASEC). "The truth is that many people retire earlier than planned due to negative circumstances, including company downsizing and medical problems." Being forced out of work before you're fully eligible for Social Security and Medicare could jeopardize your retirement. Some experts caution people younger than age 50 not to pin their hopes on Social Security income.

+ Saving without a plan. You won't know if you're on track for the kind of retirement you have in mind if you don't figure out how much money you'll need. Meyer suggests using a tool like the ASEC Ballpark Estimate calculator, available online at *www.choosetosave.org.*

+ Letting your debts get the best of you. Carrying balances on high-interest credit cards costs you interest each month. But that's not all, Meyer cautions. "Debt also affects your credit rating and can keep you from getting a good job or buying a home."

## Collect on your investments — without paying taxes.

Now may be the time to invest in a Roth IRA (Individual Retirement Account). You can contribute about the same amount as you can to a traditional IRA, but you can take out Roth earnings tax-free. That's because the money was already taxed as income when you earned it. If you're still in a fairly high tax bracket after you retire, that can make a big difference. You can take the money out when you wish rather than having to start by age 70-1/2, as with some other retirement accounts.

Another benefit of a Roth IRA is that — as long as you're still working, even part-time — you can contribute to it at any age. Still hard at work for a company that offers a 401(k) plan? Look into a new option, the Roth 401(k). It offers many of the same benefits of a Roth IRA.

### Rescue your benefits from the tax man

You don't have to pay federal income tax on your Social Security retirement benefits if your total income is less than the base amount ($25,000 for singles and $32,000 for married couples filing jointly in 2007). But if your income is more, you'll owe Uncle Sam. Make things easy and have taxes withheld from your Social Security benefit checks next year. You'll need to submit IRS Form W-4V, Voluntary Withholding Request, to the Social Security Administration.

## Safeguard retirement from common 401(k) blunders.

Ray Dunlap, a certified financial planner and president of Dunlap Wealth Strategies in Peachtree City, Ga., warns against putting your retirement in jeopardy through these common errors.

+ Not contributing enough to get your company's 401(k) match. "That's free money," Dunlap says. Claim it by making at least the matched contribution.

+ Leaving your money in a 401(k) plan after you retire. If you don't roll the money into an Individual Retirement Account (IRA), you won't get the many investment choices available with an IRA. Besides that, your heirs won't have the tax advantage of a "stretch IRA," which can spread out taxes over decades.

+ Expecting good financial advice from the 401(k) plan administrators at your company. They can explain your options, but they're legally banned from giving advice on how to divvy up your investment money.

+ Picking an investment based only on fees. "If everything else were equal, then fees would be extremely important," says Dunlap. "But the reality is that not everything is equal. So you have to look at net investment performance," or how much a fund grows when fees are included.

Dunlap encourages people to get help from a financial adviser when it's time to take money from a company 401(k) plan. "This is one of those enormous life decisions that probably shouldn't be done alone," he warns.

## What to do before taking money from a 401(k). When it's time to take money from your 401(k) plan, do it carefully.

"A lump sum from a 401(k) is great if you do it in the form of a rollover into an IRA," Dunlap says. "There's no tax consequence and the money continues to accumulate with a tax deferral. But if you cash out and take the money with a check payable to you personally, it's very expensive."

That's because if you take the money directly, you'll have to pay at least 20 percent in taxes right off the bat — more if it's a really big chunk of money. Instead, open an IRA even before it's time to take your 401(k) money. You can open the account with no money in it, get your account number, and have the information you need to do a rollover.

## Here's a great reason to keep working

Don't fret if you don't have the money set aside to retire early. Staying on the job may be the best thing for your health. A study of Shell Oil Company retirees found those who left work at age 55 were more likely to die within 10 years after they stopped working than those who continued working until they were 60 or 65. And you won't be alone. A recent survey found 24 percent of seniors are continuing to work after they officially retire.

**Stock up to outsmart inflation.** Retirees often think they should sell their stocks and other high-risk investments to buy safer choices like bonds. But going too safe may not be safe at all.

Ask your financial adviser about putting a quarter of your portfolio in stocks to keep inflation from eating away at your nest egg. Since stocks and bonds often move in opposite directions — when one goes up in value, the other goes down — owning both gives you a safety net against rough times.

**Keep your nest egg growing a little longer.** Two big boys of investments have figured out how to let your money grow while you take out funds on a regular schedule. Fidelity's Income Replacement funds will send you monthly payouts, gradually using up your investment over time. That's a big change from a traditional mutual fund, which grows until a certain maturity date. Similarly, Vanguard's Managed Payout funds give you monthly payouts without dipping into your principal.

**Annuities provide peace of mind — at a price.** With guaranteed pensions going the way of the dodo, people are looking for surefire ways to finance retirement. An annuity, or investment in which you make an initial large payment to an insurance company in return for monthly income, may solve that problem. In particular, an income-for-life annuity guarantees you get a check every month — no matter how the stock market fares. Some company 401(k) plans are starting to offer annuities within the plans, so you can decide to shelter a portion of your retirement savings.

But annuities have their drawbacks. Annuities tend to be complicated and expensive. You'll probably pay fees that are two or three times what you'd pay for a mutual fund. When you get money out of an annuity, you'll be taxed at your income tax rate rather than the lower capital gains rate that often applies to mutual funds. Maybe worse, if you die sooner than you expect, your heirs get nothing from your income-for-life annuity.

**Get the pension you deserve.** Find guidance through the maze of pensions with these aids.

+ You may qualify for an annuity or other funds through the Pension Benefit Guaranty Corporation (PBGC), the federal agency that stands behind pensions. The PBGC guarantees pensions that are ended due to company financial problems and other reasons. Search for your name or former employer in the PBGC database of lost pensions at *www.pbgc.gov* or call 800-400-7242.

+ An organization founded with help from consumer advocate Ralph Nader wants to get you the pension you deserve. The Pension Rights Center offers counseling and help with your company or government pension. Find assistance online at *www.pensionrights.org*, or call 202-296-3776.

+ U.S. veterans or their survivors can get help applying for the VA Improved Pension program through Project VetAssist. This free service is for needy or disabled veterans 65 years or older who served during World War II or the Vietnam, Korean, or Gulf wars. Access Project VetAssist at *www.vetassist.org*.

**Don't stumble into retirement with no plan.** Many online tools and calculators can help you make the most of your retirement years and savings. Try these three to get an idea of where you're headed.

✦ Answer the questions at *www.livingto100.com* to predict your life expectancy. Knowing how many years you need to plan for can help you spread out your savings.

✦ Get an estimate of your Social Security benefits at this Web site — *www.ssa.gov/OACT/quickcalc/*. Enter your specific earnings information for best results.

✦ Find out how long your nest egg is likely to last. Just enter seven bits of information into T. Rowe Price's retirement-income calculator at *www3.troweprice.com/ric/RIC/*.

## Self-employed? Don't lose out on retirement savings.

Working for yourself means you can set your own hours and make your own decisions. But it also means you can't save for retirement in a company 401(k) plan.

Check out a Keogh plan, a favorite of doctors and lawyers who want to sock away big bucks for later. You can contribute up to 25 percent of your earned income with a current annual maximum of $45,000. That's a lot more than you can put into an IRA (Individual Retirement Account).

## 4 reasons to delay taking Social Security. You may be

eligible to receive Social Security retirement benefits as young as 62 years old. Hold your horses — starting that early is not always the best choice. You may win in the long run if you wait until you reach full retirement age or even 70 years old. Consider these reasons to wait.

✦ You want to get the largest possible check every month because you haven't saved enough.

✦ You're still working and you don't want to pay taxes on Social Security benefits or pay an earnings penalty.

✦ Your husband or wife is much younger than you are. He or she may need a larger benefit for a longer time, and delaying benefits until age 70 will raise your monthly payment.

✦ You come from a long line of long-lived folks. If you expect to be hale and hearty into your 90s, it may be wise to wait until you can receive the largest payment.

## Defend yourself against Social Security errors.

Everyone makes mistakes — even Uncle Sam. If you receive a Social Security payment that's higher than you should get, you'll need to pay it back. But there are exceptions. If the mistake was not your fault and having to pay it back would be a financial hardship, you may get to keep the money. Contact the Social Security Administration at *www.ssa.gov* or call 800-772-1213.

### What to do when you lose your job

If you find yourself pushed into an early retirement by down-sizing or other factors, it may be for the best. Handle it right, and you may find success you never imagined. That's the message in Harvey Mackay's book *We Got Fired! and it's the Best Thing That Ever Happened to Us*. Mackay describes a number of well-known people who were pushed out of work — only to reach greater heights, including poet Walt Whitman, entertainer Shirley Temple Black, and football coach Lou Holtz.

Here are some of the tools Lou Holtz used when he was fired as head football coach of the University of Arkansas, going on to find greater fame and success.

* Be honest about why your situation has changed. Don't wallow in self-pity.

* Don't express bitterness. You may need help from your co-workers later.

* Look on the bright side. Losing your job could be a ticket out of a career rut or dead-end situation.

**Protect your future — check your Social Security Statement.** The Social Security Administration sends you an annual Social Security Statement a few months before your birthday. Check it to be sure your personal information is correct and all your earnings are included. That way you won't have any nasty surprises when you apply for retirement benefits.

To request a statement, complete the form *Request for Social Security Statement* (SSA-7004-SM), available online at *www.pueblo.gsa.gov.* You'll get your new statement in about four to six weeks.

**Steer clear of Social Security scams.** Where there's money to be had, there's a con man out to get some. That's certainly the case when it comes to Social Security. One swindle involves a promise to get you a refund of all the Social Security tax payments you made while you were working — for a small fee of around $100 and a percentage of your refund. Don't fall for it. Social Security tax payments are never refundable.

**Smart way to plan for life after work.** You may have the money part of retirement figured out, but that's not all you need for a smooth transition out of your career. Brothers Jonathan and David Murray, authors of *Two for the Money: The Sensible Plan for Making it All Work*, say you need to make an effort to get your head around life after work. Some of these suggestions need planning long before you say sayonara to your boss.

+ Make friends away from work. After you retire, you'll need companions who share your other interests.

+ Take time for your hobbies. Some people succeed in making a life-long interest into a retirement job.

+ Reconnect with your spiritual side, which you may have neglected while working.

+ Volunteer in an area that interests you. If your grandchildren live too far away to play with regularly, consider coaching or refereeing for kids' basketball or soccer.

166

✦ Rent an office if you plan to build a new business after you retire. Having a set space will help you develop your new identity.

**4 amazing ways to beat burnout at work.** Everyone has stress at work sometimes, but don't let those feelings send you rushing into retirement before you're truly ready. Avoid work burnout by reconnecting to the meaning and joy in your job. Try these mind-changing tactics from Pat McHenry Sullivan, author of *Work With Meaning, Work With Joy.*

✦ Ask yourself questions you can answer — "What can I learn from this?" or "How can I serve here?" Listen to your answers. Thoughts such as "Pay attention to this" or "You need to commit to this aspect of the job" may help you find out what is important in what you're doing.

✦ Lighten up. Choose a problem that is bothering you at work, and try to find something funny about it. Practice developing a sense of humor about obstacles. You may be able to drain them of their power and open yourself to more creative approaches to your work.

✦ Imagine taking your car in for a tune-up and cleaning. Try to picture your brain with all the things that are misfiring and cluttering the space. Then imagine a team of workers reconnecting loose wires, putting away messes, and doing an overall cleaning of your brain. Let your mind get cleaned, rewired, and ready to go on.

✦ Close your eyes. Picture a wise person who has all the answers you need. Visualize taking a walk until you come upon this person and ask all the questions you can't seem to answer yourself. Then listen for the responses.

**Revamp an old resume for a new career.** Re-entry. That's what they call it when you try to get a job after being retired or out of work. If you're moving from your long-term career field to the job of your dreams, like teaching or something related to a hobby, you may need a new resume. It needs to show you can fill the bill for the new job — even if you haven't actually done the work before.

Try these resume tips from career coach Wendy S. Enelow, author of *Best Career Transition Resumes for $100,000+ Jobs.*

+ Include highlights of your job history on the resume, and save the small details for an interview. You can't put it all in one document.

+ Show how you fit in. Although you're moving between career fields, demonstrate how your experience can relate to the new position.

+ Choose the right keywords for your chosen field. Nowadays, computers often sort through a stack of resumes before people do. If your resume doesn't include the specific words and phrases an employer thinks are important to the job, it won't make the cut.

+ Aim for perfection. Typos, spelling errors, and grammar slip-ups show carelessness.

Enelow's book also includes examples of resumes that have been revised to help land jobs in specific fields.

## *Mix and mingle to beat the blues*

Depression is common among seniors, and being lonely can make the problem worse. Even more startling, a recent study found seniors who are lonely have a higher risk of developing Alzheimer's disease. Instead of sitting alone watching TV, consider taking a part-time job to meet others. Or find a way to share your favorite hobbies or games, like playing cards or creating scrapbooks, with a group of like-minded people. You'll all benefit from new friendships.

## 3 reasons to keep working — even after you retire.

Just because you're retired doesn't mean you have to stop working. Consider working part-time in an area you enjoy to ease the transition from career to retirement.

+ You can continue adding money to your IRA as long as you have earned income.

+ Many people can collect a pension from their previous employers while they work.

+ Staying active and involved as you age may help you avoid boredom and depression.

---

### Take advantage of scholarship program for older adults

The AARP Foundation has money available to people older than 40 who want to go back to school but don't have the funds. Preference goes to women and grandparents who are supporting their grandchildren. Get information at *www.aarp.org*.

---

**Volunteer to put your knowledge to work.** Volunteering lets you stay useful without the obligations of a paying job or losing Social Security benefits. These groups would love your help.

+ ElderWisdomCircle.org. Young people who need advice post questions to this free Web site. Then someone from a crew of 600 seniors gives advice — without leaving home.

+ Peace Corps. You're never too old, but you must pass the same physical exam as other volunteers. Lillian Carter, mother of a former president, joined the Peace Corps in her 60s.

+ Experience Corps. If you're over 55, you can volunteer to tutor elementary school students in 19 cities. Get the details at *www.experiencecorps.org*.

**Pick your perfect second career.** Even if you must continue working for financial security, try to select work that's right for you. Consider these questions as you pick your next job so you can look forward to the daily grind.

+ Does the job fit your personality and use your skills?

+ What do you really enjoy doing that you can get paid to do?

+ Are you more in need of status, money, or personal freedom at work?

+ Can you find a position with a small group of coworkers for a better sense of community?

**Enliven your mind with long-distance learning.** You finally have the time to go back to school, but you don't feel like getting out of the house. No problem. Your home computer makes it easy to get involved in long-distance learning. Whatever your reason for getting more education, there's a way to do it from home.

+ Gear up for a second career or even pursue a college degree. Online learning through colleges like the University of Phoenix online *(www.phoenix.edu)* or Walden University *(www.waldenu.edu)* make it possible.

+ If you don't have a career goal in mind but you've always wanted to learn more about about, say, physics, poetry, or Asian history, you can sample college courses for free through MIT's Open Course Ware *(ocw.mit.edu)* or Yale Open Courses *(open.yale.edu)*.

+ Explore your hobby or even turn it into a business. Learn more about gardening, woodworking, or needlework with online learning. At *www.quiltuniversity.com* you can take online quilting classes with respected instructors for about $25–$50 per course. If knitting is your bag, check out *www.knittinghelp.com* for free online instructional videos.

If you'd rather learn in person, contact your local senior center or community center for a schedule of upcoming classes.

## Learn while you travel with Elderhostel

With programs starting at less than $500 for a three-night stay, lectures, activities, food, and transportation, Elderhostel lives up to its motto, "Adventures in Lifelong learning." You can choose from trips near or far, with programs that include outdoor adventure, classroom lectures, crafts, and even study cruises.

Dee H., veteran of four Elderhostel trips, says the greatest benefits are meeting people and learning while she travels. "Without Elderhostel, I couldn't afford to schedule individual lectures and tours provided by experts," she says.

If money is tight, consider applying for an Elderhostel scholarship of up to $800. Get more information at *www.elderhostel.org*.

**Settle on the best place to settle down.** Do your homework to find your perfect retirement spot. Consider these factors, based on advice from *U.S. News & World Report.*

- ✦ population above 15,000
- ✦ good health care facilities
- ✦ low cost of living
- ✦ low crime rate
- ✦ opportunities for continuing education
- ✦ plenty of cultural and recreational activities

# Foolproof ways to foil fraud

**Protect your identity from thieves.** Concerned about identity theft? You should be. In 2004 alone, about 10 million Americans were victims. And in 2005, it's estimated that an identity was stolen every four seconds. In his latest book, *Stealing Your Life*, Frank W. Abagnale, author of the best-selling memoir *Catch Me If You Can*, explains this common crime.

The scary thing about identity theft is that it can happen to almost anyone. Possible victims include anyone who has a credit card, bank account, mortgage, car loan, debit card, driver's license, Social Security number, phone service, health insurance, or a job. Paying bills and using the Internet also puts you at risk.

Once someone steals your identity, they can use it to wipe out your bank account, take out loans in your name, or adopt it as an alias while committing other crimes. You may be denied credit, charged for purchases you didn't make, harassed by collection agencies, or even arrested.

Learn how to prevent this costly crime with these tips from Abagnale's book.

- ✦ Check your credit report regularly.

- ✦ Don't give out your Social Security number.

- ✦ Protect your computer. If you use a wireless connection, make sure it's encrypted.

- ✦ Keep track of billing cycles. A missing bill may mean an identity thief changed your address.

- ✦ Examine financial statements carefully to make sure all the purchases are legit.

- ✦ Guard your mail from theft. Get a post office box and put outgoing letters in a drop box.

- ✦ Invest in a shredder.

- ✦ Practice safe shopping online.

+ Avoid sketchy ATMs, like the portable kind in delis and hotel lobbies.

+ Be suspicious of calls or e-mails from a business asking for personal information.

+ Put strong passwords on your accounts.

+ Keep your credit card close when shopping or eating out. Make sure salespeople and waiters don't have a chance to copy your card.

+ Use safe checks, from your bank, and use them sparingly.

+ Store your Social Security card, passport, and all financial and tax records in a safe spot in your home.

+ Cancel credit cards you don't use.

+ Opt out of marketing lists that get sold and resold.

+ Read privacy policies for your bank and other businesses, and choose all the restrictions available to you.

+ Place fraud alerts on your credit reports.

While nothing is foolproof, Abagnale points out, making things more difficult for thieves may prompt them to give up on you and target someone else.

## Drive away with your identity intact

Be careful at car dealerships. Instead of getting a new car, you may lose your identity. When you take a car out for a test drive, the salesman will ask to make a photocopy of your driver's license. That's so they have proof you're licensed in case of an accident. Make sure to get that photo-copy back when you leave. Otherwise, a shady salesman could pass the information along to identity thieves.

**Safeguard your Social Security number.** For identity thieves, Social Security numbers are like the numbers on a winning lottery ticket. Make sure no one hits the jackpot with yours. Know the law. Many may ask, but only these three must know your Social Security number.

+ your employer

+ your bank or any institution involved with taxes or income

+ credit bureau, when you're requesting a copy of your credit report. Also, if you're opening a credit account, the company might want to check your credit record and will need your Social Security number.

If your state puts Social Security numbers on driver's licenses, ask if you can use a different number. Other companies might ask for your Social Security number, but you're not legally compelled to give it to them. Keep in mind they can refuse to do business with you if you decline.

**First aid for medical ID theft.** A robber may demand "your money or your life" — but crooks who practice medical identity theft could cost you both. Thieves use your health insurance identification or Social Security number to get medical care or make phony insurance claims for reimbursement. Often, they pay employees at hospitals or doctor's offices for this information.

Like all identity theft, this crime takes a financial toll, but it can also mess up your medical history and health care records. If someone else's information finds its way into your records, it could appear as if you've been treated for conditions you never had. You could even be given the wrong blood type during a transfusion. Here are some ways to protect yourself from medical ID theft.

+ Guard your health insurance card. Don't loan it or show it to anyone except trusted health care professionals.

+ Be suspicious of clinics that advertise aggressively, promise to waive co-payments, or provide transportation.

+ Ask to view your medical records.

✦ Shred any health care or insurance documents you don't keep.

✦ Read your insurance company's explanation of benefits letters carefully, and question any claims for services or drugs you don't understand.

✦ Request a yearly list of benefits paid by your insurer, so you can spot fraudulent claims, even if the thief changed your billing address.

✦ Access your insurance billing statements online rather than receive paper mailings. Keep track of your account.

## Let relatives rest in peace

Identity thieves want you — dead or alive. When a relative dies, stop crooks from using his identity by contacting the credit bureaus and having a "deceased" alert put on his reports. You can also report the death directly to Social Security. Include a copy of the death certificate. The Direct Marking Association also has a "Deceased Do Not Contact" list, which will eliminate telemarketing calls or direct mailings to your deceased relative.

**Freeze credit report to foil fraudsters.** If you're hot under the collar about the possibility of identity theft, try this cool option. Freeze your credit report. This makes it impossible for thieves to open new lines of credit in your name. In fact, it keeps all new creditors from accessing your credit report. To put a freeze on your credit report, write a letter to each of the three major credit bureaus. It could cost as much as $10 per request. But if you can prove you've been a victim of identity theft, it's free. If you plan to apply for new credit, you'll need to "thaw" your report a few days ahead of time — and this also comes with a fee. Then you'll need to pay again to put the freeze back on. Credit freezes work best for people unlikely to need new credit.

Another option is a fraud alert. Anyone can request this free service, and you just need to contact one of the credit bureaus, which will then alert the other two. In theory, lenders and merchants call you or take extra steps to verify an applicant's identity before opening a new account. But not everyone abides by the alert, which expires after 90 days.

## Simple way to spot fraudulent charges

You'd think it would be easy to spot fraudulent charges — just look for the costliest ones. But thieves don't just buy deluxe stereo systems. They also use your financial information to pay for everyday items, like groceries and fast food. Examine your financial statements carefully to catch these small charges.

**Shield yourself from check washing scams.** The red flag on your mailbox doesn't just alert your mailman that you have out-going mail — it also tips off thieves. If you pay your bills by check, it can leave you vulnerable to a scam called "check washing." Frank W. Abagnale, author of *Catch Me If You Can* and the recent identity theft book *Stealing Your Life*, explains how it works.

Criminals may drive through your neighborhood early in the morning, spot the red flag, and steal the envelope containing your check to the phone company. They can take the check home, put a piece of Scotch tape over your signature, and use an everyday household chemical to wash off all the information on the check other than your signature. Then they can make the check out to themselves, fill in any amount, and cash it. Protect yourself by mailing your checks at the post office, but avoid mailboxes that are too stuffed, which allows thieves easy access. You should also use pens with permanent ink.

**Beware of your own family.** It may not be a slick, professional con artist who swindles you out of your money. For many seniors, financial swindles come from their own children, grandchildren, nieces, nephews, brothers, and sisters. Be suspicious if a relative you've trusted to handle your finances keeps you from checking your accounts.

Also, watch out if a relative seems eager to take you to a lawyer to sign a power-of-attorney or talks to you about changing a will, deed, or beneficiary designation on insurance policies. If you do set up a power-of-attorney, keep your relative honest by designating a lawyer, accountant, or another family member to receive regular account updates.

## Why you should check out charities before giving.

It's better to give than to receive — unless you're giving to a scam artist rather than a legitimate charity. Follow these suggestions to make sure your money goes to a worthy cause.

+ Question cute kids who go door-to-door. You may feel tempted to buy magazines or other products to support youth programs, but these young salespeople may work for a for-profit company. Ask for verification of the organization's name, address, and purpose.

+ Support firemen and policemen, but don't fall for phone or direct mail appeals. Usually, these come from outside solicitors who get 70 cents or more of every dollar they raise. Your donation might not even go to firemen or policemen at all, and it may not be tax deductible.

+ Never give money by phone, and don't let callers pressure you into making a donation. Request literature to find out more about the organization. Send a check directly to the charity instead.

+ Play the percentages. Find out what percentage of funds go to the services the charity provides and how much goes for fundraising and other costs. Sometimes, you'd be surprised how little money reaches the people in need.

+ Learn more about specific charities at Web sites like *www.charitywatch.org, www.guidestar.org, www.give.org,* or *www.charitynavigator.org.* You can also check with the IRS at *www.irs.gov.*

### Short-circuit jury duty scam

You get a call, allegedly from your local court, saying a warrant has been issued for your arrest because you failed to report for jury duty. You try to explain that you were never notified, and there must be some mistake. The caller asks for your Social Security number and date of birth to check the records and straighten out the mess. Of course, that's all he needs to swipe your identity — and create a real mess. Don't fall for this trick. Real courts respond by mail and would not ask for your Social Security number.

**Action plan for ATMs.** Use caution when using an automated teller machine, or ATM. Thieves may be lying in wait — or using technology to steal your card number and PIN. Here's how to protect yourself.

+ Examine the ATM for any suspicious attachments or extra cameras. Devices called skimmers capture information, while crooks set up cameras to spy your PIN.

+ Do not use an ATM when people are lurking nearby, and never accept a stranger's help to retrieve a stuck card.

+ Memorize your PIN. Do not write it down anywhere, especially on your ATM card.

+ Shield the keypad with your body when entering your PIN.

+ Do not linger. Have your card out as you approach the machine. Take your receipts with you, and put away your money right away. If you're making a deposit, sign the check ahead of time.

+ Avoid using an ATM at night. If you must, park close to a well-lit ATM and bring a friend with you.

+ Stick with bank ATMs. Other machines may be rigged to gather customer information.

**Fend off Medicare crooks.** Beware of scammers posing as approved Medicare Prescription Drug Plan providers. They may call you and request your checking account number for an automatic withdrawal of the $299 enrollment fee. Do not provide it — or any other personal information. Do not let any door-to-door salesmen peddling drug plans into your home, either. For more information on legitimate plans, call 1-800-MEDICARE or go to *www.medicare.gov*.

**Identify insurance fraud.** Insurance gives you security and peace of mind — but only if it's legitimate. Fraudulent companies take your premiums, but don't pay your claims. Here's how to spot insurance fraud. Watch out for companies that accept everyone or whose policies cost far less than what other companies are charging.

Avoid agents who pressure you to act quickly, discourage you from getting advice from a lawyer, demand cash payments, or ask for personal information that has nothing to do with insurance — like your bank PIN or password. Make sure the company and agent are properly licensed in your state before doing business with them.

### Shred your paper trail

Identity theft doesn't have to be high-tech. In fact, it's more likely to occur when you complete paper forms by mail or in person than over the Internet. Protect yourself by tearing, cutting up, or burning documents that contain your personal information. Or buy a document shredder to safely dispose of things like bills, bank statements, pre-approved credit card applications, ATM receipts, pay stubs, medical or dental records, and tax forms when you no longer need them.

# Top tactics for safe computing

**Shop safely online.** You can't beat the convenience of shopping online from your own home. It's a great way to avoid the hassles of crowds, parking, and driving all over town. But you must be careful. Here are some easy tips for safe online shopping.

+ Look for "https" and the closed padlock symbol in your browser's toolbar before giving your credit card number online. These are signs that you're on a secure site that encrypts, or scrambles, your private information.

+ Shop only with stores you trust. Beware of companies without a physical address or phone number to make it easy to handle disputes.

+ Seek out seals, like the Better Business Bureau Reliability Program, VeriSign Secured, or TRUSTe. But even if a site displays these seals, it could be shady. Check out the seal issuers' Web sites to verify that the company is legit.

+ Pay with a credit card. It offers more protection than a debit card.

+ Be especially careful with auction or classified-ad sites, like eBay or Craigslist. For eBay, if a seller has poor or little feedback, reconsider dealing with him. For Craigslist, only deal locally with people you can meet in person.

**Virtual credit card provides real security.** You can shop online without using your credit card number. Some companies, including Citibank, Bank of America, and Discover, offer "virtual credit card numbers." These 16-digit numbers link to your real account, but keep your real account number a secret. You set constraints, like a spending limit or expiration date, for further protection. Your best bet is to use a different virtual credit card number for each transaction. That way, even if a thief steals the number, it will be useless in the future. See if your credit card company offers this feature.

**Proven password precautions.** A good password can keep hackers away from your personal information. Experts recommend changing passwords every 30 to 90 days. The key is choosing the right password. Avoid proper names or obvious numbers, like your birthday or anniversary. Stay away from common or foreign words, even if they're spelled backward.

Make your password at least eight characters long, and use a mix of letters and numbers. Alternate between uppercase and lowercase letters. You can use a less cryptic password for things like online newspapers, but use a tricky password for online banking and other important transactions.

## Get Internet access for free

Most people pay large monthly access fees, but you won't have to — as long as you don't mind some restrictions. Internet service providers like Juno and NetZero offer free access for occasional Internet users. That means no more than 10 hours per month. Besides the limited hours, other drawbacks include advertising banners and a steep $1.95 per minute fee for technical support. You can also find cheap plans for $9.95 per month or less.

**Best bets for online bill paying.** These days, you don't have to bother writing checks and buying stamps. You can just pay your bills online, but you should take some precautions. Try to pay your bills through your bank, rather than a third-party service or the biller's Web site. The fewer companies that have your financial information, the better.

Make sure you have a strong password to thwart hackers, and review your monthly statements to spot fraud. Never leave your computer unattended while banking. Sign off and close your browser if you need to step away.

**Simple tips to cut down on junk e-mail.** E-mail may be fast and convenient, but it comes with a price — spam. This junk e-mail can flood your inbox if you're not careful. Here's how to combat spam.

+ Set up two e-mail addresses. Give one only to family and close friends, and use the other for anything else.

+ Consider a disposable e-mail address service, which creates a separate e-mail address that forwards to your permanent account. If one of the disposable addresses starts receiving spam, simply shut it down.

+ Filter out spam. Your e-mail account should provide a spam filter or a way to funnel all bulk e-mails into a separate folder. You can also install anti-spam software, but be careful. Some Web sites offering free downloads are actually disguised spammers.

+ Never reply to spam or unsubscribe to unwanted newsletters. That just lets the spammers know they reached a real person and may lead to more spam.

### Practice e-mail etiquette

Still getting used to e-mail? Here are some guidelines to keep in mind when using this new form of communication. Always assume everything you send will be forwarded — but never forward anything without permission. It's OK to use multiple exclamation points, emoticons, and abbreviations, like LOL for "laughing out loud." However, you don't want to reprimand or apologize to anyone via e-mail. Do it in person or at least use the phone.

**Foil phishing scams.** You get an e-mail from your bank that says you need to update your account. It comes with a link that takes you to a Web page where you're asked to provide information. The only problem is the e-mail isn't really from your bank — and you'll be giving your personal information to hackers. This trick is known as "phishing," and if you're not careful, it can reel you in. Here's how to protect yourself.

✦ Beware of any e-mail requests to update or validate an account, especially when the sender makes it sound urgent. Legitimate businesses will usually contact you by mail.

✦ Never click on the link provided. If you think the request may be legitimate, contact the company directly, either by phone or through a Web site you know is valid.

✦ Spot spoof Web sites by paying close attention to the URL. The part that matters comes just before ".com" or ".net." Anything that comes after a slash just represents a page on that site.

✦ Be alert. Phishers will ask for information the company should already have, like your username, password, or credit card number.

**Halt hysteria over hoaxes.** In addition to spam and phishing e-mails, your inbox can be flooded with hoaxes. Some, like the famous Nigerian letter scam, try to trick you out of your money by promising a large sum later. Others, like computer virus warnings, cause panic or otherwise encourage you to forward the e-mail to everyone you know.

Before you waste your time and energy, check it out. One good place to look into hoaxes is the Web site *www.snopes.com*. You can find the current top urban legends as well as other hoaxes organized by category. You can also search the site for specific topics.

**High-tech tips to stay safe online.** Smart behavior can help you stay safe online. But you also need some high-tech help. Make sure your computer has what it needs to ward off potential threats.

✦ Anti-virus software guards your computer from viruses that destroy data, cause crashes, or even steal your information. This software, which must be updated regularly, scans incoming e-mail for viruses and deletes them.

✦ Firewalls guard your computer from hackers trying to access your information. Make sure your firewall is configured properly and updated regularly. Your operating system may come with a firewall, but you may have to turn it on.

✦ Anti-spyware software counteracts spyware that monitors your online activities and collects personal information when you surf the Web. This software, which must be regularly updated to counter the latest threats, scans your computer and gives you a chance to remove any spyware it finds.

✦ Your operating system and browser should be set up properly and updated regularly. Change the settings to maximize online security, and update your operating system with "patches" as they become available to fix problems.

## Sidestep strains and pains

Using a computer can take its toll on your body. Prevent neck and shoulder strain by keeping your shoulders relaxed. Make sure your mouse and keyboard are on the same level as your elbows. Rest your arms on padded armrests while reading something on the screen. Remember to take breaks. You don't want to sit at a computer for too long at one time. Get up and move around a little now and then.

**Protect your privacy online.** It's alarming how public your private information can be. With just a few strokes of a keypad, anyone with an Internet connection can find your address, phone number, and birth date. People can also dig up more sensitive information with a little more effort. Make things more difficult for them.

Opt out of online people finder services whenever possible. You may have to do this repeatedly, whenever they update their listings. Limit the personal information you disclose in discussion groups, chat rooms, or blogs. Do not sign up for supermarket loyalty cards, mail in warranty cards, or enter sweepstakes. Your private information could end up in the wrong hands — and online.

## Meet friends without leaving home

A computer seems cold and impersonal, but it can introduce you to your new best friend. According to a recent study, the Internet helps build friendships by broadening your geographic networks. You can chat with people all over the world about shared health concerns, hobbies, and other interests. Simply use a search engine to find a group that interests you. You can also join social networking sites like MySpace or Facebook. Just be careful. Beware of people who ask too many personal questions too soon, do not respond to direct questions, or overreact to innocent comments.

## Find false information with background check.

Background checks can reveal deep, dark secrets — and faulty information. You may be denied credit or turned down for a job because of something you didn't do. Running a background check on yourself can help uncover and fix serious mistakes.

Start with a credit report from the three major agencies, Experian, Equifax, and TransUnion. Companies such as ChoicePoint Inc. and LexisNexis offer screening services, and ReputationDefender.com searches the Internet for unflattering postings about you. You can find other companies through the National Association of Professional Background Screeners at *www.napbs.com*. You'll have to pay for these services, but it could save you even more in the long run.

**Change settings to crumble cookies.** Don't let your computer turn into a cookie monster. Cookies, short text files that attach to your computer when you visit Web sites, can track your Internet browsing habits. Some cookies can be helpful because they save your information so you don't have to retype it every time you visit a site. But in many cases, you'd rather avoid cookies. Set your browser to prompt you whenever cookies appear. That way, you can decide whether you want to accept them or not.

**Easy ways to wipe your hard drive clean.** When you sell or donate your old computer, you're also giving the new owner access to your personal information. To be safe, you need to purge your hard drive. If you're giving your computer to a friend, you could just reinstall the operating system and format the hard drive. Your information will still be there, but it will be tougher to find.

You can also use wipe software to overwrite all or parts of your hard drive. Find these products by searching for "file wiping" in an online search engine, and choose those that meet Department of Defense specifications. At the other end of the spectrum, you can remove the hard drive and drill holes in it to destroy it.

# Head-to-toe healthcare

**Clever trick cuts your hospital bill.** You can save money if your doctor orders tests as part of a hospital stay. Before you leave your doctor's office, ask how many tests can be done on an outpatient basis — and don't forget to ask about lab tests, like blood work. Make a list of those tests and call your insurer. Ask whether they cover the tests for outpatients and how your out-of-pocket costs would differ from in-hospital testing. The same test often costs less when done "outpatient," so this simple change could save you a lot. If your insurer confirms that out-patient testing will cost you less, lock in your savings. Call your doctor back and ask him to order outpatient testing.

**Spot billing errors that cost Americans millions of dollars annually**. As many as 9 out of 10 medical bills may contain errors, according to Medical Billing Advocates of America — errors which may lead to more than $10 billion in overcharges But you can learn how to find the errors in your medical bills and get your money back. Here's how to start.

Ask for an itemized copy of your bill, a copy of your medical chart, and — if you were in the hospital — your pharmacy ledger. You're entitled to all these documents, so don't be afraid to request them. Also, be sure to save the explanation of benefits (EOB) sent by your insurer. Compare your medical chart, pharmacy ledger, and EOB with your itemized bill. Keep an eye out for errors like these.

+ Check the dates of your doctor visit or hospital stay. They should match up on all the documents.

+ Compare the list of services you're being charged for. If the medical bill lists any tests, treatments, medications, or other services that aren't shown in at least one other document, you may have found a mistake.

+ Watch out for keystroke errors. The bill may charge for two doses of medicine when your medical chart or pharmacy ledger only mentions a single dose.

187

✦ Your EOB should tell you what charges are allowed for each service. Compare the billed charges to these amounts. If you find a big difference, call and ask for an explanation.

If you catch an error in a regular medical bill, notify your doctor's office and insurer right away. If you find an error in your hospital bill, contact the hospital billing department, request an investigation of the error, and ask for a hold on the bill until the dispute is settled.

## Call 211 when you don't know where to turn

Everyone knows to call 911 for a medical emergency, but 911 can't help if you need respite care, Medicare information, Meals on Wheels, or other vital services. That's where United Way's 211 number comes in. This number connects more than 65 percent of Americans in 41 states to a one-stop shop for community services. Here are just a few examples of these services.

◆ medical information lines

◆ home health care

◆ support for older Americans and persons with disabilities

◆ crisis intervention services

◆ support groups

◆ adult day care

◆ counseling

◆ rehabilitation

◆ health insurance programs

◆ transportation services

When you call 211, you'll speak with a person trained to find the organization or agency that can help you. To learn more and find out whether 211 is available in your area, visit www.211.org.

## Get smart about routine medical tests

To protect yourself from heart disease, cancer, osteoporosis, and other serious health problems, doctors recommend screening tests. Unfortunately, the sheer number of screenings makes it difficult to remember when to have them and how often. Use this handy chart to keep it straight.

| Test or exam | When and how often |
| --- | --- |
| complete physical | before age 45: once every five years<br>ages 45–65: every other year<br>age 65 and up: every year |
| eye exam | every other year if you wear glasses, contact lenses, or have eye health concerns; otherwise, every other year starting at age 40 |
| blood pressure | overweight or have a family history of high blood pressure, ask your doctor; otherwise, at least once every other year |
| cholesterol | at least once every five years |
| electrocardiogram | once before age 40; ask your doctor how often you should have the test done after your first test results come back |
| skin check | ages 20–39: once every three years<br>ages 40 and up: every year |
| colon | age 50 and up: digital rectal exam and sigmoidoscopy once every five years |
| fecal occult blood test | age 50 and up: once a year |
| breast exam | ages 20–39: every three years<br>ages 40 and up: every year |
| mammogram | age 40 and up: every year |
| pap smear and pelvic exam | every year |
| bone density | ask your doctor |

## New Medicare policy cuts hospital dangers

You could catch a dangerous infection while you're in the hospital. In fact, the Centers for Disease Control and Prevention report that hospital-acquired infections cost $27 billion each year. But your risk of these infections may soon plummet. Medicare has announced it will no longer reimburse hospitals for infection-related costs.

Because Medicare has also forbidden hospitals from passing costs on to patients, the entire financial burden of these infections now falls squarely on the hospitals. Medicare policy makers hope this will inspire medical centers to be more diligent in preventing these infections. As if that weren't enough, Medicare also no longer covers costs related to bed-sores, surgical instruments left inside patients, and several other medical errors. Hospitals may be safer from now on.

**Untangle your medical bills.** Mountains of medical bills — or just bills from several different doctors — can contribute to insurance snarls and may keep you from catching billing errors. Even worse, some bills may get lost in the shuffle and might not be paid on time — and that could mean collection agency calls and financial troubles when you need them least.

Fortunately, several companies offer software or Web sites to help track and organize medical expenses. Users of these medical expense trackers say the products have helped resolve insurance issues, cut through paperwork confusion, and nab billing and insurance errors. Some of these services even help you record the medical services you've had.

If you'd like to try a medical expense tracker at no cost, visit *www.smartmedicalconsumer.com*. The site is free, but your information will be kept private unless you give permission for someone else to see it. The site not only stores and organizes your billing information, but its error-nabbing feature may also spot billing errors.

You'll also get extra peace of mind and here's why. Unlike many Hurricane Katrina survivors, you won't lose all your medical and billing information if a disaster strikes. That means you'll be less likely to have delays or mistakes in medical treatment while recovering from a catastrophe.

If you're still uncomfortable about keeping your medical billing information on the Web, buy software — like Intuit's Medical Expense Manager — that you can use on your home computer. Just be sure to leave a spare copy of your records with an out-of-town relative in case disaster strikes.

**What to do when Medicare won't pay.** You might think you're stuck with the bill if Medicare refuses to pay — but that's not true. You can appeal many Medicare decisions, including refusal to pay or insufficient payment. Start by examining your paperwork. The company that sends you Medicare billing information has probably mailed you an Explanation of Medicare Benefits or a Medicare Summary Notice. Find it and read up on why Medicare refuses to pay this bill and how you can appeal. If you are under a Medicare managed care plan, ask your plan how to appeal. They must tell you in writing.

Make your case as if you were a lawyer like Perry Mason. Write a very detailed letter explaining why Medicare should reverse its decision. You should also provide supporting documents, if possible. If waiting for a particular medical test or treatment will endanger you or put your health at serious risk, ask for a fast decision on your appeal. If you are under a Medicare managed care plan, you should get results within three days.

**Do this before shopping for health insurance.** You've never had problems getting health insurance before, but insurance companies are suddenly avoiding you like the plague. You've even been rejected. If you can't imagine why, check your medical records for accuracy.

Insurers may mistakenly think you're a high risk because someone forgot to note that your high blood pressure has been brought down. Or a simple typo can make insurers believe you've had a serious illness when you were actually diagnosed with a mild ear infection. Before you shop for health insurance or switch to a new insurance company, check your medical records, find any errors, and get them corrected. Not only will insurers be far more interested in your business, you may get lower rates as well.

**Where to go when you can't get insurance.** No matter how many health insurers have turned you down, that doesn't mean you're uninsurable. In their book, "You, the Smart Patient," Michael Roizen and Mehmet Oz offer three ways you could still get insured. First, call your state insurance board. Many states offer some kind of insurance to the "uninsurable" who have a low income. If you have Web access, visit *www.covertheuninsuredweek.org* and *www.patientadvocate.org*. Help may be waiting for you there.

**Collect on denied health insurance claims.** If your health insurance has refused to cover a recent medical test or treatment, you can appeal. Studies suggest as few as 30 percent of insurance appeals may be denied. Appeal correctly and insurance might pay after all. Start with these tips.

✦ "Make sure you read your plan booklet," recommends Lin Osborn, director of Health Plan Navigator, a patient advocate firm. Learn what's covered, what isn't, and how to appeal. If you don't have a paper copy of your insurance policy, check your insurer's Web site. Also, find the claim denial form or letter you received and read it.

✦ Call customer service. Ask why your claim was denied. "Be very specific," recommends Osborn. "Why did this not pay? Under what

192

circumstances will you pay?" Ask how to appeal, what information and documents to provide, how to get them, and what deadlines you must meet.

✦ Keep a log of every phone or written contact with your insurer. Write down the date, who you spoke or wrote to, and a summary of what was said.

✦ Write a letter explaining why your claim shouldn't be denied. "Pretend that you're writing this out for an 8-year old," says Osborn. "You need to make it clear — really, really clear, step by step." Include documents with the letter to support your points. For example, if your letter explains why your treatment was medically necessary, you might include a letter from your doctor, supporting medical records, and your log of contacts with your insurer. Send the letter with a "confirmation receipt" so you'll have proof your insurer received it.

Most insurance companies respond within 30 days, so keep checking your mailbox for possible good news. If you're still denied, call your state insurance department to find out where to appeal next.

### Know when the "best health plan" isn't right for you.
Some health plans seem great until you get sick. That's when some people have discovered coverage gaps and high out-of-pocket costs that sent them deep into debt. That's why the policy with the lowest premium isn't always the best health plan. To protect yourself, ask these questions when shopping for health insurance.

✦ How do the copays and deductibles compare with your current insurance?

✦ What coverage can you expect for hospitalization, surgery, medical tests, and other costs that are likely during serious illness or injury?

✦ Is there a lifetime cap on benefits? If the answer is yes, don't accept a number below $2 million.

+ What is the deductible? Does it go up after the first year?

+ How do copays apply to the deductible and out-of-pocket limits?

## When to call 911

No one wants to call 911 without good cause, but if you experience the symptoms or problems listed below, don't hesitate to call for emergency help right away.

| | |
|---|---|
| heart attack | Symptoms include chest pain; pressure like a heavy weight against your chest; extremely rapid, strong, or irregular heartbeat; sudden, intense weakness; profuse sweating; and sudden shortness of breath. Women may not experience chest pain. |
| stroke | Symptoms include sudden, intense overall weakness or dizziness; trouble speaking or understanding; weakness in an arm or leg; seizure; and possibly a headache. |
| severe bleeding or pain | Call even after the bleeding has stopped, especially if there is weakness or drowsiness. |
| choking | Call even if the victim is conscious. |
| serious burn | Any burn larger than 2 to 3 inches across; any burn located on the hands, feet, face, groin, or buttocks, or around a major joint; any burn that involves all layers of skin; any burn that is dry and white or black. |
| severe allergic reaction or asthma attack | Wheezing or noisy breathing; difficulty breathing or speaking; blue tinge to lips, skin, fingertips, or fingernails. |

**Beware these HMO tricks and traps.** Your HMO's representative may promise you'll always get the right treatment from the right doctor, but some HMOs secretly limit your options. Before you sign up for an HMO plan, read the contracts and other documents carefully and ask the HMO representative about these issues.

✦ Some HMOs pay doctors a flat fee annually for each patient. That means your doctor makes less money if he sees you more often. Find out whether doctors are paid this way. If you consider two or more plans, call your doctor's office and find out how they are paid by each plan.

✦ HMOs may place restrictions on which treatment options your doctor can tell you about. These are called "gag rules." Read carefully to see if you spot any gag rules in your plan.

✦ Ask your doctor how she receives approval for treatment decisions and referrals to specialists under the HMO plans you're considering. If she has to go through a lot of effort or red tape, you should probably consider a different HMO plan.

✦ Get detailed information about the HMO policies and pricing for using doctors or treatments outside the plan. Also, get specifics on policies and pricing for treatment of long-term illnesses.

To avoid problems after you've chosen your HMO, keep every document they send you and file any disputes in writing. And if you have a good reason for needing a treatment or specialist not covered by the HMO, ask your doctor to draft a letter explaining why.

**Speedier, cheaper alternative to the ER.** You could wait up to eight hours to see a doctor if you go to the emergency room for a problem that isn't life-threatening. Even worse, the bill will be exorbitant. But if you go to an urgent care center, you could pay up to 50 percent less and wait a fraction of the time. You may even be pleasantly surprised by all the things an urgent care center can do.

Many centers are equipped to do X-rays and blood tests. They also handle broken bones, sprains, flu, animal bites, minor burns, mild asthma, minor injuries, ear infections, skin rashes, coughs, and sore throats. They may even set fractures, suture injuries, and write prescriptions for many common illnesses. If you need medical care during weekends or evenings, consider an urgent care center. Both you and your wallet will feel better faster.

**Make your surgery safer, easier, and less scary.** A little research on your upcoming surgery could give you big advantages. You can find out exactly what will happen, how to make the surgery easier on yourself, and learn about the risks and ways to protect yourself. How? First, ask your doctor plenty of questions. But if your doctor visit ends too quickly or you're too shaken to know what to ask, the Web can help. Try these surfing solutions.

+ Visit *www.preopguide.com* for an insider's guide to surgery. This site helps explain what happens before, during, and after surgery — and why.

+ Find the Web site for your hospital or surgery center and learn what they say about surgery. You may even find information about your particular operation.

+ Surf to *www.facs.org*, the site for the American College of Surgeons. Click "Patients" and then "Patient Resources." This will take you to a list of links filled with valuable information about surgeries. Check out as many as you can. You'll find both general information to help prepare for surgery and details about specific kinds of operations.

+ Visit the site for the Agency for Healthcare Research and Quality at *www.ahrq.gov*. Click the "Surgery" link listed under "Consumers & patients." Click "Having Surgery? What You Need to Know" for a guide that helps you prepare for surgery and learn about a range of operations.

+ Visit the Web sites of organizations dedicated to your condition or illness. For example, if you need knee or hip surgery, you may find answers at the Arthritis Foundation's site at *www.arthritis.org*. When you visit sites, be sure to check "Site Map" if you have trouble finding the surgery information. You'll usually find "Site Map" links listed at the very top or bottom of the page or along one side.

## Cut through medical jargon

Your doctor was speaking English a moment ago, but now he's using words that sound as if a computer made them up. Those strange-sounding syllables are called medical jargon. While you can't learn every medical term your doctor knows, understanding the most common ones can help considerably. Start with these.

| Medical jargon | English translation |
| --- | --- |
| acute | A condition or illness that's severe enough to need treatment right away. Some acute conditions are serious and some are not. |
| BP | The abbreviation for blood pressure. |
| chronic | A condition or illness, such as diabetes, that doesn't go away but can be treated. |
| contraindicated | This means "thou shalt not" for doctors. For example, if a drug or treatment is contraindicated, doctors think it would not help you. |
| indicated | This treatment or drug is recommended to help your problem, and your doctor will probably treat you with it. |
| edema | Most of us would call this "swelling," but this kind of swelling occurs because too much fluid accumulates in part of your body. |
| –itis | When you hear this at the end of any word, it means some part of your body is inflamed. For example, gastritis means your stomach is inflamed. |

**Crack the billing code for cheaper surgery.** The bad
news is you need surgery, but the good news is you can comparison shop
to get the best price. Start by asking your doctor which CPT (current
procedural terminology) code will be used for this surgery. The CPT
code is a five-digit code used to identify what medical service you're billed
for. Every hospital uses the same code for your surgery, so call several of
them and ask for the price of the particular CPT code you need. You'll
soon know where your cheapest option is.

To shorten your list of places to call and to eliminate "clunkers," remember these two tips.

+ Deep discounts and good service don't always go hand in hand, so
   ask your doctor or surgeon if you should avoid any particular hospitals — and why.

+ If you want to stick with a particular surgeon, ask where she has
   hospital privileges. Those are the hospitals where she can perform
   surgeries so they may be the only ones you'll want to call.

**3 secrets you should know about hospitals.** In his
book *How to Get the Most From Your Hospital Visit*, Mahmoud
Elghoroury, a medical doctor with a master's degree in health care
administration, reveals three things hospitals may not want you to know.

+ Hospital bills can unexpectedly soar into the thousands with surprising speed. Some bills are so high a middle-class family can lose
   their home because they can't pay. Protect yourself. Get a hospital
   insurance policy. Because the benefits are limited to hospital
   charges, the monthly premium is very reasonable.

+ Don't automatically think you need a teaching hospital for every
   treatment or surgery. While it's true teaching hospitals have the most
   highly trained doctors, the latest medical knowledge, and the most
   advanced equipment, you may not need those for routine surgeries
   and treatment. Teaching hospitals also cost more. Do a little research

into the hospitals available to you. You may find teaching hospitals best for surgeries and illnesses that are serious, complicated, or unusual, while many local community hospitals can give nearly equivalent care for routine surgeries and treatments.

+ Hospitals are under financial pressure to release you as quickly as reasonably possible. They are rarely required to keep you until you've fully recovered, and you may still need medical care when you're sent home. That's why you should pay careful attention to your discharge papers. They contain your doctor's plan to safely complete your recovery at home and may even include instructions for medical care outside the hospital. Read the discharge plan carefully. Make sure it matches what your doctors have told you, and if it doesn't, ask why. In fact, ask questions if you find anything you don't understand. Your health and recovery could be at stake.

## 2 simple tricks for better communication

You didn't get to voice all your questions and concerns at your last doctor visit, but you will the next time if you remember these two tricks.

* Before you leave for your appointment, make a list of your questions and concerns. Write them down in order of importance and take the list with you. Doctors are frustrated by people who don't mention their most crucial issues until the appointment's tail end, so they'll appreciate your efforts.

* Plan ahead for interruptions. Doctors usually interrupt patients within 23 seconds. When the inevitable happens, say you have more to add and pick up where you left off. If the doctor still interrupts, ask if you can revisit your topic before your appointment ends or if another health professional can speak with you about it before you leave.

**Get the most from your doctor visits.** What you say in the doctor's office may determine how quickly your doctor finds the right diagnosis and treatment. Here's how you can prepare yourself to get the best possible results.

+ Start keeping a symptom diary several weeks before your appointment. Include information about things that may influence your symptoms, such as stressful events or foods that affect how well you feel. Take this diary with you to the doctor's office.

+ Write down all the prescription medications, over-the-counter drugs, and supplements you're taking. Include how often you take them and the dosage for each. Give the nurse a copy of this list to put in your medical file or take all your medicines with you.

+ Ask a friend or family member to come along to help take notes or ask questions. Tell that person ahead of time if you'd like them to step outside during the physical exam.

+ If you see any other doctors, write down their contact information and give it to the doctor or nurse. If you've had recent, important test results, scans, or X-rays from another doctor, call ahead and ask if you should bring copies of those to your appointment.

+ Be ready to provide a list of all past hospitalizations, if needed. Keep a list in your purse or pocket if you're afraid you'll forget one.

+ Know your family history. Gather information on any important or serious medical conditions your parents, siblings, or grandparents have had.

**Insider's tip for scheduling a doctor's appointment.** You're not feeling well. You need to see your doctor soon, but he doesn't have an opening until next week. Here's what to do.

"Clearly explain why you feel you need to be seen that day or the following day. Most practices allow a block of time each day for what are called add-ons. These are generally reserved for true emergencies," says Rita DiGiovanni, a former medical office manager with 20 years of experience.

If you feel it is urgent you be seen, tell the doctor's receptionist. If you're not satisfied with her answer, ask to have a nurse contact you for advice on what to do until the doctor can see you. "Quite often a nurse or medical assistant will be able to ascertain how urgent the problem is and will either work you into the schedule or advise you what to do until you can be seen," DiGiovanni says. Either way, you can rest a little easier knowing a medical professional has reviewed your problem.

**Smart way to schedule more time with your doctor.** If your doctor visits never seem to last long enough, pay close attention to how you schedule your appointments. What you say can make a big difference.

Doctors allot different amounts of time for different kinds of appointments. "When you call, we say, 'What are you coming in for?' and then you tell us if it's an acute illness — something that you just woke up with that morning — or if it's a recheck or if you need a complete physical," says the office manager for The Doctor's Office in Peachtree City, Ga. "Once those questions are answered, then we know which time slots to give you."

"A new patient appointment is specifically for a patient who is new not only to the practice but to the individual doctor he or she may be seeing," says Rita DiGiovanni, a former medical office manager with over 20 years of experience. "This type of appointment requires more time," she says. So does a full physical exam. On the other hand, if you're coming in for a follow-up on an earlier problem, that only requires a quick appointment.

When you schedule an appointment, be sure to tell the receptionist why you need to see the doctor — even if you're only coming to learn the results of a test. If you think you may need extra time to ask questions or explain your problem, tell the receptionist that, too. In most cases, says DiGiovanni, people who explain that they need more time can expect to get extra time. If the receptionist says time isn't available that day, ask to schedule your appointment for a different day when more time is available.

**Take advantage of free health info and advice.** You can have access to the world's top health experts 24 hours a day — free. Here's how you can contact 13 of the best ones with your mouse and keyboard.

+ *www.PDRhealth.com* — from the experts behind the Physicians' Desk Reference

+ *www.intellihealth.com* — from the Harvard Medical School

+ *www.mayoclinic.com* — from Mayo Clinic experts

+ *www.healthfinder.gov* — health information and resources from the U.S. Department of Health and Human Services

+ *www.medhelp.org* — from doctors and medical institutions

+ *www.webmd.com* — popular health information site

+ *www.medlineplus.gov* — from experts at the National Library of Medicine and National Institutes of Health

+ *www.medicinenet.com* — articles written and reviewed by doctors and other health professionals

+ *www.safemedication.com* — prescription and over-the-counter drug information from the American Society of Health-System Pharmacists

+ *www.mypillbox.com* — drug information and help identifying pills

- ✦ *www.ismp.org* — Institute for Safe Medication Practices; helps prevent drug errors and alerts you to drug dangers

- ✦ *www.rxlist.org* — detailed drug information for questions other sites may not answer

- ✦ *www.drugdigest.org* — information about drugs, vitamins, and herbs

## Get free medical testing

A little-known government program could help you get blood work, MRIs, X-rays, or other tests for free or nearly free. If you can't pay for health care and don't have health insurance, call toll-free 888-ask-hrsa or visit this Web site — *http://ask.hrsa.gov/pc* to learn whether you qualify. You may discover centers near you that provide emergency exams, lab tests, immunizations, and X-rays at little or no cost.

**The pros and cons of medical tourism.** The average American can expect to pay $70,000 for heart bypass surgery, but a medical tourist may only pay $12,000. What's more, a $43,000 hip replacement surgery may only cost the medical tourist $12,000.

Medical tourists are people who have discovered that certain hospitals in Thailand, India, and other countries can perform the same operations cheaper than American hospitals — even after travel costs. Some state-of-the-art surgery centers also offer 24-hour nursing services, luxury rooms, and Western-trained doctors who speak English. On top of that, nearly 130 foreign hospitals are accredited by the Joint Commission International (JCI) — the international subsidiary of the group that certifies hospitals in the United States. Yet, medical tourists may also encounter risks like these.

- ✦ Many overseas hospitals are not accredited by the JCI and may not provide the quality and safety you seek.

- ✦ Some hospitals depend on interpreters and may have few staff members who speak English.

- ✦ If complications, problems, or a need for follow-up surgery occurs after you get home, you can't visit your original surgeon — unless you return to the overseas hospital.

- ✦ Not all overseas doctors are fully qualified.

- ✦ Checking your doctors' qualifications can be tough because they may not be certified with any American organization.

- ✦ You may have little or no legal recourse if you believe a doctor is guilty of negligence or malpractice.

In spite of these risks, approximately 500,000 Americans participated in medical tourism in 2006 — sometimes at their insurer's request. If you are considering medical tourism, be prepared to do a lot of research about the risks and how to protect yourself.

## 11 ways to protect yourself from medical tourism dangers. Start with these tips to protect yourself from medical tourism risks.

- ✦ Seek advice from your doctor at home. Ask whether the treatment you need is considered low-risk, routine, and uncomplicated. Also, ask whether recovery time is short and if on-site, follow-up care is typically brief. If the answer to any of these questions is no, medical tourism may not be safe for you this time.

✦ Consider using a health travel agency to help you find skilled doctors and reputable hospitals. Be aware that some agencies receive fees from the hospitals they recommend.

✦ Find out if your health insurance will help pay for treatment outside the United States.

✦ Learn whether your hospital is accredited and how many of your particular surgery they perform each year. Eliminate any hospital that isn't accredited.

✦ Get information about your doctor's licensing and other credentials. Find out his experience or success rate with this kind of surgery. Using e-mail, mail, or the phone, interview the doctor you're considering. Watch out for communication problems.

✦ Ask what kind of help you may need during recovery and how the hospital will provide it.

✦ Ask the hospital for a written statement of all services. This should include what your rights are if you're harmed by a medical error or negligence.

✦ Double-check the prices you expect to be charged.

✦ If possible, speak with others who have had treatment at the hospitals you're considering or who have had surgery overseas.

✦ Find out what medical records you should bring and which records to bring home.

✦ Ask a family member or friend to travel with you as your health advocate — particularly during those times when you won't feel well enough to be on the lookout for problems.

## Chart your past to save your future

If crystal balls could see into the future, think what they could do for your health. After all, if you could learn what health problems you'll probably have, you could take steps to prevent them. You might even avoid cancer or a fatal heart attack.

Charting your family history is like having that crystal ball because many diseases run in families. That means your risk of a particular problem is often higher if your parents, grandparents, or siblings already have it. Start talking to your relatives about their health — and yours — and take notes. To help you record your family history, the Surgeon General's office offers My Family Health Portrait. Just visit *https://familyhistory.hhs.gov*. It's easy, free, and it might save your life.

# Pay less at the pharmacy

## Put the brakes on runaway prescription costs.
Imagine paying less for your prescriptions because you don't need a medication you've been taking. It happens more often than you might expect and here's why.

"Patients and prescribers often don't think about a new symptom as possibly being a drug side effect," says Tom Clark, director of Clinical Affairs at the American Society of Consultant Pharmacists. In fact, the new symptom is usually blamed on old age or a chronic health problem the person already has. "So what often happens is the new symptom gets treated with another drug," Clark says. He even recalls one case where a commonly prescribed drug caused symptoms that strongly mimicked Alzheimer's Disease.

But that's not all. In some people who take several medications, two or more drugs may work together to cause new symptoms. Those may be even harder for a doctor to diagnose correctly. Fortunately, switching to a safer — and sometimes cheaper — drug may help. The trick is to recognize the problem.

To find out whether you're experiencing medication-based problems, talk to a senior care pharmacist. You can find one by visiting *www.seniorcarepharmacist.com*. Call the one nearest you and ask how to arrange a brown bag checkup to evaluate your medications. Check whether the pharmacist charges for this service, too. If a senior care pharmacist isn't available nearby, call your regular pharmacist about a brown bag checkup. You might end up feeling better, taking fewer pills, and saving money.

**Don't let your Part D savings get away.** Holding on to Medicare Part D prescription drug discounts can be like trying to grab a greased pig. The longer you hang on, the more slippery things get. Every year Part D plans can raise premiums and copayments. Some plans do, some plans don't, and some plans may lower them only for certain drugs.

What's more, the number of drugs a plan covers may expand or shrink. That's why the prescription drug plan that was perfect for you last year may be a poor choice now. Even people on one of the Extra Help plans may be affected. To keep your discounts, shop around for the best-priced Part D plan every year.

**Part D plan picking made fast and easy.** Finding the most economical Part D plan doesn't have to be like hiking up Mount Everest. Just visit *www.medicare.gov* and let their online comparison tool do all the hard work for you. Just type in a list of your medications and the software shows you cost figures for deductibles, monthly premiums, and copays. You'll immediately see which plans can save you money. You can also compare pharmacy networks, determine how a plan's coverage gap may affect you, and see how the plan's customer service rates. When you use Medicare's online comparison tool, picking the perfect plan could take just a few minutes.

### 7 common antibiotics available for free

If your doctor prescribes any of the following antibiotics, take your prescription to your local Publix grocery store. Their pharmacy will provide up to a 14-day supply of these prescription drugs at absolutely no charge. If you don't live near a Publix grocery store, check with the grocery stores in your area to see if they offer the same benefit.

* amoxicillin
* ampicillin
* cephalexin
* ciprofloxacin (except ciprofloxacin XR)
* erythromycin (except Ery-Tab)
* penicillin VK
* sulfamethoxazole/trimethoprim (SMZ-TMP)

**Go "clubbing" for deeper drug discounts.** Even if you don't have a membership at Costco or Sam's Club, these warehouse stores could help you save up to 75 percent on prescription drugs. That's because you don't have to be a member of either club to buy prescription drugs from their remarkably low-priced pharmacies.

**Uncover hidden prescription bargains.** Just because insurance doesn't cover your prescription doesn't mean you have to pay the full price. You can easily save up to 50 percent off mail order medications or up to one-third off drugs from your local pharmacy. What's more, you won't have to pay money, prove your age or income, or give information about your health. Just find out if your county offers the NACo prescription drug discount card.

Sponsored by the National Association of Counties (NACo), this card covers your entire family and offers an average savings of around 20 percent. Over 800 counties and 57,000 drugstores already participate, so find out if your county does, too. Visit your county's Web site, call your county health department, or talk to your pharmacist for more information.

If your county doesn't offer the NACo card, you can still cut your pill bill with these tips.

+ Ask your pharmacist if your drug has a long enough shelf life to allow you to buy in bulk. If it does, you might save with bulk discounts. Just don't forget to ask your doctor to adjust your prescription amounts accordingly.

+ Shop around by phone. Call drugstores, supermarkets, and discount department stores about the price of your prescription drug. Also, check the online versions of these stores because online prices may differ from regular store prices.

+ Ask your pharmacist about less-expensive alternatives to your doctor's prescription. Sometimes pharmacists know more about what's available than doctors do. Call your doctor with this new information so you can get your prescription changed and your drug costs down.

## Little-known risk from beta carotene supplements

If you take high doses of beta carotene supplements, talk to your doctor. One study suggests high doses may promote lung cancer in former smokers. Other studies say high doses may raise your risk of health problems, while still more studies showed exactly the opposite. Your doctor can tell you the latest news and help you determine what's safe.

Meanwhile, experts say you shouldn't cut back on foods containing beta carotene, like carrots, sweet potatoes, spinach, and cantaloupe. And don't stop taking any vitamin or mineral that your doctor prescribed without getting her approval first.

**More prescription drugs available for $4.** Just because Wal-mart didn't offer your prescription for $4 last month, doesn't mean you can't get this super discount today. Wal-mart has recently added more drugs to its $4 program and hints that even more may be coming in the future. Talk to your Wal-mart pharmacist or visit *www.walmart.com* to find out if you can start paying less for your prescription today. And check other stores in your area, such as Kroger, for similar discounts.

**Follow the safe path to big online savings.** Legitimate online pharmacies can slash your drug costs — but be careful. Some pharmacies aren't ready for prime time, while others are shady operations that can damage your health — and your wallet. Take these steps to defend yourself.

✦ If you've never bought from an online pharmacy before, don't worry. The U.S. Food and Drug Administration offers a consumer safety guide packed with great how-to tips. Just visit *www.fda.gov/buyonline*.

✦ Some online pharmacies may not have the software to handle your insurance copayments. Before you try an online pharmacy, check with your insurance company.

✦ Only use pharmacies that display the Verified Internet Pharmacy Practice Sites (VIPPS) seal of approval. This seal certifies that a Web site complies with the quality and privacy standards required by the National Association of Boards of Pharmacy (NABP.) The seal also means the pharmacy is licensed, but seeing the seal isn't enough. Some sites display the seal even though they've never been certified by the NABP. To find out if a seal is valid, click on it. This should take you to a site that verifies the legitimacy of the pharmacy. If it doesn't, try a different online pharmacy.

✦ To find a VIPPS-certified pharmacy, visit *www.nabp.net.*

✦ Only use online pharmacies that have licensed pharmacists available to answer your questions and avoid any site that doesn't require a prescription for prescription medicine.

## Surf to find coupons and rebates

Before you pick up your new prescription — or even one you've been taking awhile — surf to the drug manufacturer's Web site. You may find coupons or rebate forms that can save you money on your prescription purchases.

**Qualify for drug assistance programs.** Prescription assistance programs don't just help people without health insurance. They may also help if you have meager prescription coverage, low to mid-range income, or a major illness requiring high-priced medicine. More than 200 programs are available, but you don't have to sift through them all. A free phone call to the Partnership for Prescription Assistance (PPA) can point you to the ones you may qualify for. To reach the PPA, call toll-free 888-477-2669.

**Catch the drug mistake many doctors make.** No matter how good a doctor is, he may still prescribe a drug that's not on your formulary list — a list of medications your drug plan will pay for — and that could cost you a bundle. Request a copy of the formulary from your insurance company and take it with you whenever you visit a doctor. Always ask the doctor to check your formulary before prescribing any medicine. Most doctors won't mind doing this. They prefer to stick to drugs on your formulary because they know you'll be more likely to fill a prescription when you know you can afford it.

**Never forget to take your pills again.** If a regular pill organizer doesn't help you remember to take your medicine, try these ideas.

+ Ask your doctor if you can take a time-released pill, so you won't have to take your medication as often.

+ Link your pill taking with another activity you do regularly. For example, you might decide to take your pill after picking up the newspaper each day.

+ Set your watch alarm, clock alarm, or cell phone alarm to remind you. If you need an extra alarm, consider buying an inexpensive travel alarm clock.

+ Switch to a pill organizer that comes with an alarm.

+ See if the manufacturer of the drug you are taking offers a reminder program. Ask your pharmacist for the manufacturer's name and check that company's Web site for information.

## Stop wondering if you took your pill

You can't remember if you took your medication, but skipping a pill or taking one too many can be dangerous. To prevent this problem, create a chart like the one below.

Include the name of the medicine, the color of the pill, directions for taking it, and spaces for each day. In each day slot, write the times you plan to take each pill. When that time rolls around, take your pill and mark through the time on your chart. Here's how your chart might look at 2 p.m. on Monday.

| Drug and directions | Sun. | Mon. | Tues. | Wed. | Thurs. | Fri. | Sat. |
|---|---|---|---|---|---|---|---|
| drug #1 (red pill) 4 times daily with food | ~~9 a.m.~~ ~~1 p.m.~~ ~~5 p.m.~~ ~~9 p.m.~~ | ~~9 a.m.~~ ~~1 p.m.~~ 5 p.m. 9 p.m. | 9 a.m. 1 p.m. 5 p.m. 9 p.m. | 9 a.m. 1 p.m. 5 p.m. 9 p.m. | 9 a.m. 1 p.m. 5 p.m. 9 p.m. | 9 a.m. 1 p.m. 5 p.m. 9 p.m. | 9 a.m. 1 p.m. 5 p.m. 9 p.m. |
| drug #2 (pink pill) 3 times daily | ~~8 a.m.~~ ~~3 p.m.~~ ~~8 p.m.~~ | ~~8 a.m.~~ 3 p.m. 8 p.m. | 8 a.m. 3 p.m. 8 p.m. | 8 a.m. 3 p.m. 8 p.m. | 8 a.m. 3 p.m. 8 p.m. | 8 a.m. 3 p.m. 8 p.m. | 8 a.m. 3 p.m. 8 p.m. |
| drug #3 (blue pill) before bed | ~~9 p.m.~~ | 9 p.m. | 9 p.m. | 9 p.m. | 9 p.m. | 9 p.m. | 9 p.m. |

**Make a large capacity pill organizer for pennies.** You might think you take far too many pills to fit into an inexpensive pill organizer. But no matter how many pills you take, you can make a pill organizer that matches your pill regimen exactly. All you need are self-stick labels and two sizes of resealable bags.

Buy one package of resealable bags labeled as "snack size" and another labeled as sandwich bags or pint-size. If you later decide snack-size isn't small enough, check office supply stores or craft shops for tinier bags. Label each of the sandwich or pint-size bags with a day of the week. Next, write down your pill schedule on paper. For example, you may take nine pills at 8 a.m., six at noon, and five at 7 p.m. Label one snack-size bag for each clock time you expect to take a pill and then fill each bag with the appropriate medications.

Drop this first set of bags into one of your day-of-the-week bags. Then fill all the other day-of-the-week bags the same way. Each morning, pick up your bag for that day and slip it in your pocket or purse so your pills can go wherever you do. Just remember to remove the bag at night and refill your convenient pill organizers every week.

## Wake up to a cheaper sleep remedy

If you thought you couldn't afford Ambien, guess again. It's now available as a generic that could save you 70 percent or more. That's why *Consumer Reports* declared it a Best Buy. Just remember to be careful when taking sleeping aids because they may have side effects or become habit forming.

**Expert help for prescription problems.** Arthritis, vision problems, or trouble swallowing can make taking medicines difficult. Fortunately, your pharmacist can offer three surprisingly helpful solutions to these prescription problems. If you have trouble opening your pill bottles, ask for a different cap. "We offer snap cap which is a lot easier to open," says Lauren Costick, pharmacy manager at Walgreens in Newnan, Ga. But you must request the easy-open cap or the pharmacist is required to give you the childproof top instead, she adds.

You don't have to settle for the tiny print on your pill bottle label either. Ask your pharmacist if you can get your labels and other drug-related information in large print. And if swallowing pills is tough for you, ask your doctor or pharmacist if the medicine is available in a patch or liquid form. Just be ready to supply your doctor's phone number. Your pharmacist will need to check with your doctor before making this change to your prescription.

**Generic drug secrets you should know.** Cheaper generic drugs may be safer than many name brands, but switching to a generic can be very risky. Here's what you need to know to save money and protect your health. According to Worstpills.org, more health problems appear with newer brand name drugs than with older generics.

This may happen because the safety of newly approved drugs has only been tested by a limited number of people in clinical trials. But after FDA approval, many more people start taking the drug. This provides the broadest possible test of its safety and reveals any dangerous effects that didn't show up during clinical trials. That's why some newly approved medications are pulled off the market after just a few years. It's also why cheaper generics may sometimes be the safest choice. By the time a name brand drug is allowed to be sold as a generic, it has been used by so many people its safety has been thoroughly tested.

Then again, generics can still house one hidden health danger. While the active ingredient in a generic drug must be exactly the same as its name brand equivalent, the inactive ingredients can vary widely. That means the generic version of a "safe" name brand drug may contain gluten, sugars, dyes, artificial flavorings, or other products that could cause a dangerous allergic or diabetic reaction. If you have diabetes, food intolerances, celiac disease, or allergies, ask about the inactive ingredients in your generic drug before you switch from a name brand. Your pharmacist can help you avoid a dangerous reaction and find another generic you can take safely.

**Avoid dangerous medication mistakes.** More people are injured, hospitalized, or killed by medical errors every year than live in Hawaii and Alaska combined. That's more than 2 million people, and you could be next. To protect yourself, learn as much as you can about your medication. Ask your doctor the following questions about any prescription you get.

+ Why do I need to take this medicine?

+ What are the risks of taking this drug?

+ What side effects are likely?

+ What should I do if I miss a dose?

+ How much do I take and how often do I take it?

+ What is the name of this medicine?

+ Should I avoid any foods, vitamins, activities, or other drugs while taking this medicine?

If you can't remember these questions, write them down and hand the paper to your doctor when he gives you a prescription. Write down the answers he gives you, too. Take them with you to the pharmacy so you can be sure you get the right medicine. Always keep them with your medicine at home.

To be even safer, read up on your medicine. If you have Web access, use the medicine-related Web sites listed on pages 202 and 203. Make it a habit to read the package insert that comes with your medicine.

You can also check your local library for a copy of the *Physicians' Desk Reference*. This guide includes useful information about your medicine that your doctor may not have time to mention. It also warns you about dangerous interactions between drugs and foods, shows pictures of commonly prescribed medications, and tells how to spot signs of an overdose.

## Become a stranger to prescription drug dangers.

"Safe health care shouldn't stop when a patient leaves the hospital or doctor's office," says Carolyn Clancy, medical doctor and director of the Agency for Healthcare Research and Quality. "Medication errors that occur at home are a serious problem." But you can help prevent them with these tips.

+ Store medications separately from any other containers, recommends Hedy Cohen, registered nurse and vice president of the Institute for Safe Medication Practices. Cohen once received a report where a person accidentally took a pet's medication because all the medicines were stored together. She adds that storing a tube of medicinal gel next to toothpaste has also led to problems.

+ Don't be tempted to take an extra pill if the normal dose of a medicine doesn't relieve your symptoms. You might become a victim of the "ceiling effect." This happens when your body's receptors for the drug have reached full. If you take more medicine then, other receptors in your body may start accepting the drug instead. That can lead to side effects that can be unpleasant or dangerous.

+ Don't stop taking your medicine because refilling the prescription is too expensive. Stopping some medicines suddenly can be dangerous. Instead, call your doctor's office, explain that the prescription is too expensive, and ask if a cheaper alternative is available.

In many cases, the difference between making a medication error at home and avoiding one starts before you get home. Ask your doctor to thoroughly explain your medication, including its name, dosage, and how to use it. "You make a difference in learning to use your prescription drugs safely by talking with your health care provider," says Clancy.

## Escape the dangers of taking the wrong drug

When your doctor "calls in" a prescription for Zantac, the pharmacist could think he heard Xanax and give you the wrong drug. The same thing can happen if a prescription is hard to read. "Errors resulting from look-alike/sound-alike drugs are a problem that spans the entire health care system," says Darrell Abernethy, medical doctor and chief science officer of the U. S. Pharmacopeia.

In fact, a recent report by the U.S. Pharmacopeia found that 1,470 drugs have names that look or sound like the names of other drugs. That makes it far too easy for pharmacists to misunderstand which drug a doctor has prescribed. To help protect yourself, ask your doctor to spell the brand and generic names of your medication. Write these down and check them against the label on your medicine when you receive it — especially if you take any of these.

| Prescription drug | Sound-alike or look-alike |
| --- | --- |
| Celexa | Zyprexa |
| Evista | Avinza |
| Paxil | Taxol |
| Prilosec | Prozac |
| Actonel | Actos |
| Allegra | Viagra |
| Aricept | Aciphex |

**Tummy-soothing trick foils antibiotic misery.** You hate taking antibiotics because they always give you diarrhea, but a trip to your grocery store could change that. A recent study found that adults over age 50 slashed their odds of antibiotic-caused diarrhea simply by enjoying a probiotic drink twice a day. If you'd like to try this, keep in mind that each drink contained "live cultures" of helpful bacteria, like *Lactobacillus casei*, *Lactobacillus bulgaricus*, and *Streptococcus thermophilus*. Look for these ingredients when you shop.

Also, remember that each drink in the study was only 97 milliliters — about 3 ounces. Shop accordingly since the per-ounce price of some probiotic drinks can be pretty high. And whatever you do, never drink your probiotics within two hours of taking an antibiotic. This prevents your antibiotics from killing your probiotics and ensures you get the most bang for your buck.

## #1 way to prevent a cold

Two items found in every kitchen and bathroom are all you need to fight 200 different viruses, including the dreaded common cold. And you're going to need the help because sneaky viruses lay in wait for you on telephones, stair rails, and many other places you touch every day. Your hands need only brush those spots to pick up viruses and bacteria.

Even worse, your hands can transmit those bad bugs into your body when you touch your eyes or nose. Not surprisingly, visiting your kitchen or bathroom regularly can break this cycle because that's where you'll find the soap and water to wash viruses and bacteria off your hands.

And here's a bonus tip. Don't use antibacterial hand gels when soap and water are available. Research shows hand gels don't remove as many of the viruses as simple hand washing. Wash your hands often and use hand gels only when you can't get to soap and water.

**Purge the perils of leftover pills.** Your doctor prescribed enough painkillers for a week, but after the third day, you no longer needed them. Traditional wisdom suggests flushing them down the toilet, but that may contaminate streams in your area. In fact, researchers have found traces of prescription drugs in fish. Don't just drop the medicine in the trash, either. Research shows some teenagers use "free" prescription pills to get high. Use these methods to dispose of leftover drugs safely.

First, call your pharmacist to find out whether your state has any rules about medicine disposal and ask whether he knows of any local places to drop off your drugs for disposal. Before getting rid of your medicine, be sure to scratch out any personal information on the label, such as your name and phone number.

If your pharmacist suggests you throw the medicine away, be sure to do it properly. Mix used kitty litter or coffee grounds in with the pills, mark through all personal information on the label, and drop the container into a sealable bag. If the bag is clear, slip it inside a small, opaque bag and tie the outer bag closed.

# Power down your power bills

**Earn cash from your electric company.** Let the electric company pay you — for a change. When you sign up for their load management program, Georgia Power will credit your electric bill $20. Other utilities may offer similar deals.

"Air conditioners cycle, meaning that they run for a certain amount of time (on), and then shut down (off)," explains Dean Harless, Marketing Issues manager for Georgia Power. When you sign up for load management, the utility company installs a radio receiver on your AC. Then, when energy use in your community starts to overwhelm the power company, they send a signal to your receiver, telling it to shut off the AC.

"For example, if your air conditioner normally runs 15 minutes, the switch will allow it to operate for 5 minutes." The temperature in your home may rise a few degrees, but the AC makes up for it later, once the switch turns off again. This, in turn, saves the company money. "Since running the air conditioner is shifted to later in the day, it takes some demand off the system during the peak hours of energy demand. This helps Georgia Power avoid having to build more combustion turbines to handle a few peak hours each summer."

Harless says the utility company typically only flips this switch a few times each summer, so you probably won't even notice it. But each time they flip the "off" switch, Georgia Power gives you a $2 credit on your electric bill. Signing up for the program and having the receiver installed is free.

**Great gadget puts money back in your wallet.** Beat the summertime heat, and power bills, with this energy-saving tip. Invest in an Energy Star programmable thermostat, and you could slash your heating bill — gas or electric — up to 30 percent.

This nifty little device keeps you snug for less by automatically adjusting the temperature based on your personal schedule. No more forgetting to turn off the heat when you leave home. The thermostat does it for you. The savings can really add up. For every degree you lower your thermostat in winter, you can save up to 5 percent on your heating bill. Use the extra money on your vacation, instead of on your bills.

If you have a heat pump, get a programmable thermostat designed especially for them. Dramatically raising or lowering the temperature by hand on a heat pump activates the inefficient electric backup heater. A heat pump thermostat saves money by gradually raising and lowering the temperature to keep the backup heater from kicking in. Also, keep lamps and televisions away from the air conditioning thermostat. It can sense the heat from these appliances, making the AC run more than necessary.

## Slash your power bill

These six easy steps can save you more than $700 a year on utilities — and you're conserving energy, too.

| Action plan | Potential yearly savings |
| --- | --- |
| Update old appliances and heating and cooling equipment with Energy Star qualified products. | $450 |
| Wash your clothes in cold water using detergents formulated for cold water. | $63 |
| Install an Energy Star programmable thermostat. It automatically adjusts the temperature at night and while you're away. | $100 |
| Sign up with your utility company for load management and off-peak rate programs. | $100 |
| Cool your home with a whole-house fan instead of AC. | $330 |
| Replace your five most-used incandescent light bulbs with Energy Star compact fluorescent bulbs. | $60 |

**Ceiling fans reap cool savings.** Research by the Florida Solar Energy Center shows turning on a ceiling fan can lower your energy bill in summer, but only if you also raise your thermostat. Fans allow you to bump up the thermostat a whopping 6 degrees and still feel just as cool. That equals big savings. Turning up your thermostat just 2 degrees in summer can shave 14 percent off your cooling bill. The higher you raise it, the more you save. On the other hand, leaving the air conditioner set low while running fans will actually increase your bill.

**2 ways to boost your HVAC's efficiency.** Two simple steps can boost the efficiency of your heating and cooling system, lengthen its life, and save you money.

✦ Check the air filter every month and clean or change as necessary. A dirty filter blocks airflow through the whole system, forcing it to work harder, use more energy, and break sooner.

✦ Hire an expert to tune up your air conditioner in the spring and your furnace in the fall. A properly tuned system runs more efficiently.

### Proven way to trap allergens

Cleaning or replacing your heating and cooling system's air filter not only helps it run more efficiently — it also reduces the allergens floating around your home. According to experts with the American Lung Association, air filters are one of the most effective ways to cleanse the air of allergens, but they only work if you change or clean them regularly. High-efficiency particulate air (HEPA) filters are the gold standard, since they catch almost all particles. Filters with accordion-like ridges have a larger surface area that may help them trap more allergens than flat ones.

**Best way to repair leaky ducts.** Heating and air ducts can be a major source of wasted energy in your home. Leaky ducts that travel through unheated spaces, like an attic or unfinished basement, can lose 60 percent of the hot air they carry before it reaches the register. It's easy to seal leaks yourself.

+ Check for air leaks. Look for holes in the ductwork and joints that have separated.

+ If you find a leak, don't bother with duct tape. It fixes almost everything except leaky ducts. Use mastic, a goo you apply with a paintbrush. Butyl or foil tapes work well, too. Buy tape marked with the Underwriters Laboratories (UL) logo.

### Get more heat from your firewood

The amount of heat firewood produces depends on its weight. Heavier wood, like seasoned hardwood, weighs about twice as much as softwood and gives off about twice as much heat when burned. White ash, beech, yellow birch, sugar maple, red oak, and white oak produce the most heat. If you have several different species in your woodpile, burn the softwoods in the warmer winter months and save the hardwoods for the coldest months.

**4 things to consider when buying new windows.** If you're looking for ways to trim your heating and cooling bill, consider replacing old, single-pane windows. Heat lost through drafty windows can account for 10 to 25 percent of your energy bill, according to the U.S. Department of Energy. Here's a basic shopping guide to the best windows for your climate.

✦ In the Sun Belt and other warm climates, buy double-glazed windows with spectrally selective coatings. These block some sunlight, keeping rooms cooler in summer and cutting your cooling load 10 to 15 percent.

✦ In colder climates, look for gas-filled windows with low-e coatings and a U-value of 0.35 or less. Low-e coatings reflect heat back into the room during winter, while U-values measure insulating ability. The lower the U-value, the better the insulation.

✦ In temperate climates with cold and hot weather, choose windows with low U-values to insulate against cold and low SHGC (solar heat gain coefficiency) to keep your home cool in summer.

✦ No matter what climate you live in, buy windows with the Energy Star, EnergyGuide, and the National Fenestration Rating Council labels. Also, look for those with air leakage ratings of 0.3 cubic feet per minute or less.

**Quick fix for a "leaky" refrigerator.** A one dollar bill can help you save money and electricity. You don't even have to spend it. Close your refrigerator door on a dollar bill, then try to pull it out. If it slides out easily, your refrigerator is leaking cold air — and precious money. Adjust the door latch so it closes more tightly, or replace the seal around the edges.

### Go green with environmentally friendly energy

More and more utility companies are offering "green" options, allowing their customers to buy blocks of energy made from renewable resources like wind and solar power. Contact your utility company and ask about buying green power. Or visit the federal government's Green Power Network Web site at *www.eere.energy.gov/greenpower*, and click on the map to see the green options in your state.

**3 easy, energy-efficient cooking tips.** Believe it or not, you can trim your energy bill while cooking, too. Try these energy-saving tips.

+ If you have three dishes that need to bake at different temperatures, don't bake them all separately. Pick the average temperature and pop them all in at once. Don't bother preheating your oven for a dish that needs to cook more than one hour.

+ Broil food when possible, since broiling doesn't require preheating.

+ During warm months, run your kitchen exhaust fan while you cook. It will suck out the hot air, cooling your kitchen more effectively.

**Maximize your refrigerator's efficiency.** Before you store foods in your refrigerator, wrap them up and cover the liquids. This keeps their moisture from escaping. Moist air forces the refrigerator's compressor to work harder.

### Smart way to keep your cool in a dry climate.

Regular air conditioners are the wrong choice for dry climates. Instead, buy an evaporative cooler. It costs less to run in dry conditions, plus adds moisture to the air rather than sucking it out as air conditioning units do.

**Pull the plug on high electric bills.** Save money by unplugging small appliances, not just turning them off. TVs, toasters, battery chargers, computers, and most other electric appliances suck up energy while plugged in, even when they are turned off. Pull the plug and you could use 75 percent less electricity around your house, plus see a big drop in your energy bill. To make it easier, plug nearby appliances into the same power strip. Turning off the power strip will cut all electricity to the appliances and save you the hassle of unplugging them individually.

## Make microwaving healthier

Microwave cooking might be better for you than you think. Consider these points.

♦ "Nuking" french fries before you fry them reduces frying time, which cuts the number of cancer-causing compounds, called acrylamides, produced by frying.

♦ Most experts agree microwaving vegetables generally doesn't destroy their nutrients, as long as you use little or no water. Cooking your veggies in water tends to leach out nutrients. Cruciferous vegetables are the exception. Zapping broccoli, cauliflower, and cabbage on high power may destroy more nutrients than steaming.

**Free money for upgrading appliances.** The government and even utility companies are literally giving away money simply to help you buy more energy-efficient appliances. Tax credits and rebates abound, if you know where to find them.

So if you need a new water heater, refrigerator, or other appliance, check these resources to see if you can get a rebate or tax incentive for buying a new, energy-efficient model. You'll save money each month on your utility bills, on top of great rebates. These sites can also point you toward home loans to help with energy-efficient remodeling.

✦ *www.dsireusa.org*

✦ *www.energystar.gov*

✦ *www.ase.org/taxcredits*

✦ *www.energytaxincentives.org*

Be sure to contact your electric and gas companies directly and ask about their current rebates. If they don't offer any deals, consider switching providers. Call competing utilities and compare their rebates and energy costs. In addition, your state may offer a sales tax holiday on energy-efficient products. Call your state's Department of Revenue or Taxation to learn more.

---

### 3 biggest energy mistakes

Correcting these can give you instant savings.

* Buying a second freezer or refrigerator for extra storage. If you need more storage, consider buying a bigger kitchen refrigerator. In general, it's cheaper to run one large model than two small ones.

* Insulating only your attic. Even though heat rises, floors over crawl spaces and unheated basements benefit from insulation, too, as do exterior walls and windows.

* Buying the wrong size heating and cooling unit. Don't listen to high-pressure salespeople. Buy the right size heating and cooling system for maximum efficiency.

---

**Simple device boosts appliance efficiency.** You know the ancient freezer in your garage is an energy hog, but you just can't give it up. Instantly boost its efficiency with a power controller. This device regulates the electricity that comes through your outlet and matches it to the motor's needs. This helps the appliance run cooler and more efficiently — and lowers your electric bill in the bargain. You'll see the most savings with appliances made before 1990. Those made after 1990 already have energy-saving features, so a power controller probably won't help.

**Get better light from fluorescent bulbs.** Compact fluorescents (CFLs), those new-fangled, energy-saving light bulbs, come in different colors and brightness, not just the bluish-white of old-fashioned fluorescents. Use this buyer's guide to get the right bulb for your rooms.

✦ Watts measure how much energy the bulb uses, while lumens measure the amount of light it gives off. Two CFLs can use the same number of watts but give off different amounts of light. Read the package label and buy a CFL with the same number of lumens as the bulb it's replacing — or more if you need more light.

✦ Like regular bulbs, CFLs can produce different shades of light, from cooler, bluish light to warm, yellowish light. For soft or warm light like that of incandescent bulbs, look for a Correlated Color Temperature (CCT) of 2700K to 3000K. For light that resembles "bright white," "daylight," or "natural" incandescent bulbs, look for CFLs with 3500K or higher.

✦ The Color Rendering Index (CRI) measures the bulb's ability to show an object's true color, when compared to sunlight. Buy CFLs with a CRI of 80 or higher.

✦ Buy only Energy Star-qualified CFLs. They must meet tough standards, and unlike other fluorescents, these are guaranteed not to buzz or hum.

## Do-it-yourself energy audit

You can audit your home's energy efficiency without hiring an expert. These three handy Web sites help you figure out how much energy it takes to run appliances or heat and cool your home and recommends simple changes to save you money.

• *www.energysavers.gov*
• *rehabadvisor.pathnet.org*
• *hes.lbl.gov*

**Turn out the lights on a common myth.** Leaving fluorescent lights on instead of turning them off won't save you money. Old fluorescent bulbs needed a lot more energy to turn on than stay on, but the new ones don't. Incandescent bulbs don't, either. To keep more money in your wallet, turn off the lights when you leave a room.

**LEDs put more Christmas cash in your pocket.** Toss your old Christmas lights and plug into LEDs — light-emitting diodes. LEDs look like the familiar strings of holiday lights, but they are cool to touch, less likely to start a fire, and can cut energy costs 85 percent compared to incandescent Christmas lights. Look for LEDs marked with the Underwriters Laboratories (UL) seal.

**4 ways to pay less for utilities.** Don't let utility companies hold you hostage. Pay the price you want with these tactics.

✦ Watch the competitors' deals, then call your current provider and ask them to match it. Have the terms of the competitors' offers in front of you so you can quote them word-for-word. Be firm but polite, and make sure you are speaking to someone with the authority to negotiate.

✦ Fight for "new customer" status. If your current company offers a great deal to new customers, call and ask for the same rate. They may give it to you if you agree to sign up for an additional year of service.

✦ Check rates through your state's public utility commission or public service commission. Many state governments offer online tools for comparing the rates of different utility providers.

✦ Web sites called service aggregator sites help you pull up the prices of different phone, cable, electric, gas, Internet, and other providers in your area. Some sites even help you make the switch then and there. Check out *www.whitefence.com*, *www.connectutilities.com*, and *www.allconnect.com*. A few charge a fee for switching your service for you. Also, not all service providers post their prices on these sites, so it still pays to shop around.

**5-step plan to resolve billing errors.** Billing mistakes don't have to end in shouting matches with a customer service agent. You can resolve the dispute without ever raising your voice.

✦ Call when the company is least busy, on a Wednesday or Friday morning, for instance. Don't try calling on Monday or the day after a holiday.

✦ Strike the right tone. Be firm but polite. Don't become argumentative or combative. Talk to the representative as though you want to work together to solve the problem.

✦ Take notes during the conversation, including the case number of your problem, the customer service rep's name and extension, and the time and date of your call. Ask when you can expect the company to fix the problem, and write down that date to follow up.

✦ Try calling at a different time of day if you can't make headway with a particular customer service agent. You may get someone more helpful. If the problem persists, ask to speak with the manager.

✦ File a complaint with your state's public utilities or service commission if you can't resolve the problem with the company. If you still aren't satisfied, complain to the Better Business Bureau.

### Insulate with special paint

A new paint does more than pretty-up a room. It helps insulate your home and lower your utility bills. Insuladd is a special ceramic powder you add to regular paint then brush onto walls or your home's exterior. Insuladd contains tiny, hollow ceramic spheres. As the paint coating dries on the wall, it forms a thin film that manufacturer's claim keeps heat from escaping in winter and entering in summer. For more information or to order the product, visit *www.insuladd.com* or call 888-748-5233.

# Smarter phone strategies

**Stop telemarketers once and for all.** You can end most unwanted telephone sales calls by registering your phone number with the National Do Not Call List. Just dial 888-382-1222 from the phone number you want to register, or go online to *www.donotcall.gov*. Registration used to expire after five years, but now the Federal Trade Commission (FTC) says it may make registration permanent, so stay tuned.

Political organizations, charities, telephone surveyors, and businesses you already deal with are allowed to continue calling you. Let them know separately if you want them to stop. Telemarketers, however, have 31 days to take you off their call lists. If they keep calling anyway, there are six ways to make them wish they'd never dialed your number. Complain to:

- ✦ the FTC at 888-382-1222 or *www.donotcall.gov*. Give them the company's name or phone number and the date of the call.

- ✦ the Better Business Bureau in the company's home state.

- ✦ the Federal Communications Commission at 888-CALL-FCC or 888-225-5322.

- ✦ your state attorney general.

- ✦ your state public utility or public service commissions.

- ✦ small claims court. If you ask the company to take you off their calling list, but they call again within 12 months, you can file a claim against them in court.

**Guard your phone bill from fraud.** Cramming happens when companies sneak charges into your phone bill for services you never agreed to or services that cost more than they led you to believe. Spotting these fraudulent fees can be tricky. They may appear on your bill as a "service fee," "service charge," "other fees," "monthly fee," "minimum monthly usage fee," "calling plan," or "membership," among others, warns the Federal Communications Commission.

Go over your phone bill carefully each month and question any charges you don't recognize or understand. Do this before paying the bill, and ask the company to adjust any incorrect charges. If they refuse, complain to the FCC by calling 888-CALL-FCC or your state's public service commission.

**Stand up to slamming scams.** When your phone service gets switched without your permission, you've been slammed. You don't have to pay for the first 30 days of slammed service. What's more, the phone company must reimburse you half of the fraudulent charges. The trick is to catch these scams in the first place.

+ If you see the name of a new preferred telephone company on your bill, call their number immediately and ask for an explanation.

+ If a telemarketer calls and asks you to switch phone or long-distance companies, you can tell them you aren't interested and ask them to take your name off their calling lists.

+ If you get a letter in the mail asking you to verify your switch to a new phone company — and you know you didn't authorize a switch — call the sender right away and tell them so. Then call your local phone company and let them know you want to stay with your current service providers.

**Make free 411 calls.** Two new services have cropped up that give you the same information — free.

+ Dial 800-FREE-411 and listen to a short, 10-second commercial before you get your listing information.

+ Call 800-GOOG-411 to get commercial-free listing information for businesses, thanks to the Internet search giant Google. This 411 service can connect you automatically and even send a map of the area to you or a text message with the listing information if you are calling from a cell phone.

---

## Protect pacemaker from mobile phones

Cell phones may interfere with pacemaker signals in some people. When your phone is on, keep it at least 6 inches away from your pacemaker. Hold it away from your body when dialing and against the ear farthest from your pacemaker while talking. Never place a phone in the shirt pocket over your pacemaker while it is still "on."

---

**Free cell phones for savvy shoppers.** Buy it online, and your next cell phone could be free. Major phone carriers, like Verizon *(www.verizonwireless.com)* and AT&T *(www.wireless.att.com)*, offer great deals on cellular phones if you purchase over the Internet and sign up for a one- or two-year contract. Independent dealers, such as LetsTalk.com *(www.letstalk.com)* offer terrific bargains on phones from all carriers for easy, one-stop shopping. Most of these deals rely on rebates — some instant, others are mail-in.

Decide which phone you want before you buy it online. Visit the phone carriers' brick-and-mortar stores so you can handle the phones and press the buttons. Find one you like, then surf the Internet for the best deal on that model. Understand the terms of your contract before you take the plunge. Most companies charge hefty cancellation fees if you decide you want out. Be sure you get a trial period during which you can return the phone and cancel service free-of-charge if you can't get reception where you need it.

**Wireless 911 warning.** Carrying a cell phone for emergencies is a good idea. "The wireless phone can be a lifesaving tool, particularly if you're out and about," agrees Patrick Halley, Government Affairs Director for the National Emergency Number Association. "In the past, you would have had no access to 911 at all" while on the go.

There's just one problem. Landline telephones are tied to a street address. When you dial 911 from a landline, the 911 operator knows your physical location, which helps police, fire, or emergency medical technicians find you faster. Your cell phone, however, doesn't have a fixed address. It goes wherever you go. When you call 911 from a wireless phone, your cell phone company estimates where you are and sends that information to the nearest 911 center. "Of course, the estimate is always going to be less accurate because it's not a physical location," says Halley.

For example, a cell phone won't tell the 911 operator your altitude. "If I call from the 17th floor of an apartment building on my landline phone," the operator gets that information, Halley explains. "Whereas, if I dial from the 17th floor on my wireless phone, they don't even know which building I'm in, much less what floor I'm on." That's why it's important to tell the 911 operator where you are. "It's easier said than done, but try to be calm, keep your wits about you, and provide your exact location." Don't hang up until you do.

### Ditch contracts and avoid hefty cancellation fees.
Getting out of a lengthy cell phone contract can cost you up to $250 per phone, thanks to phone companies' outrageous cancellation fees. Luckily, new Web sites like *www.cellswapper.com* and *www.celltradeusa.com* can help you beat the system. These services help you find someone to take over your phone contract for the rest of its term, while avoiding the phone company's hefty cancellation fee.

### Escape costly text messages.
Unwanted text messages can send your cell phone bill skyrocketing. Ground it by blocking them. Companies sometimes send unsolicited text messages, called cell spam, that can run up your bill. It's illegal. If you get messages like these, call your cell phone company and ask them to subtract the cost of them from your bill. Texts from well-meaning friends or wrong numbers also contribute to sky-high charges. Your cell phone company may let you block several phone numbers from sending you text messages. Some service providers will turn off the texting feature on your phone altogether. Call your carrier for details.

### *Latest buzz on cell phones and cancer*

The American Cancer Society (ACS) says cell phones don't increase your risk of brain cancer. However, new research may link long-term use with rare tumors called acoustic neuromas. More studies are needed, but the ACS says you can protect yourself by keeping cell phone conversations short and talking through an earpiece while holding the phone away from your body. Both time spent on the phone and closeness to it may affect your risk of acoustic neuroma.

**ICE can save your life.** Emergency room doctors and first responders often use your cell phone to locate family members and friends when you are injured and cannot speak for yourself. Those close to you can tell doctors your drug allergies, medical history, current prescriptions, and special needs. Open your cell phone's address book, and type the letters ICE — an acronym for "in case of emergency" — in front of the names of people you want contacted in an emergency.

# Simple fixes for plumbing problems

**2 steps to saving more water.** Spend five bucks at the hardware store and cut your water use by thousands of gallons a year, just by installing an inexpensive faucet aerator. First, check to see if your faucet already has an aerator. Look for tiny numbers printed on the mouth of the faucet. These tell you the flow rate. The lower the numbers, the better. If they are higher than 2.75 gpm (gallons per minute), install a new aerator. If you don't see any numbers, you don't have one. Stick your finger inside the faucet mouth and feel around. If you can feel "threads," then your faucet can accept an aerator.

Also, consider replacing old, leaky shower heads with low-flow models. These water misers use only 2.5 gallons of water per minute. You can easily tell if you have a water-wasting shower head by placing a 2-quart sauce pan on your bathtub floor. Turn the shower on full blast and situate the pan in the middle of the spray. If it fills up in less than 12 seconds, you need a low-flow shower head.

**Quick faucet fixes.** You don't need a plumber to fix these common faucet problems. You can do it yourself with a little know-how.

+ Faucets that spit rather than spray probably have a clogged aerator. Simply unscrew the mouth of the faucet and rinse out the screen inside, removing all mineral buildup.

+ Kitchen sink sprayers with low water pressure probably need their diverter cleaned. Unscrew the head on the main faucet and look for a small valve in the faucet's stem (base). Pop it out with a screwdriver and soak it in a hot, half-vinegar, half-water bath.

+ Leaky shower heads most likely need a new O-ring, a small rubber or plastic ring. Unscrew the shower head from the wall pipe.

Remove the O-ring from inside the shower head. Take it with you to the hardware store and buy a new one the same size, along with Teflon tape. Wrap the tape around the threads of the shower head and insert the new O-ring. Screw the head back onto the wall pipe by hand.

## Drinking "hard" water guards your heart

The same hard water that stains your toilet can actually help your heart. Drinking natural mineral water lowered blood pressure in one study and slashed heart attack risk in another. In fact, researchers found the harder the water, the lower the heart attack risk in men. Magnesium seems to lower blood pressure, while fluoride reduces heart attack risk. Iron and copper in water, however, may boost your chance of a heart attack.

**Easy repairs for common toilet problems.** The phantom flusher. The toilet that never stops running. The unexpected overflow. All plumbing problems you can fix yourself with this advice and a little elbow grease.

+ Think fast to stop an overflowing toilet. Take the lid off the tank, grab the floating ball inside, and pull up. This will stop water from flowing into the bowl. Reach down with your free hand and turn off the water valve connecting the toilet to the wall.

+ Put an end to running toilets. Sometimes the chain inside the tank gets caught under the flapper valve inside the tank. If that's the case, try this no-cost trick. Thread the chain through a plastic straw. Cut the straw down to size, if necessary. This will keep it from getting sucked under the flapper.

✦ Replace the flapper valve. If the chain isn't the problem, the flapper valve probably is. This rubber piece at the bottom of the tank drops closed after you flush, but over time, it may start to crack and leak. Take the old one with you to the hardware store to get the right replacement.

**Unclog your drains with vinegar.** Clear clogged drains like a Roto-Rooter with this three-ingredient drain opener. It's natural, safe, and won't damage pipes, either. Pour half a cup of baking soda down the drain, followed by a cup of hot vinegar. Let the two bubble and break apart the debris. After a few minutes, flush the drain with a quart of hot water. Try these other natural remedies for nasty clogs, too.

✦ Sweep sink drains clean by dropping three Alka-Seltzer tablets down them followed by a cup of white vinegar, then flush with hot water.

✦ To remove grease buildup in drains, dump half a cup of salt and half a cup of baking soda down the drain, then a kettle of boiling water. Allow it to sit overnight before rinsing.

✦ Maintain free-flowing pipes with this weekly treatment. Combine 1/4 cup of baking soda, 1/4 cup salt, and 1 tablespoon cream of tartar, and stir thoroughly. Pour the mixture down the drain, then immediately follow with a cup of boiling water. Wait a few seconds, then rinse with cold water.

**S.O.S. for septic systems.** Septic tanks need tender loving care if you want them to last a lifetime. Zane Satterfield, engineer scientist with the National Environmental Services Center, offers his expert advice.

✦ Don't install a garbage disposal. "The biggest mistake homeowners can make is installing a garbage disposal. That's one of the hardest things on a septic system," he explains, because the food scraps disrupt the bacteria in your septic tank from breaking down human waste.

+ Ignore additives that claim to boost your septic system. "We would rather you not use those. Some people put too much additive down the septic system." This causes the solids in the tank to break down too fast and clog your leach bed.

+ Check cleaning labels for key phrases. "'Septic safe' is probably the best phrase to look for," he says. "Environmentally safe" is not the same, nor is "biodegradable." "Something biodegradable can still be hard on your septic tank, like food scraps," he points out.

+ Don't sweat the small stuff. Household cleaners, even ammonia and bleach, are safe to flush down your pipes in small amounts. "That's the key word — in small amounts." For instance, the amount of bleach you use to wash a load of whites won't hurt, but don't use more than the package recommends.

+ Avoid flushing wet wipes. "Unless they say otherwise on the container, they do not break down like toilet paper. Even if they say biodegradable, they can still take longer to break down than regular toilet paper," warns Satterfield.

**Say goodbye to frozen pipes.** You can prevent your pipes from freezing in winter with these inexpensive ideas.

+ Insulate both hot and cold water pipes in unheated areas, like your basement, crawl space, and garage. Inexpensive pipe sleeves and heat tape can help prevent freezing. In your attic, simply tuck the pipes under regular attic insulation.

+ Insulate with newspaper if you live in an area with mild winters. Wrap 1/4-inch of newspaper around exposed pipes in unheated parts of your house.

+ Open cabinet doors under the sinks in kitchen and baths when the temperature drops. This lets warm household air circulate around the plumbing.

+ Set your thermostat a little higher on nights when you have a hard freeze. Your heating bill may cost a few dollars more, but you'll protect your pipes from bursting.

+ Leave the heat on when you go out of town in winter, and don't set the thermostat lower than 55 degrees.

**4 ways to thaw pipes.** Hopefully, all the insulating steps you take will protect the pipes in your home from freezing. But if the worst happens, the American Red Cross gives this advice for thawing pipes.

+ Wrap an electric heating pad around the frozen section of pipe.

+ Aim an electric hairdryer at the pipe until it has thawed.

+ Set up an electric space heater near the frozen areas.

+ Soak towels in hot water and wrap them around pipes.

Keep applying heat by one of these methods until you regain full water pressure. Be sure to open a faucet while you thaw the pipes. Running water helps thaw the ice inside pipes. Never use a blowtorch to thaw pipes. The intense heat could boil the water inside and cause the pipe to explode. Don't thaw them using any kind of heater with an open flame, including kerosene, propane, or charcoal heaters.

**Why you should test your water for toxic substances.**
Your water utility tests and controls the quality of your drinking water. Every year, the utility should send you a water-quality report that tells you if any contaminants were found in the water and whether they are dangerous. What this report won't tell you is the quality of water inside your home.

The plumbing in your house can leach lead, copper, and other contaminants into otherwise clean public water. That's why it's a good idea to test the water coming from your faucet. If you drink well water, you should test for coliform bacteria, nitrates, total dissolved solids, and pH levels every year.

Call your municipal water authority or department of health and ask if they do in-home testing. Some do it free — others charge a small fee. You can also buy do-it-yourself test kits, ranging from about $15 to $150 each.

Unfortunately, most DIY kits only test for one contaminant at a time. You will probably need more than one kit to test for multiple contaminants. You can also have a state-certified, independent lab test your water. This option sometimes costs more but lets you test for multiple contaminants. Contact your local health department or the EPA's Safe Drinking Water Hotline at 800-426-4791 for a list of certified labs.

**Make your home water safer to drink.** "Many people in the United States are fortunate to have high-quality drinking water, without any contaminants above levels of concern," says Richard Andrew, NSF's operations manager in their Drinking Water Treatment Units Program. But, occasionally, harmful compounds creep into water supplies. "Lead can be an issue in older community water systems," he points out, while "inorganic contaminants, such as arsenic, are the most common in individual wells. All can be dangerous, especially for individuals with compromised immune systems."

You can choose from five at-home methods for treating your water — adsorption filters (such as charcoal filters), reverse osmosis systems, distillation systems, ultraviolet disinfection products, and water softeners. Some remove certain compounds better than others. For instance, NSF recommends adsorption filters for removing cancer-causing compounds called PCBs, while either adsorption, reverse osmosis, or distillation can get rid of lead.

The best way to figure out which system to buy is to visit the NSF Web site at *www.nsf.org/Certified/DWTU/* and look up each contaminant you know is in your water. NSF will tell you which filters are certified for removing that pollutant. You can also call the NSF Consumer Affairs Office toll-free at 877-NSF-HELP for advice.

Whichever method you choose, Andrew offers this advice. "People should make sure that the system is NSF Certified for treating the contaminants in their water. Beware of any products or claims that are not certified. Some noncertified products may have little basis for the claims they make."

## Go tankless for greater savings

Need a new water heater? Consider the super-efficient tankless model. This device heats water only when you need it, instead of heating and storing a whole tank of water. The result — lower energy bills. In fact, experts say replacing a water heater tank with a tankless model can shave 10 to 40 percent off your hot water heating costs. These devices are available in electric, natural gas, and propane-powered varieties. They cost more to install but cost less to run. Plus, they last longer — up to 20 years, compared to 10 to 15 for tank heaters.

# Pathway to perfect plants

**Extend gardening season for pennies.** Imagine making a season-extender that won't blow away or break the bank — no matter how many you use. All you need are 2-liter bottles and duct tape. Place one bottle as your center marker and form a circle of bottles around it. Wrap duct tape around the outside of the circle to bind all the outer bottles together. Then remove the center bottle, and you have a new cloche.

For best results, position the cloche around the plant in the morning and fill each bottle with water and a pinch of salt to help hold the heat. The sun will heat the water during the day. That will keep your plant warmer during chilly nights because water retains heat better than air does. For extra protection from frost, throw a sheet of clear plastic or a transparent old shower curtain over the cloche.

**7 bargains and freebies for gardeners.** You could spend loads of money on planters, plants, and garden supplies, but you'll probably like these bargains and freebies better.

+ Ask your county extension agent how late you can plant spring bulbs so they still bloom this coming spring. If the right time is after the New Year, buy during spring bulb closeout sales when you could get up to 75 percent off.

+ Don't buy garden tools or equipment if you only need them a few times each year. Instead, borrow or trade tools with other gardeners. For larger, rarely used items, renting may be cheaper than buying.

+ Check local dairies, horse farms, and other farms for free manure.

✦ Don't buy fresh annuals every year. If you live in the southern half of the country and your annuals don't reseed, dig them up, pot them, and keep them in your garage until replanting time. Get advice on overwintering annuals from your local county extension agent.

✦ Don't spend loads of money on a composter. Make a compost pile in your backyard instead. If pests or other problems make a composter necessary, check with your local trash company. They may sell quality composters at far more reasonable prices than your garden supplier.

✦ Organize a plant swap to trade plants you don't need for new plants you want. Seed swaps can work equally well.

✦ Shop flea markets and yard sales for plants and garden supplies. Also, try the bargain bins at home improvement stores. Just be sure to check the health or quality of the product carefully before you buy.

And don't forget reusables. "Items like older pots, colanders, or pitchers that you no longer use in the kitchen can easily be planted up to find new life as whimsical, inexpensive planters," says Colleen Vanderlinden, freelance writer and creator of *www.inthegardenonline.com*.

**Spend less for quality trees and shrubs.** Get the best deal possible if you're buying from the plant nursery. Bypass that tree in the 10-gallon container and buy the smallest size available instead. Not only will you get a dramatic discount, but your tiny tree will probably be the same size as the 10-gallon version in just a few years.

That may sound unlikely but consider this. Because a 10-gallon tree is container-bound for several years, it can't grow as rapidly as a younger tree planted where roots can spread out. So buy small when shopping for trees, shrubs, and perennials. Your new plant may become just as big and impressive as its older brothers in a few years, but you'll save big today.

**Get free plants for landscaping.** "Ask garden centers for plants they are throwing out," recommends The Frugal Wench. "This seems to work best at local places. Most of the big box stores have strict policies against giving plants away, but the local places sometimes will just direct you to their trash pile and say "help yourself." This saves them money on dumping fees when they have to dispose of them, since dumps charge by the pound."

For more ideas on how to supply many of your gardening and landscaping needs for free, visit *www.frugalwench.com* and click the "Frugal Gardening 101" link. You'll not only discover ways to get free plants but also free mulch, free pots, free tools, and much more.

**3 offbeat paths to garden savings.** You can avoid paying full price on many garden items. Here's how.

+ Check your local farmer's market for perennials. Not only will you find plants proven to survive in your climate, but you may get lower prices than at the plant nursery.

+ Stock up on garden supplies at end-of-season sales. Don't buy anything that's not on sale. You can always try again when the season resumes next year.

+ Find out which trees and plants can be put in the ground near the end of the growing season and which ones you could successfully overwinter inside. Those are the trees and plants to buy at end-of-season discounts.

**End the misery of lugging a heavy sprayer.** To you, "heavy metal" is that five-gallon pressure sprayer you have to lug around the garden. End the misery. Take a couple of bungee-style cords and strap your heavy sprayer to a wheeled luggage cart or a dolly. Then let the good times — and your sprayer — roll.

246

**Keep cut flowers fresher longer.** Your cut flowers can look lovelier and last longer with these secrets.

+ Snip most flower varieties in late afternoon or early evening. Not only will each flower be thoroughly supplied with water and food when you cut it, but you'll also get a longer-lasting display. Cut roses and irises while they're still buds.

+ Don't cut with scissors. They crush the stem and cripple the flower's ability to drink. Use a very sharp knife, pruning shears, or florists' shears instead.

+ Make a slanted cut. A flat cut rests against the bottom of the vase so the stem can't easily take in water.

+ To help flowers retain their beauty and freshness, mix one cup of regular lemon-lime soda with three cups of very warm water and one-quarter teaspoon of bleach. Add one-quarter teaspoon of bleach every five days. For a simpler solution, mix one-quarter cup of Listerine mouthwash with a gallon of very warm water.

### Make a garden kneeler for pennies

Buy a slab of 3-inch foam and wrap it in thick plastic bags. Some of the thinner discount store bags won't hold up well, so stick with department store bags or outdoor garbage bags. Consider putting one inside the other for added durability. When you're done, use duct tape to secure the bags snugly around the foam.

**Rescue your houseplants from softened water.** You've finally installed a water softener, but now your potted plants are struggling.

That's because softened water is saltier than hard water even if you can't taste the difference. To fix this salty problem, find out whether your outdoor hose faucets are attached to the water softener line. If not, collect hose water for your houseplants. Otherwise, try one of these.

+ Buy gypsum from your garden center. Before watering your plants, thoroughly mix one-half teaspoon into a gallon of softened water.

+ Replace the soil once a year and scrub away any salt deposits you find on the pot.

+ Collect rainwater to water your plants.

**Turn trash into compost treasure.** Pretty flowers, lush foliage, tasty vegetables. These are the things gardens are made of. But getting your garden to grow doesn't have to cost you a bundle. Household items you already have can work just as well. All you need to know is what throw on the compost pile. Use this list to help.

+ tea leaves and coffee grounds
+ sod and soil
+ toadstools
+ shredded corncobs
+ shredded leaves
+ crushed eggshells
+ grass clippings
+ uncolored human hair
+ pet hair
+ hay and straw
+ fruit and veggie peels
+ citrus fruits
+ sawdust

**Free coffee grounds for your garden.** Some Starbucks stores offer several pounds of spent coffee grounds to gardeners for free.

Call your local shop to see if they participate in this Grounds for Your Gardens program. If they don't, call around to other coffee or donut shops. You may get free grounds from one of them.

Sprinkle these coffee grounds around evergreens, roses, azaleas, camellias, and rhododendrons. Use them in your worm bin or compost bin. A coffee-grounds mulch can even help outdoor containers that stay too water-logged, but mulch lightly or your plant won't get water at all. Coffee can also cause caffeine poisoning in dogs, so avoid using it if dogs frequently pass through your yard.

**Grow tastier tomatoes and beat blossom end rot.** If you constantly battle blossom end rot, you could grow your tomatoes in extra large tomato cages. Caged plants resist blossom end rot better than staked tomatoes. But there's a better solution. For the sweetest, juiciest tomatoes ever, add powdered milk to their water. It nourishes your tomatoes with calcium, so they're far more tantalizing and delicious. That extra calcium can also defeat blossom end rot before it starts.

**Change kitchen waste into plant food — with no composting.** Use banana peels to grow beautiful flowers and tasty vegetables. But don't stop there. You can find many more ways to reuse the things you usually throw away. Start with these.

+ Save your banana peels year round. Air dry them on an old window screen until they're slightly crunchy. Then store them in a sealed container until you need them. Spread whole or shredded peels around tomato roots, rosebushes, staghorn ferns, veggies, and more. Their phosphorous and potassium make plants healthier and happier.

+ Crushed eggshells are great for potted plants and outdoor plants. Press them into the soil and watch your plants flourish.

✦ Don't throw out that pickle jar. Pour the leftover juice around your gardenias and other acid-loving plants.

✦ Save the water from boiling potatoes or spaghetti, let it cool, and use it to water your plants occasionally. Plants adore this "starchy" water.

**Beware the dangers of wood ash.** Sprinkle potassium-rich wood ash around your flowers, and you might get bigger blooms — but sometimes it can do more harm than good. This ash can turn acidic soil more alkaline in just a few days. But if your soil is already alkaline, it could damage your plants and deprive them of vital nutrients.

On top of that, wood ash adds salt to your soil, which can harm some plants even more. So don't use wood ash if your soil is neutral, alkaline, or already has plenty of potassium. A soil test can tell you whether your soil is acid or alkaline and what its potassium levels are if you're not sure. Consider doing this inexpensive test every other year. Your plants will thank you.

**Rev up your roses with a secret ingredient.** Brew up your own "liquid gold" for your roses. Here's how. Shop for alfalfa pellets or alfalfa meal. You'll need at least one-third cup of alfalfa for each rosebush, so be sure to buy enough. Pour the alfalfa into a container and add one gallon of water for each bush you'll feed. Let this alfalfa tea brew several days before using it to water your roses. Repeat this process once every three or four months. If you don't have time for tea, push a handful of alfalfa pellets into the soil around your rosebushes instead. Roses will devour it and reward you with luscious blooms.

## Stretch your growing season

Extend your growing season farther into autumn with this easy-to-make hot cap. Cut the bottom off a 2-liter plastic bottle, soak the label to remove it, and place it over the plant you want to protect. Push it down into the soil a little to keep the wind or animals from pushing it over. If the plant is too bushy for a two-liter, try a bottomless plastic milk jug.

Unlike some hot caps, you don't need to remove these bottles from your plants every day. Instead, just remove their caps. This lets hot air vent up and out of the bottle so your plants don't overheat on warm, sunny days. Just be sure to put the caps back on at sunset to keep your plants toasty all night long.

**Grow herbs indoors even in poor light.** You'd love a window herb garden during winter, but your windows don't let in enough light. Instead of expensive grow lights, tack a fluorescent light fixture to the underside of a shelf. Stock it with one "warm" fluorescent tube and one "cool" one and place your herbs 5 inches beneath it. Give your herbs about 16 hours of this "daylight."

If you used a fluorescent light fixture that has a cord and plug, attach it to a light timer, and you won't have to turn the lights on and off yourself. Just keep in mind that your herbs could use a few hours of real daylight, too. If you can't fit all the herbs you want under your lights, move your chives and parsley to an indoor windowsill permanently. They accept less light than other herbs.

**Seed starting for tightwads.** You can make most seed-starting kits cheap or free. Here's how to create a seed-starting station that provides warmth, light, humidity, and the best odds of success.

✦ Don't waste your money on plastic pots. Instead, poke holes in the bottom of cleaned out avocado skins or eggshells. Now you have free "pots" for your seeds.

✦ Seeds thrive on humidity, so place your "pots" inside clamshell plastic containers. Once closed, these containers keep humidity inside. You get these containers any time you order take-out food. Just save them and rinse them out.

✦ The inside of your refrigerator may be very cold, but the top is nice and warm. Set up your seed starters there.

✦ Seeds demand light, so place fluorescent lamps above them.

**Pick the right tree every time.** Buy the wrong tree and you could waste a lot of money on a plant that can't survive. To bark up the right tree, remember this advice from Wayne Juers, horticulturist and plant doctor for Pike Family Nurseries headquartered in Norcross, Ga.

✦ Decide whether you want quick shade or a slower grower. "Fast growth always provides a fast shade, but at the same time, it provides a very brittle tree that is easily blown over or breaks in strong winds and ice," says Juers. Slow-growers are more likely to survive bad weather.

✦ Figure out how much sun and shade your tree will get. Do a little research to determine which tree varieties grow well in that light and then eliminate the ones that grow too fast or too slowly for your needs.

✦ If you're planting the tree yourself, choose a tree with a trunk diameter — called a caliper — of 2 inches or less. Trees with larger calipers can be tough to plant on your own. "You need a professional or you need a crew to help you dig the hole and get it in," Juers explains.

✦ Only choose trees with a straight trunk.

✦ Bypass trees with scars, exposed bark, or peeled bark. These are signs of damage during unloading.

✦ Avoid any container tree that has very loose dirt or looks as if it fell out of its container. Check balled and burlapped trees closely, too. "Make sure it has a nice size ball," says Juers. "It shouldn't be square or odd-shaped, and the ball must be firm. If the ball is loose, that means it was dropped and soil has moved away from the roots, and the tree probably won't live."

**Become a bulb expert.** The next time you shop for spring or summer bulbs, remember these tips from Wayne Juers, horticulturist and plant doctor for Pike Family Nurseries headquartered in Norcross, Ga.

✦ "Make sure the retailer has them displayed in a somewhat of a cool, dry place," says Juers, "because if they've been exposed to sun or moisture, they will start to rot."

✦ Look for bulbs that are firm, never mushy.

✦ Larger bulbs may cost more, but consider the benefits. "You're going to get more plants out of the bigger bulbs, Juers says. "But sometimes for value, the little bulbs are fine. Just buy more of them, and you might get a better deal."

✦ For spring bulbs, Juers offers two extra pieces of advice. "Make sure there's lots of paper-like skin on the outside," he says. And, instead of buying bagged bulbs, look for single bulbs packed in Styrofoam or shredded straw. "You get a better quality bulb when you can hand select," he explains.

Be careful after buying bulbs, too. Plant them at the right time and the right depth. "People make a lot of mistakes because the bulbs become available much too early to plant," says Juers. Plant spring bulbs by September and October if you live in the colder areas like the Northeast, but wait until November or December if you live farther south. Cold-area gardeners should plant summer-flowering bulbs in late May or June, while Southern growers can plant their bulbs in April.

## How deep to plant your bulbs

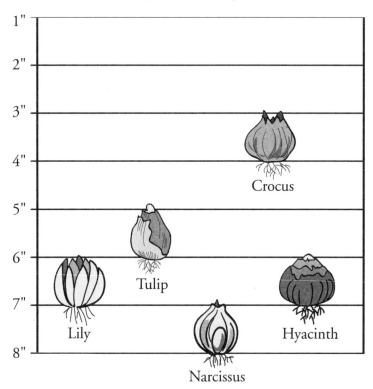

**Super solution for muddy shoes.** If you've ever forgotten to take off your muddy gardening shoes, you know gardening can become a case of mud, sweat, and tears when you try to clean a muddy carpet. But shedding your shoes every time you go inside for supplies can drive you nuts. Solve both problems with ease.

Just find an inconspicuous spot near your door and keep two shower caps or plastic grocery bags there. Whenever you need to come inside, slip the shower caps or plastic bags over your shoes. If you use plastic bags, tie them around your ankles like a ballerina's toe shoes. Either way, you'll never need to wrestle with this mud problem again.

**Prevent container stains on your deck.** Before you put containers on your deck, try this inexpensive stain preventer. Check recycling centers, yard sales, flea markets, and other secondhand stores for burner grates from old gas stoves. Ask friends and family to keep an eye out for these, too. Once you collect a few, you'll have charming "stands" to rest your containers on.

Even if the containers drip on the wood, the water won't stay long enough to cause a stain. If the grates look unattractive to you, check your local home improvement store for spray paint that can be used on metal. Turn your grates a bright, modern silver; a country-style copper; or any other color that suits your taste.

**Simple secret for early veggies.** Plant borage in pots throughout your vegetable garden. You'll attract bees that can help bring you an earlier crop. If you're short on pots, don't plant borage straight into the ground. It can be as invasive as mint. Instead, check yard sales and flea markets for discounted pots in good condition.

**Water your plants while on vacation.** Water your houseplants while visiting Europe or enjoying the beach in Jamaica. You can do it if you start a few days before your departure. You'll need a bucket, a stool or crate, and an old mop head made of rayon or another synthetic fabric. Fill the bucket with water, put it on the stool, and place your plants in a tight circle around it. Turn the mop head upside down and put it in the water.

For each plant, take one mop strand and bury its end deep in the soil near the roots. Keep the plants lower than the mop head so water can seep down the strand. Also, make sure that part of the mop head will stay beneath the water while you're gone. Check your plants once each day until you leave to be sure they are getting enough water. If they are, just add extra water to the bucket before you go. Your well-watered plants will be waiting when you come home.

**Get the most blooms from your rosebushes.** Before you snip that gorgeous rose, be sure to cut at the right spot. Otherwise, your plant will produce tiny, weak stems that won't hold up your stunning rose. When you're pruning or clipping, cut back to a stem with at least five leaves. Your rosebush will thank you by putting out a stronger stem that can support the weight of more rose blossoms.

**Unleash more power from your fertilizer.** Soil that's too alkaline or acid can prevent your plants from absorbing the fertilizer you give them. That's like pouring fertilizer money down the drain. Fortunately, soil testing is easy and inexpensive. Just dig up a few samples and ask your local cooperative extension agent how to get them tested. The test results will reveal whether your soil is acid or alkaline, which nutrients it needs, and how to fertilize or amend it so your plants and lawn flourish.

But remember, your soil test results are only as good as the samples you take, so be careful to do it right. Don't mix samples from the vegetable garden with samples from the flower bed, shrubbery bed, or lawn. After all, the kind of soil that grows a perfect lawn can differ greatly from the ideal soil for veggies. Pick which areas you want tested and take one group of soil samples for each. You'll be surprised how easy it is.

For example, go to your veggie garden, dig up several 5-inch-deep plugs of soil, and mix them together. Remove anything in the soil sample that isn't soil. Drop the sample into the container recommended by the testing lab and label accordingly. Follow the same process for the lawn or any other area you want tested. When you're done, you'll have perfect soil samples that may lead to the most dazzling yard and garden you've ever had.

## Choose the perfect container

Walk into a garden center and you'll find all kinds of containers made of different materials. Use this table to help you find out which one is right for your needs.

| Material | Advantages | Disadvantages |
|---|---|---|
| concrete | durable, can grow moss and lichen on their sides | heavy |
| glazed ceramic pots | retains moisture well | may dry out too slowly or be too airtight for root growth |
| hypertufa troughs | durable, can grow moss along their sides | hard to find |
| metal | durable and attractive options include cast iron, aluminum, copper, or steel | small ones heat up too much, especially in the sun; poor insulators in cold weather |
| plastic and fiberglass | lightweight, inexpensive, durable, and resistant to staining | dry out slowly |
| stone and artificial stone | durable | expensive and may be heavy |
| terra cotta | great for root growth and good air exchange | heavy, dries out rapidly |
| wood | keeps soil temperature from fluctuating too much, good insulator in cold weather | wood rots |

**Plot the perfect garden layout every year.** Find an empty squeezable ketchup or mustard bottle or an empty drink bottle that has a pull-up "sipper." Clean it out, let it dry, and fill it two-thirds full with flour. Now, go out to your garden bed and use this squeezable marker to mark where each plant should go.

For best results, "draw" a shape that matches the plant's mature size and leave a gardener-size working space between plants. You can even mark spaces for walking paths or garden art. When you're done, you'll have the perfect garden layout for your space. This clever trick also saves money because you'll never buy more plants than your garden can hold.

**Avoid pruning mistakes that disfigure trees.** Don't make the unkindest cut of all. Prune your trees skillfully so you won't lose the extra branches — or the whole tree — to disease. Before you cut, find the node, the place where one branch or twig connects to another. Cut near the node, but don't cut too closely or peel bark off the tree.

These mistakes — called bark-ripping, flush-cutting, and stub cutting — can leave the tree open to damage, disease, and dead branches. But if you prune correctly, the neatly pruned branches make great stakes for flowers and vegetables. Not only do they provide a charming, natural look, they also help you spend less money on stakes.

**Bark ripping**

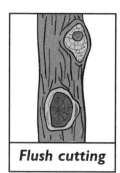

**Flush cutting**

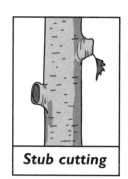

**Stub cutting**

**Beat damping off and blackspot.** Simple ingredients from your kitchen pantry can stop these two fungal bullies from picking on your yard and garden. If damping off is the problem, drink some chamomile tea and drop the used tea bag into 3-3/4 cups of water. After the tea bag has soaked awhile, remove it, and pour the water over your seedlings. For severe cases, use a fresh tea bag straight from the box. Damping off fungi hate it when you do that.

When the problem is blackspot tainting your lawn, fight back by sprinkling cornmeal right over those little brown patches. It's cheap, easy, and you may be surprised at how well it works.

**No more weeds in driveway cracks.** You've finally killed the weeds that set up housekeeping in your driveway and sidewalk cracks, but they'll grow back if you're not careful. Fill the cracks with sand, so the weed seeds can't get enough light to grow. For smaller cracks, try masonry sand, or stone dust. Here's another idea — scuttle weeds in the cracks of driveways and sidewalks with boiling water. Follow up by salting the cracks.

---

### Low-salt de-icer keeps you and your plants safe

De-icing salt can compact your soil, cripple root growth, and damage your plants, but here's the good news. You can protect your plants by reducing the amount of salt you normally use and mixing it with sand or kitty litter. Some experts say you can get safe traction by using as little as 1 pound of de-icing salt for every 50 pounds of sand. But if that sounds too scary, just try to use more sand than salt. Your wallet and your plants will appreciate it.

---

**Kill weeds and their seeds naturally.** You wouldn't expect a common household ingredient from your pantry to work like an expensive weed killer, but white vinegar does. Just heat it up, pour it in a spray bottle, and take aim. It's cheap, easy, and poison-free.

Expect young weeds to die quickly, but stubborn or well-established weeds may require another round or two of spraying. If that's a few sprays too many for you, try a single dose of pickling vinegar. It's more powerful than household vinegar and hits weeds harder. But aim very carefully or you may accidentally kill nearby plants.

Once you've wiped out your weeds, prevent future weed wars with these tips.

- ✦ Raise your mower blade. Taller grass blades keep light away from weed seeds, so they never start growing in the first place.

- ✦ Keep weeds out of your beds for good. Cover them with landscape fabric and a light coating of mulch.

**Defend your plants from weed-killing sprays.** Whether you're spraying your weeds with vinegar or something more toxic, you don't want to damage the surrounding plants. Here's a simple solution. Trim off the bottom of a plastic 2-liter bottle and do the same to a 16-ounce bottle. Store them both with your garden supplies. When you're ready to spray a weed, pick the appropriate size bottle. Place the bottle over the weed, slip the sprayer nozzle into the mouth of the bottle, and spray. Give the chemicals 30 seconds to sink in and then move on to the next weed. Your plants will remain safe, but your weeds won't live to tell the tale.

# Gardening shortcuts

**Get trellises, mini-pots, and a raised bed for free.**
Turn useless old things into great homes for plants. Use these ideas to
get started.

+ A chipped or cracked coffee mug can be a free planter for
your windowsill.

+ An old fireplace screen or bed headboard can become a trellis. So
can those lighted wire frame Christmas reindeer when their lights
stop working.

+ The sandbox your kids don't want anymore can be turned into a
raised bed.


**Turn your trash into garden treasures.** There is no shortage of items you can repurpose in the garden," says Colleen
Vanderlinden freelance writer and creator of "In the Garden Online" at
*www.inthegardenonline.com*. "Some of my favorites are items that would
normally end up in the landfill or in my recycling bin."

The mesh bags that oranges or onions come in are a good example. "Put
freshly dug tender bulbs in them, hang the bag in your shed or basement, and let your bulbs dry out a bit before storing them," suggests
Vanderlinden. She also recommends putting one bag inside another.
"Fill with potting soil, and sift over newly planted seeds," she says. And
at the end of the season? "Ball them up and use them as a great scrubber
for cleaning out flowerpots." But that's not all.

"Use old, worn serving spoons as garden tools. They work especially well
in planting up container gardens, when typical trowels are often too
large for such a small space," advises Vanderlinden.

"Another item I use in the garden is small, single-serving plastic yogurt
containers," she adds. "I use them to start vegetable seeds indoors by

washing them thoroughly, drilling or poking several holes in the bottom for drainage, filling with soil, and planting seeds. Tomatoes, peppers, and eggplants all do wonderfully grown this way, because they develop large root systems in a short amount of time. You can also use yogurt containers as measuring scoops when mixing up homemade potting soil. For example, if your recipe calls for eight parts peat to one part perlite, you'll know to add eight containers full of peat and one full of perlite, and your mixture will be perfect every time."

## Beware thirst-free dehydration

You can be dehydrated even if you're not thirsty — especially as you age. So drink plenty of water when you garden and watch for these signs of dehydration.

♦ dry lips and tongue

♦ rapid heart rate and breathing

♦ dizziness

♦ confusion

♦ dry, taut skin

♦ dark-colored urine

If you notice these symptoms, see your doctor right away.

**Make a seed-storing catalog.** An inexpensive photo album or old CD wallet can be the ideal place to keep your seed packets. Slip the packets in the pockets and you're set. For extra convenience, you can use sticky notes to make index tabs for each "page" or to tack notes on an individual pocket.

**Dig up ideal seed keepers that cost nothing.** An empty, plastic pill bottle from your last prescription is an ideal place to store seeds. Unlike seed envelopes, the bottles keep your seeds visible and in one place if the container tips over. They'll also keep your seeds dry and protected. So when you're done using a pill bottle, just clean it out, let it dry, and drop your seeds in. You can even label the bottle. If you don't have enough pill bottles, ask friends and family members to pass along their empty bottles when they no longer need them.

**Lighten heavy containers the easy way.** "You can use plastic grocery bags to fill space in the bottom of a large flowerpot or window box, which will save you soil and make the container lighter and easier to move," says Colleen Vanderlinden, freelance writer and creator of "In the Garden Online" at *www.inthegardenonline.com*. If you're short on plastic bags, use leaves or packing peanuts instead. Fill the bottom third of the container and then add soil. Your back and your wallet will thank you.

**Raise hard-to-grow flowers with ease.** Finally, you can enjoy flowers that are high maintenance or hard to grow successfully. You can also add plants that are usually killed by a freeze or heat wave every few years. Here's how. Select containers large enough for several flowers. Plant one or two varieties that you already grow successfully without much work, but leave open space for other flowers.

Next, buy silk versions of the flowers you wish you could grow. Choose only those that can easily pass for the real thing. Insert these into the spaces between the live plants. The casual observer will never know the difference, and you'll get to appreciate plants you thought you could never have. Just be sure to replace your silk flowers every few years. Not only will that keep your silk plants from becoming tattered, it will also give you the opportunity to try different flower varieties.

**Never hunt for missing garden items again.** Easily organize hand tools, plant labels, and other items you need for gardening. Get a hanging shoe organizer with clear plastic pockets. Drop your trowel and similarly sized items into the pockets. Then slip clear plastic cups, resealable baggies, or other small, transparent containers into the remaining pockets. Fill each one with twist ties, garden pegs, or other small items. You can even label the pockets so you can find everything at a glance.

### Stop freeze damage cold

Protect plants from an overnight frost or freezing temperatures with kitchen garbage bags or old pillow cases. Once you tuck a pillow case over a plant, it will be as toasty "in the sack" as you are.

**Water without wasting a drop.** Use the right watering tool at the right time to make sure all the water gets to your plants. If you water with a sprinkler, do it in the morning. Up to 40 percent of the water can be lost to evaporation if you run the sprinkler during the warmer, sunny afternoon hours. On top of that, morning watering allows leaves to dry before evening when damp leaves are more likely to "catch" fungal diseases. But if you water with a soaker hose or drip system, do it at night so the water has more time to sink into the soil.

**Make tomato stakes that water roots.** You could install both tomato stakes and root-watering pipes, but you'll like this clever two-for-one trick much better. For every tomato plant you plan to grow, cut a 5-foot length of 2-inch PVC pipe. Make a mark about 10 inches away from one end of each pipe. Next, use a post hole digger to make holes near each spot where you plan to place a tomato plant. Dump the displaced dirt on a plastic bag near each hole.

Drop the first pipe into one of the holes. Push it down into the soil as far as you can. Place a 2-inch thick piece of board over the top of the pipe. Hammer the board directly above the PVC pipe to push the pipe further into the soil until the mark on the PVC pipe is even with the ground. Roughly 4 feet of PVC pipe should remain above the dirt. Fill in the space emptied out by the post hole digger and dump any leftover dirt back down the pipe. Repeat this process for all the other poles. When you're done, you'll be ready to plant tomatoes. Just make sure each tomato plant is only a few inches from a pipe.

When you're ready to water, turn the hose on extra low and put the nozzle end in the pipe. Allow the pipe to fill and move on to the next pipe. Check back on the first pipe a few minutes later. If the water drains quickly, you may need to refill the pipe a few times. As the tomatoes grow, tie them to your PVC stakes. Wrap your tie around the stake first, knot it in place, and then tie the remaining lengths to the tomato plant.

## Avoid expensive prescriptions with oatmeal

Instead of prescription antihistamines or creams, soothe the itch from poison ivy with this clever trick. Run a warm bath and add a colloidal oatmeal product like the ones available from Aveeno. Enjoy a nice long soak. You'll be delighted by how economical and effective a 20-minute soak can be.

Homemade versions of colloidal oatmeal have been used for chicken pox and may work for poison ivy, as well. To make your own, put one to two cups of uncooked oatmeal in a blender or food processor and turn it into as fine a powder as you can. Stir the powder into your bath while the water is running and then soak the itch away.

**Pick a better garden hose.** Choose a rubber or rubber-vinyl garden hose, and it will last longer, advises Trey Rogers, lawn expert and author of the book, *Lawn Geek*. Rogers also suggests buying the highest ply hose you can.

**7 tips for gardening without pain.** If you're occasionally — or frequently — stiff and sore from gardening, now is the time to take action. Try these tips to ease the stress and strains of gardening.

+ Consider lighter tools with a fatter, longer, or more muscle friendly handle if you notice back, knee, wrist, elbow, or other strains. For example, choose a rake with a bent handle to prevent wrist strain.

+ Take a short walk and a few stretches to warm up your muscles before doing yard work. Then alternate among tasks to keep from overworking any single set of muscles.

+ Avoid stooping or bending over whenever possible. Instead, get closer to the ground by sitting on an upside down crate or use a kitchen stool.

+ Choose a shovel that matches the height between your arm and the ground. You can find them as short as 38 inches long.

+ Start gardening in small, raised beds. Make sure the center of the bed can be easily reached without straining when you sit on the outer rim. If raised beds won't work for you, consider container gardening instead.

+ Plant perennials, bulbs, or annuals that reseed themselves without your help. You'll still get beautiful flowers, but you won't have to replant every year.

+ Give climbing veggies their own trellis to limit the reaching and stretching you must do.

**Don't let injuries take you out of the garden.** Injuries from lawn and garden tools send over 200,000 people to the emergency room every year. Make sure you never become one of them. Take these steps to protect yourself.

✦ Prevent surprise sprains and strains. Don't try to lift a heavy flowerpot by yourself. Fill it after you place it and get help from friends and wheelbarrows when you need to move it.

✦ Wear sturdy shoes to protect your feet, especially if you have diabetes. Avoid sandals, flip-flops, shoes with open backs or open toes, and bare feet.

✦ Keep your tetanus shot up to date by getting a new booster shot every 10 years.

✦ Wear protective gloves and clothing anytime you use poisonous sprays. Wash yourself and your clothes thoroughly afterward.

✦ Wear protective goggles when using power tools and equipment.

## *Play in your garden to avoid arthritis*

Lower your chances of arthritis without resorting to drugs. Australian researchers found that women in their 70s who did just over an hour of moderate exercise every week were less likely to develop frequent arthritis symptoms during the following three years. Women who got more than two hours of moderate exercise had even higher odds of preventing arthritis symptoms. But there's even more good news. Exercise doesn't necessarily mean running or working out at a gym. Mowing, raking, and working in your yard or garden counts, too.

**Keep outdoor seat cushions spotless.** Pollen, dust, and pet hair can seem to magically attach themselves to your outdoor seat cushions. Put a stop to it by covering the seat cushions with old pillowcases when you're not sitting on them. If the pillowcases get dirty, just throw them in the wash.

**Make an ugly tree stump fade away.** Get rid of an unsightly tree stump without digging it up. This no-fuss method works wonders and saves you a boatload of cash. Drill large holes deep into the stump, especially near the edges. Fill them with sugar and soak the stump and its holes thoroughly with the hose. Cover with a foot of mulch and wait. Your tree stump will simply decay away. Or drill a few holes in the center of the stump and dump your leftover coals from the barbecue grill after every cookout. You'll burn the stump away from the inside out.

**Save your plants from poison ivy vines.** If you've just discovered a poison ivy vine wrapped around one of your favorite plants, don't panic. The Louisiana State University Agricultural Center recommends this method for saving your plant. Instead of spraying — and killing — your plant and the poison ivy with herbicide, break out your loppers and buy an herbicide made from triclopyr. Garden center staffers can help you find this herbicide.

Use your loppers to clip the poison ivy vine near its base and then treat the base with the triclopyr. The vine will wither away, and the triclopyr will kill the base and roots. Unlike some poison ivy treatments, you can try this one any time of year. Just remember to clean your loppers thoroughly afterward and don't try to remove the dead vine without wearing protective gloves and clothing. Wash yourself, the gloves, and the clothing as soon as you're done.

**Take the thrifty route to a garden path.** You can make an inexpensive garden path from locally available products. Depending on where you live, this may include buckwheat hulls, mushroom compost, pine straw, cherry pits, or delicious-smelling cocoa shells.

Check your local garden center. If you don't find what you're looking for, ask the garden center staff or a landscaping service where to go. You may also be able to get path materials for cheap or free from a local business or processor. For example, if buckwheat is grown in your area, a local processor may welcome the chance to get rid of some buckwheat hulls.

But if you're unfamiliar with the material, ask whether it's safe to use in all gardens. For example, The American Society for the Prevention of Cruelty to Animals reports that cocoa shells are toxic to dogs and recommends that pet owners avoid using them.

# Grass roots guide to lawn care

**Easy leaf-bagging for the one-person yard crew.**
Leaf-bagging has always been a two-person job, but now two clever
tricks can help you go it alone. If you only need to fill one plastic bag,
loop the bag's ties over your wheelbarrow handles so the mouth of the
bag faces into the wind. Now the bag is rigged for hands-free operation.
Just scoop the leaves in, and you'll soon be done.

If you expect to fill several plastic bags, lay out a tarp or shower curtain
and rake the leaves on to it. When you have enough to fill a bag, roll the
tarp up like a sleeping bag.

Put one end into the bag, turn the
tarp up on that end, and shake it so
the leaves fall into the bag. When
you've emptied the tarp, remove it from
the bag and repeat the process for the
next bag. No fuss, no muss, and no
help needed.

**Bypass the #1 lawn mowing mistake.** Mowing your lawn
to a short height may mean fewer mows per season, but it's the worst
mowing mistake you can make. In fact, this short cut may force you to
spend extra time and money fighting weeds, insects, and grass disease.
And here's why.

Lawns that get regular buzz cuts naturally have shorter blades and shallower roots. Because the size of each grass blade determines how much
sunlight it absorbs, shorter blades take in less. This sunlight shortage
makes your lawn more susceptible to disease and insect damage.
Meanwhile, the shallower roots can limit each blade's water supply,

making the grass even weaker. As if that weren't bad enough, a short lawn invites weeds to grow because more light reaches weed seeds and seedlings. That gives weeds extra fuel to help them choke out your grass.

You could beat these problems by constantly weeding and spraying during every month your grass grows, but that's hard work. Instead, keep your lawn at a height between 2 and 3 inches and never chop off more than one-third of the blade. Your lawn may reward you by smothering weeds and turning itself into lush green carpet your neighbors will envy.

## Pick the best grass for your yard

When sinking a bunch of money into a new lawn, don't plant the wrong seed. Instead, consider what conditions your grass can expect to face and choose a variety that's built to handle those conditions.

| Problem | Grass variety |
|---------|---------------|
| heat | Bermuda, bahiagrass, bluestem, zoysia |
| cold | Kentucky bluegrass, Supina bluegrass |
| drought | buffalograss, blue grama, bluestem, chewings fescue, bahiagrass, zoysia |
| shade | bahiagrass, chewings fescue, creeping red fescue, St. Augustine |
| wear | Bermuda, bluegrass, bahiagrass, zoysia |

**Defend your turf against drought.** You may not be able to end a drought, but you can arm your lawn against it. To help fortify grass so it recovers from drought quickly, start with five simple steps.

✦ Adjust your standard mowing height upward. Add a half-inch if your mowing height is 2 inches, 3/4 inch if it's 3 inches, or a

271

full inch for 4 inches. You'll encourage a deeper root system and natural chemical reactions that help your grass tolerate drought stress.

+ Avoid shallow and frequent watering. Instead, wait until the first signs of wilt show up and then water deeply.

+ Keep off the grass whenever possible. The less people and pets walk on it, the better off your lawn will be.

+ Keep your mower blade sharp. The rough cut made by blunt mower blades causes grass to retain less water.

+ Avoid using pesticides on your grass until the drought improves. They'll just add stress to an already-weakened lawn. By simply storing your pesticides until the drought breaks, you'll buy fewer containers of pesticide and your lawn will be more resilient.

**Say sayonara to sticky grass clippings.** You can forget about cleaning your mower. Spray WD-40 on its underside so grass clippings can't stick there anymore. Then, when you're hot and tired after mowing, you won't need to pry clippings off your mower deck. Instead, you can check that deck, smile at how clean it is, and go inside for a cold, refreshing drink.

**End your mowing pains.** Lawn mowing is aerobic exercise that can cause sore muscles, sore joints, and even back pain, a recent study says. But mowing should be light to moderate exercise, not an exercise in misery. If your lawn mower requires strenuous effort to move and steer, look for a lighter mower. Also, look for features you can tailor to your needs. Good examples include wheels that make the mower easier to turn or adjustable handles to prevent arm, hand, and shoulder strain.

## Powerful new sun protection lasts longer

A new sunscreen ingredient can block harmful ultraviolet A (UV–A) rays better than ever before. It's called ecamsule or Mexoryl SX, and it's just been approved by the FDA. Unlike other UV–A protectors, ecamsule isn't easily broken down by sunlight after a couple of hours, so it lasts longer. This could mean fewer wrinkles and less risk of skin cancer. To get this heavy–duty protection, you can buy Loreal's Anthelios sunscreen or Lancome's UV Expert 20, but both are pricey. Keep an eye out for new and less–expensive products that may soon contain this powerful sun guard.

## Lightweight reel mowers packed with advantages.

Your old gas-powered mower finally conked out, and you'd like a less-expensive mower that requires less maintenance. Maybe it's time to take a new look at the reel push mower. "I think a lot of people are under the misconception that they're really hard to use," says Lars Hundley, owner of CleanAirGardening.com. He explains that modern reel mowers are far less heavy and much easier to push than older push mowers. Some even weigh as little as 17 pounds. Consider these other advantages.

+ You won't have trouble starting a push mower, and you won't need to haul it to the repair shop for maintenance. "With a push mower, you push and it mows," says Hundley. "It's pretty mechanically simple, and there's really not that much that can go wrong with it."

+ The reel mower is better for your lungs and sinuses because it creates no smoke and pollution. Gas-powered mowers are heavy polluters. "Even though they're only burning a little bit of gasoline, they're putting out more pollution than an automobile for every hour you push one," Hundley explains.

✦ "You don't get the noise," adds Hundley. "You can actually carry your cell phone or your cordless phone when you're mowing with a push mower and hear it when it rings."

Of course, reel mowers aren't perfect. Their blades still need sharpening every few years, and they don't mow well in yards full of rocks, sticks, or tall weeds. And if your yard is quite large, you might need a self-propelled power mower. But otherwise, you may find that you prefer the new reel push mowers. Not only do they have all the advantages Hundley describes, but their cleaner cutting style is also better for your grass.

**How to water a slope successfully.** Watering downhill is an uphill battle. That's because water usually rushes down the slope before it has time to seep into the earth. You could buy soaker hoses, but here's a cheaper alternative. Water for a few minutes — or until you see runoff — and then stop so moisture can sink in. Return a little later for a few more minutes of watering and then stop again. Repeat this process until you're satisfied you've watered enough.

# Take aim at pesky pests

**3 ways to stop deer in their tracks.** You've always wondered why some people can keep deer out of their gardens while you can't. Now you can learn their secret. "If you're going to try to do any kind of pest control with one tool, you're doomed to failure," says Steve Tvedten, author of the free, nontoxic pest control book at *www.thebestcontrol2.com*. So don't try one way to block deer. Try three.

First, grab your blinking Christmas lights. "Christmas lights that are set up on a motion detector will keep things out," Tvedten explains. He also recommends spraying fruit trees, shrubs, and flowers with a mixture of several eggs stirred into a gallon of water. But if your deer are too hungry or too numerous to be stopped by these tricks alone, place netting over smaller plants. Or surround your garden with lightweight plastic mesh fencing tall enough to keep leaping deer out. This nearly invisible fencing won't be an eyesore to you — but deer will hate the sight of it.

**White House secret ends squirrel damage.** After years of struggles, White House groundskeepers suddenly reduced squirrel damage by more than 90 percent. They tempted the squirrels away from plants with six nut-filled squirrel feeding boxes. You can do the same thing — but more cheaply. Just fill up a few plates with nuts, leave them out near your plants, and enjoy the results.

But if squirrel feeding isn't for you, plant squirrel-resistant bulbs, like narcissus, alliums, and Spanish bluebells. If you still plant bulbs squirrels like, clean up the papery skins after planting and lay a window screen on the ground over the bulbs. Weight the edges down with rocks or boards and remember to remove the screens before your flowers emerge from the ground.

## Keep squirrels out of your bird feeder permanently.

Feed the birds, not the squirrels, by using these clever tips.

+ Find a Slinky that a child no longer wants. Using staple or wire, fasten the top of the Slinky to the underside of your bird feeder so it surrounds the pole from top to bottom. Squirrels will be completely frustrated by this simple barrier.

+ Cut the bottom off a 2-liter soda bottle or 5-gallon water bottle. Drill holes through the neck of the bottle and use part of a coat hanger to hang the bottle from the bottom of the bird feeder. The resulting umbrella shape makes pole climbing impossible for squirrels. You can also get the same effect with an old bucket. Just cut the bottom off and drill holes through the sides of the bucket near the base. Use the coat hanger to attach it to the bottom of the bird feeder, and squirrels will seek easier pickings elsewhere.

+ Ask someone at the home improvement store to help you find an HVAC reducer. This is a short metal cylinder designed to connect a small duct to a larger one. You'll also need screws and small pieces of wood — called shims — to fit between the inner wall of the reducer and the bird feeder pole. Slip the reducer over the pole, jam the shims in the empty space between the pole and the reducer, and attach the entire contraption to the bird feeder pole with nails or screws.

## Wily ways to keep your garden animal free.
Pesticides can be both expensive and toxic. But using safer remedies like these may keep animals out of your garden, protect your health, and help you spend far less.

+ Raccoons. "If you have bright lights that come on when something moves in the garden , they're not going to like that," says Steve

Tvedten, author of the free, nontoxic pest control book at *www.thebestcontrol2.com*. So pick up a flashing light that's activated by motion detectors and put it in your garden. You can also surround your plants or garden with a yard-wide perimeter of chicken wire laid flat on the ground. Raccoons won't cross it. "They don't like the way it feels," Tvedten explains.

✦ Cats and dogs. Tvedten recommends spraying these furry intruders with a stream of water. A child's rifle-size water gun is ideal for this, but the hose works well, too.

✦ Woodchucks. Put blood meal on the soil, and they will look for better eats elsewhere.

✦ Moles. Use a spray of castor oil around mole holes and your garden. Moles don't like it one bit.

✦ Voles. Plant your bulbs with crushed oyster shells so these little rodents won't eat them anymore.

**Turn up the heat to save bulbs.** Raccoons and squirrels may love your bulbs, but one trip to the kitchen could fix that. Sprinkle cayenne pepper or Tabasco sauce on the soil around the bulbs and neither coons nor squirrels will stick around. You can also try black pepper. Just remember, you'll need to "reheat" the area with a fresh round of pepper or Tabasco after each rainfall.

**Scare away birds with computer castoffs.** Collect damaged or outdated computer CDs from friends and neighbors and you may finally get to eat your tomatoes before the birds do. Just be sure nobody will ever need those CDs again. Here's how to use them.

When you plant tomatoes, tie string between the tops of your tomato stakes and thread a CD on to each section. When you're done, all your tomato stakes should have a shiny CD hanging between them. If you don't have CDs, don't worry. Just use pie plates or wide strips of foil with a hole poked in the middle. For extra protection, stick a few children's Mylar pinwheels into the surrounding ground.

## Latest buzz about West Nile Virus

You're more likely to come down with dangerous symptoms if you catch West Nile Virus after age 50. That's why you should take every opportunity to protect yourself. Wear mosquito repellent outside and take extra care to avoid mosquito bites. And since mosquitoes often catch West Nile Virus from birds, don't touch a dead bird if you find one. Instead, contact your local health department and ask them what to do.

**Keep bunnies at bay for good.** Sprinkle blood meal on the soil to keep rabbits out, recommends Steve Tvedten, author of the free, nontoxic pest control book at *www.thebestcontrol2.com*. But if you have unusually persistent rabbits, head for the hardware store and ask about hardware cloth.

"Plant" a cylinder of hardware cloth around each small tree or shrub you need to protect. Bury the bottom 2 to 3 inches in the soil, but make sure it's tall enough to rise at least 2 feet above the ground or future snowfalls. To protect an entire garden or bed, check the area for rabbits first. Then put up a fence of either chicken wire or hardware cloth.

**Repel pests with free mulch.** Save your money. Instead of buying expensive cedar mulch at the garden center, ask local friends and family for pruned branches from their eucalyptus, cedar, juniper, and arborvitae. Put these branches through a chipper shredder, and you'll have your own pest-repelling mulch. Just remember, only local plants will do.

**Make your own insecticidal soap for pennies.** Mix 3/4 teaspoon of Murphy's Oil Soap into one quart of water and then show insects who really owns your plants.

---

### Hollywood movie-making tip keeps spiders away

The next time a spider sits down beside you, grab your Lemon Pledge can. The insect trainer for the movie "Arachnophobia" used Lemon Pledge to keep his spiders from straying out of their assigned paths. Apparently, spiders don't like to walk where Lemon Pledge has recently been sprayed.

---

**Ban bad bugs from blooms and seedlings.** "If you cut the bottom off of small yogurt containers, you can slip the bottomless yogurt cup over any tender seedlings in the garden to protect them from slugs and cutworms," says Colleen Vanderlinden, freelance writer and creator of *www.inthegardenonline.com*. "Just slide it over the plant, press it about an inch into the soil, and your plant will be protected."

Here are three other great ways to beat bugs cheaply.

✦ Thrips and aphids can bring viruses that damage your plants. But, according to Mississippi plant pathologists, you can keep the viruses out just by spreading aluminum foil around tomatoes, basil, peppers, and squash.

✦ Knock aphids right off your plants with a strong spray of water.

✦ If fire ants are coming between you and your garden, pour an inch of Epsom salts over their mounds. Surround the mounds with another inch, so the ants don't escape to cause trouble elsewhere.

**Make horticultural oil spray at home.** Common household ingredients can defend roses and hydrangeas from disease-causing bugs and mites. Mix 1 tablespoon of biodegradable dishwashing liquid with a cup of corn oil, safflower oil, peanut oil, sunflower oil, or soybean oil. Then add 2 cups of water. This horticultural oil spray will snuff out pests so your flowers can flourish.

**Stop slugs without paying a penny.** Capture slugs by putting cabbage leaves or old pieces of board in your garden. Since slugs like to hide under these during the day, visit your slug traps during sunset or early evening. Flip the boards or cabbage leaves over, swipe the slugs off, and dump them where they'll never reach your garden again. If you're short on boards and cabbage leaves, surround your plants with a barrier of crushed eggshells instead. Slugs don't like to crawl over the eggshells' rough edges, so they'll stay away.

**Invite pest eaters to patrol your garden.** Imagine a garden where you never need pesticides because your own personal pest police constantly sweep it clean. You can have that garden if you attract bugs and animals that eat your pests — and you can grow charming plants to do it.

✦ Grow angelica, dill, morning glories, anise, fennel, sunflowers, or yarrow to tempt ladybugs into your garden. They'll make short work of aphids, thrips, whiteflies, and other soft-shelled insects that ravage your plants.

+ Plant holly, elderberry, dogwood, barberry, or cotoneaster to invite insect-eating birds for a snack.

+ Grow borage or sweet alyssum among your flowers or vegetables. Aphid eaters love them.

Just remember that pesticides will harm your insect eaters, so avoid using them.

## Pesticides pose Parkinson's danger

Using pesticides may raise your risk of Parkinson's disease. Researchers from the Mayo Clinic recently discovered that men with Parkinson's were more likely to have been exposed to pesticides than men without the disease.

**Frogs help garden pests croak.** Frogs feast on many of the same bugs you're trying to chase off. In fact, if you stop using pesticides and herbicides, frogs could help wipe out your pests for pennies. Here's how to invite these helpful hoppers for a snack.

+ If you have a pond, add native plants around the sides to give frogs a place to hide from trouble. Let some algae grow to nurture baby frogs. Don't add goldfish, or your frogs won't live long.

+ Make frog houses from piles of rock, wood, or leaves. Be sure to leave a doorway and frog-size space inside. If you have an old flowerpot — or half of one — turn it on its side so a frog can call it home.

+ If you don't have a pond or water nearby, tuck a few water-filled terra cotta saucers under bushes or other shady, protected spots. Be sure to include a little dirt in the bottom to make them more pond-like. These saucers give your frogs a watering hole to visit. Just remember to keep them filled.

**Dress for mosquito-busting success.** Here's what to wear to turn off mosquitoes. Choose heavyweight long sleeves, long pants, socks, and shoes as your anti-mosquito armor. Thinner fabric may be cooler, but mosquitoes can bite right through it unless you spray the clothing with insect repellent containing DEET. Also, avoid wearing bright colors, shiny jewelry, perfume, or cologne. These bright sights and sweet smells attract bugs the same way an ice cream truck attracts kids.

**Encourage plant-damaging gnats to scat.** Gnats and fruit flies aren't just a nuisance. Their larvae feed on plant roots, stunting a houseplant's growth and causing its poor leaves to yellow and wilt. But getting rid of these pests can be easy. Just add a spoonful of honey and a teaspoon of dishwashing liquid to either a cup of warm water or a cup of apple cider vinegar.

This bait mixture draws gnats and fruit flies and often drowns them. If a few stragglers seem to be escaping, sit by the jar with a spray bottle of rubbing alcohol and spray the gnats as they appear. Do this daily until the tiny troublemakers vanish for good.

# Deals on wheels

**Go online to save time and money.** Want to save big bucks on a new car? Then spend some time on your computer before heading to the dealership. Thanks to the Internet, you can save hundreds — even thousands — on a new car. It's the secret weapon car salesmen don't want you to know.

Spending more time online can save you time — and money — at the dealership. A recent study found that people who researched their car online spent an average of 80 minutes less at the dealership and 25 minutes less taking test drives and negotiating prices. Another study found that people who studied price-related information online paid about $400 less than other buyers.

That's because when you come to the dealership armed with information, you're in a better position to make a deal. And you can find a wealth of automobile information online. You can compare prices and features of different models, read reviews, and discover the true value of a vehicle by looking at the dealer cost or invoice price.

Some helpful automobile Web sites include:

✦ Edmunds Car Buying Guide at *www.edmunds.com*

✦ Kelley Blue Book at *www.kbb.com*

✦ Autobytel Network at *www.autobytel.com* or *www.myride.com*

✦ Cars.com at *www.cars.com*

✦ AutoTrader.com at *www.autotrader.com*

Explore these sites to find out all the information you need before buying a new or used car. It may take some searching, but it's better and, ultimately, cheaper than getting all your information from a fast-talking salesman.

## Sit up straight to fight high blood pressure

When using your computer to research your next car purchase, make sure to use the correct posture. A recent study has found a link between your neck muscles and a part of your brain that plays a key role in regulating your heart rate and blood pressure. According to researchers, hunching over a computer for hours may raise your blood pressure. To keep your blood pressure under control, you should also exercise regularly, maintain a healthy weight, quit smoking, and limit alcohol.

**Slow down to find the best deal.** Never shop for cars when you're in a hurry. You might get your car quicker, but you'll also likely pay more for it. Shop around for the best price, and compare models and prices at different dealerships — not just the nearest one. There's no sense rushing things. Take the time to shop right, using these helpful strategies.

- ✦ Never go to the dealership unprepared. Do some research, either online or at the library, first.

- ✦ Never let on how much you like a car. Once the salesman knows you're hooked, he'll be less motivated to negotiate.

- ✦ Never settle. If you don't find what you're looking for, consider ordering a car with just the features you want.

**Find the perfect time to buy a car.** When you buy a car may affect how much you pay for it. One rule of thumb is the later the better. Do your car shopping at the end of the month, and you may get a deal because the dealership wants to boost its sales figures for that month. The same logic applies to the end of the year. Shop for your car right before the next year's model is due to come out, and the dealership may be eager to clear the lot — and make a deal.

You may even save just by shopping near the end of the day. The salesperson may want to hammer out one more sale before heading home for the night. If you don't mind rain or snow, you can snag a sunny deal. That's because new car sales usually drop when the weather is lousy. Brave the elements, and you just might find a desperate dealer willing to negotiate.

**Leave flashy clothes in the closet.** Dressing for success does not mean wearing fancy clothes or expensive jewelry — at least when it comes to car shopping. If you look too well-to-do, the salesperson may assume you're a big shot and steer you toward more expensive models or take a harder line in negotiations. Pulling up in a luxury car may also hurt your chances of getting a good deal.

**Watch out for dealer tricks.** Going to a car dealership is like entering a lion's den. If you're not careful, you could end up in big trouble. Follow these tips to avoid being ripped off.

✦ Do not hand over your driver's license. Some dealers will hold your license hostage as a way to keep you at the dealership longer. Make photocopies instead.

✦ Say no to unnecessary add-ons. You have better things to spend your money on than gimmicks like rust proofing, fabric protectant, lifetime wax protection, or VIN etching.

+ Refuse to be bullied into an extended warranty. Even if you think you may want one, you can always buy it later — even if the salesman is pressuring you to say "yes" right away.

+ Look at the big picture. When it comes to financing, look at the total cost, not just the monthly payment. Longer loans mean more interest charges.

+ Divide and conquer. Don't let dealers group your trade-in and financing in with the price of the car. Negotiate a fair price for each separately.

**3 cheers for 4 cylinders.** Hybrids may be great for the environment, but they're not so great for your wallet. In fact, hybrid vehicles can cost anywhere from $3,000 to $9,000 more than the gas-only version of the same car. Luckily, you can save money by opting for a car with a four-cylinder engine. Although not as powerful as six- or eight-cylinder engines, four-cylinder models cost less and give you better gas mileage. They're also among the cleanest available engines. Check out which cars are the best — and worst — for the environment at *www.greenercars.org*.

**Get financing before buying.** Your car loan doesn't have to come from your car dealer. Often, you can find a better rate before setting foot on the lot. First, check your credit report to make sure everything is accurate — then try to improve your credit score. Next, shop around for the best rate through online lenders, banks, and credit unions. You can even pay for your car with a home equity loan or line of credit. After settling on a fair price for the car, let the dealer know you have your financing. Then see if he will beat your lender's best rate.

**Refinance your auto loan.** Refinancing isn't just for your mortgage. If you will be paying your auto loan for several more years, look into refinancing it. Just make sure the savings from the lower interest rate offsets any closing costs, as well as your local Department of Motor Vehicles' fee to transfer the lien.

## Release yourself from your lease

Don't feel trapped by your car lease. If you want to get out of a lease early, you can find someone else willing to take it over. For a fee, Web sites such as *LeaseTrader.com*, *Swapalease.com*, and *TakeMyPayments.com* allow you to post a listing. Just make sure to check your leasing company's transfer policy to see if there's a fee.

**Get the lowdown on leasing.** Leasing can be a smart and affordable alternative to buying a car. If you have good credit and don't drive too many miles in a year, leasing may be for you. Randall Farnsworth, CEO of Randall Farnsworth General Motors Automotive Group in Canandaigua and Victor, N.Y., points out the benefits — and possible pitfalls — of leasing a vehicle.

"As a general rule, you purchase assets that are going to appreciate in value and lease assets that are going to depreciate in value," Farnsworth says. Cars definitely fall into the latter category, which is one reason leasing makes sense.

"Leasing can be a smart option when you want to pay a lower payment but get more equipment than if you bought a car," Farnsworth says. Indeed, you can pay much less per month to lease a car than you would to buy the same model. As a bonus, only with a lease does the car come with a guaranteed future value, called the residual. At the end of the lease, you have the option of buying the car for that value.

But Farnsworth admits leasing can be tricky if you're not careful. "You can get turned off to leasing very quickly if you're an uninformed consumer," he says. That's because leasing comes with obligations to stay within a predetermined number of miles and to maintain the car so it's returned with only normal wear and tear. Failure to do so can be costly.

"A common mistake is not taking the time to understand the legal requirements of a lease agreement versus a buy agreement," Farnsworth says. "It's just like when you rent an apartment. You're legally responsible to leave the apartment in good condition. If you trash it, at the end you're going to owe them money. It's no different on a car."

Farnsworth recommends reading your contract or asking enough questions so you understand it. Ask the dealer for a copy of a blank lease agreement so you can familiarize yourself with the terms and conditions.

You should also know your driving habits. A low-mileage lease that limits you to 10,000 miles per year may look like a bargain — until you drastically exceed your mileage. Then you'll get a big bill.

"You have to run through how many miles you're going to drive in a year," Farnsworth says. "You have to be realistic and not take advantage of a lower payment now and be charged a lot at the end." While a standard lease allows 15,000 miles per year, you may buy additional mileage for 10 cents per mile up front. Otherwise, those same miles could cost 15 cents or more at the end of the lease.

One advantage to leasing is that the warranty should cover all repairs. But make sure to perform routine maintenance, like changing the oil and rotating the tires. You may be charged for four new tires if the tread doesn't meet minimum standards.

As long as you understand and stick to your responsibilities, a lease lets you drive more car for less money. "When you want to get the lowest possible payment with a guaranteed future value, the only thing you can do is lease," Farnsworth says. "If you want to get more vehicle for a specific payment, then you'd want a lease."

**Sweet way to sidestep lemons.** A simple background check on a used vehicle can save you from buying a lemon. Go to CarFax at *www.carfax.com* to trace a car's history. Discover if the car has been in a major accident, flooded, or damaged by fire. You can also check for odometer fraud. You'll need the vehicle identification number, or VIN. Your trusty mechanic can also give the car a once-over and may not even charge you. Despite your precautions, if you do end up with a lemon, you can find a lawyer to handle your case at *www.lemonlawamerica.com*.

**Crash safety test results at your fingertips.** The Internet does more than help you find good deals on new or used cars. You can also find out which cars are the safest. Two Web sites provide helpful crash safety test information for a variety of vehicles.

At the Insurance Institute for Highway Safety's Web site, *www.iihs.org*, you can find ratings based on front, side, and rear impact. See if the car you're considering ranks as Good, Acceptable, Marginal, or Poor in these situations. You can also find a list of the safest cars by year and class.

Go to *www.safercar.gov* to view the National Highway Traffic Safety Administration's crash safety ratings. Using a five-star system, it measures how cars stack up in front and side crashes, as well as the car's risk of rolling over during an accident. Although not every car has been tested, these sites can help narrow your search for a safer vehicle.

**Car color affects crash risk.** When it comes to safety, silver cars get the gold medal. A New Zealand study found that silver cars were least likely to be involved in a crash causing serious injury. On the other hand, driving brown, black, or green cars may put you at higher risk.

## Modifications make cars safer for seniors

Just because you have a few more candles on your birthday cake doesn't mean you have to give up driving. With a few modifications, you can make your car safer and more comfortable. Put an oversize mirror over your rearview mirror for a bigger field of vision, give yourself a boost with pads on the seat, use pedal extensions to reach the floor, install a bar in the door frame to support you as you get in and out of your car, or add a seat belt handle so you don't have to stretch to buckle up. If you need to pay for more extensive modifications, such as a ramp or a lift, automakers have programs that can help.

# Keys to selling your car

**Top tips for trade-ins.** When you buy a new car, it's easier to trade in your old one than sell it yourself. But it's also easier to get short-changed on the deal. Here's how to make the most of your trade-in.

+ Know your car's value. Use the Internet to research trade-in values for your make, model, and year. That way, you'll know if you're getting a fair offer.

+ Make sure your car is in good shape and looks good. Bring maintenance records as proof of your tender loving care. If you don't value your car, why should the dealer?

+ Shop around. You may get a better offer at another dealership. But don't insist on an unrealistic price for your car.

+ Don't be fooled. Dealers may act disinterested in your car, but they can earn big profits from reselling trade-ins.

+ Keep negotiations for your trade-in and your new vehicle separate so you get a good deal on both. As a bonus, most states only tax you on the difference between the new car's sale price and what you received for your trade-in.

**Super strategies for selling your car.** It may take more time and effort, but you can get a better price selling your car yourself rather than trading it in at a dealership. Here's a quick guide to selling your vehicle.

+ Get a feel for the market. Research the value of your make and model with tools like Kelley Blue Book. Look at local classifieds for similar cars to see what the going rate may be.

+ Set your price accordingly. You'll also want to take into account mileage, condition, location, gas mileage, and any special features or improvements. Boost your price by a few hundred dollars to leave room for negotiation.

✦ Advertise your car. You can do this simply by putting a "For Sale" sign in your window. You can also place classified ads in local papers, tack up signs on neighborhood bulletin boards, or list your vehicle online. Make sure your ad includes important information like the year, make, model, color, mileage, condition, color, and price. If you're open to negotiations, include "OBO," for "or best offer." If you're set on your price, include the word "firm."

✦ Show off the car. Park your car, with its "For Sale" sign, in places where it may generate the most interest. Remember that your appearance counts, too. If potential buyers want to test drive your car, ride with them so you can answer any questions. Feel free to bring a friend along if you're uncomfortable.

✦ Once you agree on a price and decide on a method of payment, close the deal. Make sure you know your state's laws regarding title transfers and any other paperwork you'll need to complete. You can usually find the necessary information on your state's department of motor vehicles Web site.

## Hot way to remove bumper stickers

You may enjoy personalizing your car with bumper stickers — but when it comes time to sell your car, they can be a sticking point. Fortunately, you can remove bumper stickers or window labels with a heat gun or hand-held hair dryer. Just be careful not to soften the car's paint along with the adhesive.

**6 ways to spruce up your car for selling.** When showing your car to prospective buyers, make sure it makes a good first impression. Try these tips from Edmunds.com to give your car more appeal.

✦ Wash, wax, and detail the car. Get rid of dents, dings, and scrapes.

✦ Make low-cost repairs yourself. Also, take care of routine service, like an oil change.

✦ Clean out any clutter from inside the car. Wipe down the dashboard and empty the ashtrays.

✦ Wipe brake dust off the wheel covers and clean the tires with a tire gloss product.

✦ Clean the windows, both inside and out, as well as all mirrored surfaces.

✦ Soothe the minds of prospective buyers. Show them the car's maintenance records. You can also have your mechanic issue a report about the car's condition or order a Carfax report at *www.carfax.com* for your car.

**Clean critters from your windshield.** Whoever buys your car won't pay extra for the bugs on the windshield. Get rid of them with this homemade windshield cleaner. Make a paste using about 70 percent baking soda and 30 percent liquid dish detergent. Dip a wet sponge into the paste, scrub the windshield, and rinse thoroughly. Don't use the mixture on other parts of the car.

# Car care secrets

**10 ways to find the best repair shop.** Car problems are bad enough. Don't make things worse by taking your car to a shifty repair shop. Instead, follow these tips from the National Institute for Automotive Service Excellence (ASE).

+ Shop for a repair shop before you actually need one, so desperation doesn't enter into your decision.

+ Ask friends and coworkers for recommendations.

+ Check out a shop's reputation through a local consumer organization.

+ Do not choose a shop just for its convenient location.

+ Look for a tidy, well-organized shop with modern equipment.

+ Make sure the shop handles your make and model.

+ Look for ASE certifications and other signs of mechanics' competence, like trade school diplomas and certificates of advanced coursework.

+ Ask questions of the staff. They should be courteous and helpful. You can even ask for names of some customers as references.

+ Look for clearly posted labor rates, diagnostic fees, and guarantees.

+ Start small. Take your car to an unfamiliar shop for a minor job first.

**Beware of shady mechanics' dirty tricks.** Not all auto mechanics are honest. Some just want your money. Watch out for these warning signs that your mechanic may be ripping you off.

✦ Recommending extra and expensive services, like engine or transmission flushes. Check your owner's manual for recommended scheduled maintenance items.

✦ Swapping multiple parts. Your mechanic may replace one part, only to find that the real problem is something else that also requires replacing. While a misdiagnosis can be an honest mistake, you should get a refund for the first repair or a discount for the second.

✦ Passing off old parts as new. A mechanic may just clean up your old part, put it back, and charge you for a new one. Always ask to see the old, broken part or receipts for new parts.

## Get wise to phony air bags

Air bags can save your life — as long as they are actual air bags. Some crooked repair shops remove valuable air bags from cars and replace them with junk, such as packing peanuts or rags. If the steering wheel color doesn't match the dashboard or gives in the center, this may be a sign of a phony air bag scam.

**Shop smart for auto parts.** When you need new parts for your car, come prepared. In some cases, it may help to take a picture of the part you need and bring that with you. But mostly, you need to know your car.

Felix Martinez, the assistant manager at Dave's Auto Part & Accessories in Hoboken, N.J., discusses some common mistakes and offers advice for customers.

"They rarely know the make and model of their car. They don't realize every car is different," he says. Bodies for similar sounding cars may be different, requiring different parts.

"Definitely know your make and model," Martinez says. "Have your VIN number handy." That can save time if he needs to call a dealer for a question about parts. You should also know how many cylinders your car has, as well as what size tires you need — and leave the diagnosis to the pros.

"A lot of people try to diagnose it themselves and don't know what the problem is," he says. They might buy a host of additives, like octane boosters or fuel injector cleaners, that could cause other problems. "Have the car checked out. See what's wrong with it. You do what you want after that."

**Drive your car longer for bigger savings.** According to a recent *Consumer Reports* survey, driving your car past 200,000 miles is cheaper than buying a new car every five years. In fact, it can save you more than $30,000. Of course, the key is to buy a safe, reliable vehicle and take good care of it. That means strictly following the maintenance schedule and using only recommended parts and fluids. It also involves keeping an eye out for problems by regularly looking under the hood. You should also keep the car clean to prevent rusting.

Yet, it doesn't always pay to hold onto an old vehicle. If it needs repairs that cost more than its value, spends more time in the shop than on the road, or has been in a flood or serious accident, give up on it.

**Collect oil with kitchen castoff.** Put that old kitchen dish drainer to work in your garage. It's a handy way to drain oil from the old filter or collect the last drops from used quart containers. Just set the drainer over an oil pan and let the containers drain overnight. If the drainer is smaller than the oil pan, you can support it with strips of wood.

**Keep your vintage car as good as new.** When you own a classic car, you must take good care of it. Here are some helpful tips to keep your older vehicle looking great.

+ Store it in a garage, away from freezing temperatures and sunlight. Cover it to keep out dust and critters.

+ Take care of the leather interior and rubber parts, including tires and hoses. They need lubrication and moisturizing.

+ Find the right parts for the car's make, model, and year — not always an easy task.

+ Protect the engine, which was designed to run on straight gasoline, not today's ethanol blends. This may involve using a fuel stabilizer, replacing old fuel lines and gaskets with ethanol-resistant materials, or replacing a damaged fuel tank.

Lastly, enjoy your car. It's important to drive at highway speeds now and then to clean out the carburetor, circulate oil, and extend the life of the engine.

**Clean greasy hands with olive oil.** Olive oil is great for your heart. It's also great for greasy hands. After working on your car, drizzle some olive oil or vegetable oil on your dirty hands and rub it in. Wash your hands in hot soapy water, and the grease will come off much easier.

**10 great gas-saving tips.** With gas prices so high, it's more important than ever to find ways to get more mileage for your money. Here are 10 easy ways to improve your mileage — and your finances.

+ Use cruise control. Maintaining a constant speed improves mileage.

+ Replace dirty or clogged air filters. This can improve mileage by as much as 10 percent.

+ Clean out your trunk and back seat. Extra weight takes its toll on fuel economy.

✦ Consolidate trips. Instead of making several short trips around town, do all your errands at once. You'll cut down on cold starts and help your engine run better.

✦ Avoid rush hour. Idling just wastes gas.

✦ Open your windows when driving in town, but use your air conditioner on the highway. Open windows create drag at speeds above 40 mph.

✦ Ditch the rooftop carrier. Your car burns gas trying to overcome wind resistance.

✦ Skip the warm-up. Start driving immediately. Your engine warms up faster that way.

✦ Ease into stops and starts. Don't slam on the brakes or floor the accelerator at green lights. Smooth driving not only saves fuel, it also extends the life of your brakes, transmission, and tires.

✦ Keep tires properly inflated. If a tire is underinflated by just 2 pounds per square inch (psi), it increases fuel consumption by 1 percent.

**Running on empty can empty your wallet.** Refill your gas tank when the needle hits a quarter of a tank. Otherwise, you can stir up sediment that collects at the bottom of your tank. This dirt can clog or damage parts, including your fuel injector and filter. It may even require an entire fuel-system flush and cleaning, which can cost $1,000. It's cheaper just to keep an eye on the fuel gauge.

**Save money at the pump.** Don't pay any more for gas than you have to. Buying a higher octane fuel won't help your car run any better — it just costs more. Unless your car requires a higher octane fuel, opt for the lowest and save money. While you're at it, don't feel like you have to buy "name brand" gas. All gasoline must meet certain standards set by the Environmental Protection Agency, so you can save money without harming your car when you fill up at lesser-known stations.

## *Stick to 60 mph for big savings*

Pay 10 to 20 cents less for your next gas fill-up. How? Just obey the speed limit. For every 5 mph you drive over 60 mph, it's like paying an extra 20 cents per gallon of gas. This simple tip improves gas mileage by up to 23 percent.

**Little-known way to protect the environment.** If you let your car idle for longer than a minute, it spews more pollution than it would if you stopped and restarted it.

**Terrific tips for top-notch tires.** You may not give your tires too much thought, but you should. As the only part of your car that touches the road, tires are key to your safety. Follow these guidelines to keep your tires on a roll.

✦ Check the tire pressure. Do this once a month with a tire gauge. For an accurate reading, check tire pressure on cold tires, or those that haven't been driven on for at least three hours. Both overinflated and underinflated tires pose dangers. Make sure you stick to the recommended tire pressure, measured in pounds per square inch (psi), listed in the owner's manual. You may also find the information on the vehicle door edge, door post, glove box door, or trunk lid.

✦ Check the tread depth. It should not fall below 1/16 of an inch. You probably know the old penny trick. Stick a penny in the tread, and if you can see the top of Lincoln's head, it's time for new tires. Recently, Consumer Reports recommended using a quarter — and 1/8 inch — as your benchmark instead.

✦ Rotate the tires. Periodically switching tires from front to back and from side to side prevents uneven wear.

✦ Buy wisely. When you need to replace your tires, shop around for the best price. You also want to get the proper size and pay attention to a variety of rankings, including speed, treadwear, traction, and temperature. Fresh tires are best. The last four digits following the "DOT" indicate the week and year of manufacture.

---

### 3 ways to improve your driving skills

As you get older, improving your physical fitness can help improve your driving. Make your neck more flexible by slowly turning your head as far as you can to the left and holding it there for 10 seconds. Move back to the center, then do the same thing on the right side. Repeat this a few times. Strengthen your hands by squeezing a tennis ball, and strengthen your legs by walking 30 minutes each day.

---

**Learn the details of detailing.** Why spend top dollar to get your car professionally detailed when you can do it yourself? Just follow these tips, and your car will shine.

✦ Start with the interior. Remove and vacuum the floor mats and treat any stains. Vacuum the upholstery or treat leather upholstery with a leather conditioner. Wipe the dash with a clean rag, then use cotton swabs to clean out air vents and other tight spots. Blasts of compressed air can clear dirt from tiny cracks.

✦ Wash the exterior with clean, cool water. Move from the top down. To avoid scratches, anything that comes in contact with your car's finish should be soft.

✦ Apply wax. Spread a thin, even coat and buff so it shines.

+ Keep it up. Washing your car once a month will do, but if your car is exposed to harsh conditions, you may want to wash it every two weeks instead.

**Mayo jar fights road tar.** Mayonnaise does more than perk up your sandwich. You can also take road tar off your car with this simple kitchen condiment. Just slather some mayonnaise over the tar. Let it sit a few minutes, then wipe it with a clean rag.

**Give your brakes a break.** Your brakes help you stop — so you should stop abusing them. Here's how to extend the life of your brakes.

+ Stick to the speed limit. It taxes your brakes more to slow down from higher speeds.

+ Get rid of unnecessary weight in the car.

+ Plan trips to avoid heavy traffic, including rush hour. If you do get stuck in traffic, leave extra room between your car and the car in front of you so you won't have to brake as hard.

+ Do not rest your foot on the brake pedal.

+ Use a lower gear on long, downhill drives rather than relying only on the brakes to control your speed.

+ Have your brakes checked regularly and keep them in proper adjustment. On some vehicles, the parking brake mechanism helps adjust the rear brakes.

**Cool way to protect your car's AC.** Once a month, turn on your car's air conditioner and let it run for a few minutes. This will keep the compressor, hoses, and seals in tip-top shape. You may get a little chilly in December, but it will be worth it come July.

# Steer clear of auto dangers

## Simple steps to take before calling a tow truck.

Your car won't start — but that doesn't mean you have a major problem. Try these simple solutions to get it started.

+ Make sure there's gas in the tank.

+ Make sure the car is in park and your foot is on the brake.

+ If you're driving a stick shift, make sure you're depressing the clutch pedal all the way.

+ Check if the front tires are wedged against the curb or turned all the way to one side.

+ Fasten your seat belt and make sure the car's alarm system is not activated.

You can also try to narrow down the problem to save the mechanic some time — and save yourself some money. For example, if the headlights, wipers, and radio work, the battery isn't dead, so the problem may be the starter.

**Learn to speak your car's language.** Whether it squeals, rumbles, clicks, or pings, your car may be trying to tell you something. Solve the mystery of strange sounds with these helpful hints.

+ A squeal may come from loose or worn power steering or a fan or air conditioning belt.

+ Clicks may mean a loose wheel cover, a loose or bent fan blade, a stuck valve lifter, or low engine oil.

+ That screech could be your brake wear indicators telling you it's time for maintenance.

+ You may hear a rumble from a defective exhaust pipe, converter, or muffler.

✦ Pings result from using a lower octane gas than is recommended for your car.

✦ A worn crankshaft or loose transmission torque converter can make a rhythmic pounding sound.

✦ Clunks or thumps could mean a loose shock absorber, exhaust pipe, or muffler.

---

### 10 essential items to keep in your car

Don't leave home without these 10 key items. They could prevent a major disaster.

- blanket
- first–aid kit
- flashlight
- ice scraper
- shovel
- jumper cables
- tire gauge
- spare tire with jack
- flares
- emergency phone numbers, along with a cell phone or prepaid phone card

---

**Steer clear of skidding.** The calm before the storm can be deadly. A recent study found that the more days between periods of precipitation, the more accidents take place when it finally rains or snows. That could be because oil on dry roads turns slick on the first day of rain, but it gets washed away with more rain. Or people could just drive more carefully after a day or two of wet weather. Whatever the reason, here's how to cope with poor conditions.

+ If your car starts to skid, turn the wheel in the direction you want the front of your car to go. Lay off the gas and brakes unless you have anti-lock brakes. In that case, brake firmly as you steer.

+ If your car starts to hydroplane, do not brake or turn suddenly. Ease your foot off the gas. Pump your brakes gently if you need to brake. If you have anti-lock brakes, you can brake normally, and your car's computer will do the pumping.

+ To prevent hydroplaning, slow down and stay away from puddles. Try to drive in the tire tracks left by the cars in front of you. Make sure your tires have good tread and are properly inflated.

**3 surprising ways to reduce your risk of injury in an accident.** You may not always be able to avoid a traffic accident, but you can limit your injuries. Here are three ways to do that.

+ Make sure your head restraint is positioned properly to avoid whiplash. The top of the restraint should line up with the top of your head or the top of your ears. It should also be no more than 4 inches away from the back of your head.

+ Do not recline your seat. Your seat belt will no longer be in the right position and may actually hurt you.

+ Secure all loose articles in your car. That way, you won't be pelted by flying objects.

**Best way to keep you and your passengers safe.**
Want to reduce your risk of an accident? Turn off your cell phone. Studies show talking on a cell phone while driving quadruples your risk of a wreck. However, just having passengers in your car also boosts your risk. In fact, your risk of an accident more than doubles with two or more passengers — so stop talking and drive.

**Surprising ways to keep your windshield clear.** A fogged windshield can cost you your life. Think about it. Here's the item to carry in your glove box to remove the haze instantly. It's unusual, but inexpensive — and it works. Just rub the windshield with a chalkboard eraser to fix the problem. You can also repel rain from your windshield. Simply dampen a cloth, dip it in baking soda, and wipe it on the windshield inside and out. To keep frost away from the inside of your windows, rub them with a solution made of two teaspoons of salt in a gallon of hot water. Then wipe them dry.

**Protect yourself from carjacking.** When driving, you need to be alert for pedestrians, other vehicles, traffic signs — and carjackers. These car thieves can sneak up on you if you're not on the lookout. Follow these tips to reduce your risk of being carjacked.

+ Park in well-lit areas.

+ Do not park near walls, dumpsters, woods, or large vehicles that obstruct your view.

+ Use valet parking or a garage with an attendant.

+ Keep your doors locked and windows rolled up.

+ Be especially alert when you slow down or stop at garages, parking lots, intersections, self-service gas stations, car washes, highway ramps, and ATMs.

+ As you walk to your car, take note of suspicious people sitting in cars, handing out flyers, or loitering in the area.

+ If someone approaches you on your way to your car, change direction or enter a busy store.

+ Do not turn your back while loading packages into your car.

+ Look under, around, and inside your car before getting in — then start it and drive away immediately.

+ Do not stop to help someone who looks like they're having car trouble. Call the police instead.

+ If you're bumped by another car filled with young males, wave the other vehicle to follow you to a gas station or busy place before getting out.

+ Try not to drive alone, especially at night.

Most important, if an armed carjacker confronts you, do not resist. Give up your car. It's not worth losing your life over a vehicle. Get away as quickly as possible and call the police. If you are forced to drive, consider crashing your car at a busy intersection where bystanders can call for help.

---

### Find a new home for old phone books

Instead of tossing out last year's phone book, keep it in your car. It can come in handy for ordering takeout, running errands, and finding business addresses. If you're short, you can even sit on it to give you a boost.

---

**Keep air in your spare.** There's nothing more annoying than a flat tire. Don't make matters worse by replacing your flat tire with another one. Whether you have a donut or full-size spare tire in your trunk, always make sure you keep it properly inflated. When you have a flat tire, pull over to a level area along a straight stretch of road to change it. Make sure your car is in park and put your flashers on. You may also want to set up flares, warning lights, or reflectors about five car lengths in front of and behind your vehicle.

**Put the squeeze on dirt and grime.** Fill an empty, clean, squeeze dish detergent bottle with water and store it in your car. Use it to wash your hands after changing a flat tire or checking under the hood. You can also use it to clean off your windshield if you're out of wiper fluid.

306

**Limit risk of lockouts.** A few simple tricks can help you avoid the hassle of getting locked out of your car. Instead of using the inside door locks, always lock the door with your key. Keep an extra key in your wallet or somewhere else where you can always get to it. If you do get locked out, your best bet is to call a locksmith. If you have an older car, you may be able to unlock the door with a bent coat hanger, but you can damage newer vehicles — and possibly injure yourself by triggering the air bag. If it's a true emergency, like a baby locked in the car, call the police.

**Quick way to replace a misplaced key.** If you have an electronic ignition key, write down its identification code number on a piece of paper and keep it in your wallet. That way, if you lose the key, it will be easier for a locksmith to make a copy.

**Sidestep speeding tickets.** Obviously, the best way to avoid a speeding ticket is to obey the speed limit. But if you do get pulled over, here's what to do.

+ Do not speak first. Respond "No" if the officer asks if you know why he pulled you over. Never admit any wrongdoing, argue, or try to make excuses.

+ Make notes at the scene. Details like the location of the stop, weather conditions, traffic conditions, names of any passengers, and any distinguishing characteristics of your car could come in handy later if you need to cross-examine the officer.

+ Show up in court and plead not guilty. That's half the battle. Many times, especially in the summer months when people take vacation, the officer will not show up — and you'll get off.

+ Be prepared to defend yourself. You can't count on the officer not showing up, so you should have a Plan B. Maybe the officer's view was obstructed, maybe he pulled over the wrong car, maybe his radar gun wasn't calibrated right, or maybe his recollection of the incident was foggy.

Even if you lose, you'll pay the same fine you would have paid in the first place. Fighting the ticket will only cost you time — and may cost you nothing.

**Keep this on hand to prevent overheating.** In an emergency, you can add plain water or antifreeze to stop your car from overheating. Keep some bottled water in your car for such a situation — and for drinking. But during routine maintenance, use a 50-50 mixture of water and antifreeze.

## Simple ways to fight car fires

Consider installing a travel fire extinguisher for your car. Some models come with straps so you can store them behind the front seat, while others require mounting a bracket to hold them. Just make sure not to use screws anywhere near the gas tank. You can also keep boxes of baking soda in your car and garage to put out a fire. The baking soda won't damage anything it touches.

**Tips for winterizing your car.** Winter brings more than holiday cheer — it also brings an element of danger to driving. Make sure you and your car are prepared. Check your car's fluids, battery, windshield wipers, headlights, heater, and defroster. Also check your tires' depth and pressure, and consider replacing them with snow tires if necessary. Keep your gas tank full to avoid condensation. Do not use cruise control in icy conditions. Practice defensive driving, especially around trucks, which take longer to stop. Put sandbags in your trunk to add weight to the rear of your car for better traction.

**Lay trunk clutter to rest with old pillowcases.** Stick an old pillowcase in your trunk to use as a handy storage bag. It can hold a change of clothes, shoes, tools, or other supplies. You can also keep your trunk clean and dry by slipping muddy shoes or a wet umbrella in the pillowcase.

# House hunting hints

**The best season for home buying.** When you think of Christmas, you may think of caroling, cookies, presents, and family — but it's also the best time to buy a home. That's because home prices reach their low point in December. You also have less competition from other buyers because most people look for homes in the summer when it's easier to pack up and move, especially with children. Plus, people are in the Christmas spirit, so the seller may come down on the price. Make an offer on Christmas Day, and you may receive a wonderful Christmas present.

**How to find the best real estate agent.** Real estate professionals vary greatly in experience, determination, and ability. Here are some tips for finding one that's best for you.

+ Ask for referrals from friends, family, and coworkers who have had success with their agent.

+ Do some research. Search online or look at print advertising to learn more about local agencies and agents.

+ Attend open houses. It's an easy way to meet agents and get an idea of how they work. Collect business cards and make notes.

+ Look for experience and commitment. Pick an agent who's been in business at least two years. Stay away from part-time agents who may not have the time to dedicate to your needs.

+ Interview at least three potential agents. Ask how familiar they are with the neighborhood or how often you'll hear from them. You'll also find out if you are comfortable working with them.

+ Make sure they can work around your schedule. This could mean working nights and weekends.

**Guard against real estate fraud.** Buying property can be tricky enough without dirty tricks. Here's how to protect yourself — and your money — from fraud.

✦ Be suspicious of investment opportunities that promise no money down and cash back at closing.

✦ Make sure the seller really owns the property. Check with the local tax assessment office or recorder of deeds.

✦ Never let someone else use your name or social security number to buy property. Be especially wary of anyone who offers to pay you for the use of it.

✦ Read and understand everything you sign. Ask your attorney for explanations if you need help.

✦ Refuse to sign any document with information left blank.

✦ Always get a complete set of the closing documents.

### Action plan for house hunters

Before you start shopping for a home, make sure to get your credit score. Then do what you can to boost it. Most lenders consider people with scores above 650 to be prime borrowers — those most likely to be approved at favorable rates.

**When renting makes sense.** Most financial experts consider "rent" a four-letter word. It's true buying a home usually makes sound financial sense, but sometimes renting can be the smarter move. For instance, if you have an unstable job situation or you're planning to move in a few years, you should probably rent. Likewise if your credit score is too low to get a good interest rate on a loan. If renting in your area costs considerably less than monthly mortgage payments and other housing expenses, it may be a good idea to keep renting. Here's a comparison of the pros and cons of renting and owning.

## Renting vs. Owning

| | Renting | Owning |
|---|---|---|
| **expenses** | rent | down payment, closing costs, mortgage payments, taxes, insurance, maintenance |
| **tax breaks** | none | can deduct interest on mortgage and property taxes, don't have to pay taxes on the gain when you sell |
| **investments** | invest the money you would spend on a down payment and monthly mortgage payments instead | your house is an investment, which grows more valuable over time |
| **mistakes** | failing to invest while renting | overpaying for the house, paying more than you can afford, paying too much interest |
| **benefits** | easier to move if you relocate, no cost or effort spent on maintenance | mortgage payments stay the same for 30 years, while rent goes up; ability to customize the home |

**The facts about foreclosures.** When a homeowner can't keep up with the payments, it could mean a housing bargain for you. That's the idea behind foreclosures, but it takes some work to find these potential deals. First, you should learn your state's foreclosure laws and procedures. You can check RealtyTrac at *www.realtytrac.com* or your local county clerk's office. Then look for foreclosures in your area. Check your local office of the Real Estate Investment Association. You can also look online at the RealtyTrac or the Bargain Network at *www.bargain.com*. But remember, wily real estate professionals and investors usually scoop up the best deals right away.

Your best bet is to buy a bank-owned property through a broker. You may not get as good a deal, but you'll have fewer hassles. If you buy at auction, you may save more — but you need to pay in cash, don't get a chance to inspect the property, and may even have to evict the tenants. Expect to pay for repairs as well, since foreclosures are sold "as is." You may be able to buy a "pre-foreclosure" directly from the financially strapped owner. This could be your best chance for a good deal.

Foreclosures aren't always bargains. If a homeowner hasn't built much equity in the property, the asking price will be pretty close to market price. When possible, look for houses owned by people who have lived there at least two years and stay away from those who bought their home with no money down.

## Breathe easier after environmental checkup

Even a low-priced home isn't much of a bargain if the surrounding air isn't safe to breathe. Learn about the environmental conditions of a community before buying a home there. Good sources include Envirofacts at *www.epa.gov/enviro* and Scorecard at *www.scorecard.org*. These Web sites provide information about an area's quality of air and water, including sources of chemicals and hazardous waste. Databases may not be completely up to date, so you should also check out local newspapers or Web sites to find out more information.

## 4 can't-miss tips for finding a good home inspector.

Finding the right home inspector can save you a lot of hassles — and money. It's important to find out as much as you can about the house you're planning to buy. You don't want to be surprised later with unexpected repairs. Follow these tips to find a good home inspector.

+ Look for a full-time inspector who has been in the business at least five years. Make sure he has professional certifications from legitimate industry organizations.

+ Don't jump at the lowest price. You may save a little money on the inspection, but it could cost you much more in future repairs if the inspector is not thorough.

+ Don't rely on your real estate agent for a recommendation. While your agent may recommend a good inspector, he could also be trying to speed up the sale with a quick, less-than-meticulous inspection.

+ Search online. Several Web sites let you search for qualified home inspectors in your area. You can also find more information about the home inspection process. Check out HomeGauge at *www.homegauge.com*, the American Society of Home Inspectors at *www.ashi.org*, the National Association of Home Inspectors at *www.nahi.org*, and the National Association of Certified Home Inspectors at *www.nachi.org*.

## 5 smart strategies to maximize your home's value.

You may think you'll make a big profit when you sell your home, but you probably already spent much of the money. When you take into account interest, insurance, taxes, repairs, and renovations, you've paid much more for your home than just the purchase price. Here's how to make the most of your biggest asset.

+ Pay as little as possible for your home for the best chance to make a profit later. Remember, your home is not guaranteed to go up in value.

+ Slash interest costs. Add a little extra to each mortgage payment so you pay down the principal quicker and waste less on interest.

+ Take advantage of tenants. Buy a two-family home or a house with a rental unit, and use the rent to quickly pay off your mortgage. Then you can sell and move into a better home.

✦ Limit renovations. Don't redo your kitchen or bathroom in hopes of boosting the value of your home. Renovations can be expensive, especially if you have to borrow to pay for them, and you usually lose money on the deal.

✦ Stay in one place. You can't build equity or benefit from rising housing costs if you keep moving.

**7 strategies for successful landlords.** Becoming a landlord can help boost your wealth, but it's not always profitable. Here are some smart tips for investing in rental property.

✦ Choose a rental house over an apartment building. A house, if located in a good neighborhood, appreciates in value more quickly.

✦ Get a thorough inspection before you buy the property.

✦ Make sure your rental income will cover all out-of-pocket expenses, including the mortgage on the property, taxes, insurance, and repairs. One rule of thumb is to charge 1 percent of the house's market value in monthly rent.

✦ Enjoy the perks. As long as you can break even, you can still benefit from the property's appreciation and tax breaks. For instance, you can write off most repairs.

✦ Set aside some extra cash for unexpected emergencies. One month's rent for each unit is a good guideline.

✦ Watch out for bad tenants and other headaches. You can hire a professional property manager, but his fee eats into your profits. Long-distance property management can be even trickier.

✦ Consider a lease option. If your tenants have an option to buy after a few years, they will probably take better care of the property. In the meantime, you get a steady stream of income from rent and the tax benefits of homeownership.

# Mortgage fitness

**Sure-fire way to get approved for a mortgage.** Before trying to purchase or refinance your home, make sure your finances are in order. Bruce Arnold, a mortgage loan originator in East Stroudsburg, Pa., offers these tips to improve your chances of being approved for a mortgage.

"One of the greatest advantages when applying for a mortgage is a good credit score," he says. "The best thing you can do for that is to keep your total liabilities under 50 percent of what's available to you. Anything over 50 percent could detract from it. And never be 30 days late on a payment."

Timing also matters when it comes to your mortgage application. "Prior to, it's not a very good idea to go out and open new credit lines. It's not a good idea to go out and buy new vehicles," Arnold says. "Because if you open a new loan, your score is going to take a little dip." New credit lines can also affect your debt-to-income ratio, which should be no more than 50 percent. This includes not just your mortgage payments, but also your taxes, homeowners insurance, and all other monthly payments. A new car payment can push you over the edge and keep you from getting a mortgage.

"Another big mistake is consolidating all your loans on an interest-free credit card and closing all your old, good credit lines. That's very damaging," Arnold says. Not only will the new account hurt your credit score because of its lack of history, but you also cancel everything your credit score was built on. If you consolidate, do not cancel your old credit lines. Just leave a minimum balance on them. Before applying for a mortgage, Arnold also recommends knowing your credit score, paying off any collection accounts, and making sure there are no judgments or liens against you.

**Go online to find best rates.** The Internet can be a great tool for gathering information about mortgages, comparing rates, and even applying for loans. Here's how it works. For basic research, visit HSH Associates at *www.hsh.com*, Bankrate.com at *www.bankrate.com*, or Mortgage Bankers Association at *www.mbaa.org*. You can also check out government sites like Fannie Mae at *www.fanniemae.com*, Freddie Mac at *www.freddiemac.com*, and the U.S. Department of Housing and Urban Development at *www.hud.gov*. To shop for a loan, you have three options.

+ Direct lender sites. Go right to the source, like Bank of America or Countrywide. But you won't get all the information you need without making a phone call or visiting in person.

+ Auction sites. Complete a loan application, and lenders compete for your business. You'll receive offers in a day or two. Examples include LendingTree.com, GetSmart.com, and RealEstate.com.

+ Multi-lender sites. Just enter the loan amount, details about the property, and other information to get current rates. You can then fill out an application, and these sites — like LoanShop.com or ELoan.com — will forward everything to the lender.

**Play it safe with a fixed-rate mortgage.** You may be tempted by an adjustable-rate mortgage, but be careful. Even if it has a lower initial rate than a fixed-rate mortgage, it may go up considerably. Opt for the stability of a fixed-rate mortgage instead. While other housing costs, like taxes, insurance, and upkeep rise, at least you'll know your mortgage payment will remain the same. If you choose an adjustable-rate mortgage, or ARM, make sure you know how much and how often the interest rate could go up — and make sure you can afford those higher payments.

**Buy a home with no money down.** Trying to scrape together enough money for a down payment? You may need less than you think. While in the past, 20 percent was the standard down payment, today's typical home buyer puts down about 2 percent. According to the National Association of Realtors, about 30 percent of home buyers purchased their homes with no money down. That number jumps to 45 percent for first-time home buyers.

For help with your down payment, look for government incentives, which can also help with interest rates and closing costs. To learn about Federal Housing Administration (FHA) loans, go to *www.hud.gov/buying/loans.cfm* or call 800-569-4287. Check with your state, city, or county government housing agencies for other programs. You can also find out about programs through USA Down Payment Assistance at *www.usadownpaymentassistance.com*.

## Sip tea to handle stress

Financing a home can be stressful. Fortunately, you can counteract the effects of stress by drinking black tea. A six-week British study found tea aids stress recovery. After a stressful situation, people who drank tea had much lower levels of the stress hormone cortisol than those who drank a placebo beverage. Platelet activation, linked to blood clotting and the risk of heart attacks, also decreased in tea drinkers. Best of all, tea drinkers felt more relaxed.

**Save big bucks and shave years off your mortgage.** Making one extra mortgage payment a year can help you pay off your mortgage faster and save thousands on interest costs. One way to do that is to make biweekly payments. Just split your monthly mortgage in half and pay it every two weeks. That way, you make 26 payments in a year — the equivalent of 13 months.

But don't fall for biweekly mortgage plans. They may be scams and often come with hefty fees or conversion charges. You can accomplish the same thing on your own, with some discipline. Simply add 1/12 of your monthly payment to each month's check. Or just make one extra payment each year, perhaps using your tax refund or a bonus from work.

**Haggle your way to a better loan.** You may not realize that you can negotiate the rates and terms of your mortgage or home equity loan. In fact, it's a smart way to pay less. Think of the mortgage process like buying a car. You want to gather information, shop around, and haggle on the price. Don't just accept what your lender or mortgage broker offers. They may be trying to keep extra income for themselves. Just by negotiating, you could save thousands of dollars.

## Curb sleep problems with carbs

All those mortgage figures whirling around inside your head at night might make it tough to fall asleep. Try eating a starchy, high-carbohydrate meal about four hours before bedtime. According to a recent Australian study, this strategy helps you fall asleep faster.

**Tips to trim closing costs.** When calculating the cost of buying a home, don't forget closing costs. They can sneak up on you and cost quite a bundle. Compare good faith estimates from several lenders — but watch out for the old bait-and-switch. Examine all costs carefully. You may discover padded or extra fees — and may be able to reduce or eliminate some of them. Some fees may be for optional services you can do on your own. Insist on seeing receipts if any work was done by outside companies. Here are some other tips for paying less at closing.

+ Close late in the month. That way, you only pay for a few days of interest.

+ Choose a zero-point mortgage. You'll pay less at closing, but the downside is you'll have a higher rate for the loan.

+ Get help from the seller. Ask the seller to credit you money for part of the closing costs. If they are going to rent from you after the sale, check if the rent can be credited to you at closing.

**When it's smart to refinance.** Paying too much for your mortgage? Refinancing can help, but make sure you save money on the move. Consider refinancing your mortgage if you can get a new rate that's at least one percentage point lower than your current rate, and you plan to keep the new mortgage for several years. You may also want to refinance to switch from an adjustable-rate mortgage (ARM) to a predictable fixed-rate mortgage. When refinancing, it helps to maintain a good credit score so you can get the best rates. Remember to take into account any extra fees, such as an application fee or closing costs, that come with refinancing.

**Why you should rethink reverse mortgages.** A reverse mortgage sounds like a sweet deal. Available to people age 62 or older who own their homes, reverse mortgages let you remain in your house while receiving monthly payments from the lender. You can also get a lump-sum payout or a line of credit. The loan doesn't have to be repaid until you sell the house, move out, or die. Your children can then sell the house to pay back the principal plus interest.

But reverse mortgages have their drawbacks — mainly high fees, which can be as much as 10 percent of your home's value. Lower fees usually come with higher interest rates. You also won't get close to full value for your house. Expect more like 50 to 70 percent of its appraised value. While reverse mortgages can be helpful, don't jump at them too soon. If you take out a reverse mortgage too early, you could outlive your resources. That's why it makes more sense for people in their 70s and 80s.

# Smart moves for home sellers

**9 simple tricks to boost your home's appeal.** You may love your house the way it is — but it's the potential buyers' opinions that matter. If you spend thousands of dollars for professional "staging" to make your house more appealing, it may sell faster and for more. But in many cases, just a few small changes can make a big difference.

✦ Clear out clutter. This includes knickknacks and photos, as well as extra furniture. You may want to put your clutter in storage because buyers may look in your closets and basement.

✦ Brighten the view. Use high-wattage bulbs to make your rooms seem bigger and more inviting.

✦ Pay special attention to the kitchen and bathrooms. You should thoroughly clean and tidy your whole house, but these rooms should be spotless.

✦ Replace your old, worn welcome mat with a new one.

✦ Clean the windows inside and out.

✦ Add a fresh coat of paint to the exterior or just touch up chipped and flaking paint.

✦ Hide flaws with textured wallpaper or faux wall finishes.

✦ Place vases of flowers on kitchen or dining room tables, bedroom dressers, or the mantel.

✦ Make sure your house smells good. Hide the kitty litter box. You may want to bake cookies for a pleasant scent.

**Do this before putting your house on the market.** A little landscaping can make a big difference. In fact, landscaping can add between 7 and 15 percent to a home's value, according to The Gallup Organization. Here are some simple landscaping tips that can help you sell your home quicker and for more money.

- Plant a tree. Choose a tree with spring flowers and colorful fall leaves, and plant it at least 15 feet from your house.

- Put big pots of bright flowers on either side of the front door.

- Use annual vines to cover chain link fences, mailbox posts, and other unsightly parts of your yard.

- Plant shrubbery around your house, but keep it short and trimmed.

- Take care of your lawn — weed, mulch, and mow. Keep your grass edged and trimmed.

**Thwart thieves at your open house.** Not everyone who shows up at your open house is interested in buying your home. Some are more interested in stealing from you. Take some simple precautions when showing your home to strangers.

- Don't display valuable possessions, like expensive art, silver, or china.

- Keep your credit cards, checkbook, and house keys with you or safely locked away.

- Hide your prescription medications. A guest using your bathroom could easily steal them from your medicine cabinet.

- Remove designer dresses, fur coats, or other expensive clothing from your closets. Hide your jewelry, too.

- Don't be too chatty. You don't want to reveal too much about your personal life or schedule. Why tell potential thieves when you won't be home?

- Always escort guests through your home. Keep them in sight at all times, and make sure they can only leave through one door. Be on the lookout for a scam where one person keeps you talking while another pilfers your valuables.

**Secrets to pricing your home.** When setting the price for your home, be realistic. Overpricing it will make it tough to sell, but you don't want to shortchange yourself, either. Look at prices of comparable homes that recently sold in your neighborhood. Web sites like *www.domania.com* and *www.realtor.org* can help. So can looking at real estate listings in the newspaper, going to open houses, or consulting a real estate agent. For the most accurate price, contact your local appraiser. You may want to set your price 5 to 10 percent above market value to make sure you get close to its true worth. Another trick is to set the price just below a nice, round number — like $179,900 instead of $180,000.

## Dirty trick improves your mood

Gardening can do more than boost the value of your home — it might also boost your mood. That's because soil contains *Mycobacterium vaccae*, friendly bacteria that increase the levels of the feel-good hormone serotonin in your brain. British researchers recently observed the bacteria's effect in mice. They say it changed the mice's behavior in a way similar to antidepressant drugs.

**A guide for selling your own home.** Real estate agents make selling your home easier. They also command a 6 to 7 percent commission. With a little hard work, you can sell your home yourself — and keep that money in your pocket. You can get help with this process at Web sites like *www.forsalebyowner.com*. Here are some steps you may want to take.

+ Price your home more aggressively. You can afford to set a lower price and sell your home faster — yet still save money by not paying a commission.

+ Advertise heavily. This includes online listings, newspaper ads, lawn signs, open houses, and brochures. Good photos and a well-written ad make a big difference.

+ Hire a real estate lawyer. This additional expense is worth it for reviewing contracts and guiding you through some of the more complicated aspects of negotiating.

✦ Get an inspection. You may want to hire an inspector before a potential buyer does so you won't be surprised by any needed repairs.

**5 things shady movers won't tell you.** The process of selling your home, packing up, and moving comes with enough hassles. You certainly don't want to make things worse by hiring unreliable — or dishonest — movers. Two Web sites, *www.movingscam.com* and *www.protectyourmove.gov*, offer good advice for avoiding shady movers and finding reliable ones. Here are some tips.

✦ Get written estimates from at least three moving companies. Make sure they come to your house and inspect your belongings, not just offer an estimate over the phone.

✦ Verify the mover has insurance and is licensed by the proper authority.

✦ Make sure the mover gives you the "Your Rights and Responsibilities When You Move" booklet.

✦ Check for complaints about the company with the Better Business Bureau or the Web sites mentioned previously.

✦ Watch out for companies that use rented trucks, demand cash or a large deposit upfront, or make unreasonably low estimates over the phone or Internet. Most likely, they'll jack up the price later — after your stuff is loaded on the truck.

### Surprising way to ease moving hassles

Leaving your home can be a daunting and emotional experience. Luckily, a senior move manager can help. These professionals help you organize, sort, and downsize. They can help you sell unwanted items, customize floor plans, and arrange shipments and storage. They can even help you find a real estate agent and prepare your home to sell. They also pack and unpack. To find a senior move manager near you, visit the National Association of Senior Move Managers at *www.nasmm.org*.

# Clothing cost cutters

**3 ways to dress for less.** Follow these simple tips to save big on clothing.

+ Time it right. Never shop for clothes when they first hit the rack. A little patience can lead to big savings. Most retailers mark down merchandise after nine weeks on the shelves. Some have even shorter shelf-lives and cut prices every four weeks. Just by waiting, you may save as much as 70 percent. Seasonal shopping also nets savings. For instance, near the end of July you can usually find bargains on warm-weather clothing, including bathing suits, as stores try to clear their shelves for "Back to School" season.

+ Deal with cards. If you have a favorite store, it may be worth signing up for the store credit card, which can yield 10 to 20 percent discounts. Be sure to pay it off every month, though, because they often have higher interest rates.

+ Dig department stores. You'll usually find better bargains in department stores than boutiques. They also feature more lenient return policies.

**Talk your way to a discount.** Price tags are not written in stone. With a little haggling, you can often walk away with a true bargain. Just ask Faye McCollum, a super shopper from Columbus, Ga. who perfected the art of haggling in Turkey.

"The important thing in this process is to get to know the managers in the stores where you regularly shop," McCollum says. "Second, you watch the number of markdowns and strike when the time is right."

"For instance, one such item was a pair of evening shoes at Dillard's, gorgeous shoes with gold lamé trim on the toes. They originally sold for $164. They marked them down to $94, and I was really tempted. I examined them very carefully, thought I'd wait for one more markdown, and then found a slight scuff mark on the inside of the left shoe. I approached the manager and asked for a further reduction. Emphasis of the defect was significant, and then I went for the kill: 'Would you take $40 for the shoes?' After a phone call to her director, the manager returned and handed me the shoes. That was three years ago, and I'm still wearing them."

She also snagged a lovely faux fur for $299. It was originally priced at $700 but reduced to $399 because it had a braided hook missing. "I got the bargain, but I had to work at it," McCollum says.

Try to haggle out of earshot of other customers. Early mornings and evenings, when stores are less busy, may be your best time to talk. If you're hesitant about negotiating, remember it can't hurt to ask.

**Beware of vanity sizing.** When you shop, always try on the clothes. You may find you dropped a dress size without any diet or exercise. That's because of a trend called "vanity sizing." Clothing makers are putting smaller sizes on larger clothes. For instance, what would have been a size 8 in the 1950s became a size 4 in the 1970s and is now a size 0. You may even run into items labeled XS, for extra small. When ordering from a catalog, check the tables showing measurements and that brand's sizes to avoid any unpleasant surprises.

**Secondhand clothing yields first-rate savings.** Browse for big bargains in thrift shops, consignment shops, or resale shops. These secondhand stores can help you add to your wardrobe without subtracting much from your budget.

"There's a ton of them if you start to look for them," says Rick Doble, editor of Savvy Discounts newsletter and book. "And it's amazing what you will find. I know a woman who bought her daughter a wet suit. My wife, she bought me a Brooks Brothers button-down formal shirt for 25 cents. She bought a silk Chinese dress, one of those red, really gorgeous dresses, for $3. It's very random. Some people have trouble with that. It is random, so you're going to have to look."

Look for quality of workmanship and materials. Often, older garments were made better than today's clothes. Also look for pulls, tears, stains, and moth holes. Make sure accessories like pins and sashes aren't hiding flaws. If you have time, research the name on the label to see what the item may be worth. And remember that tailoring isn't included in the price.

## Right combo holds key to weight loss

Trying to slim down to that next lower size? Eating the right combination of foods may be as important to losing weight as how much you eat.

While popular low-carbohydrate diets may promise quick weight loss, the key is to lose weight gradually and keep it off. To do that, choose healthy sources of fats, whole grain products, and protein and cut down on refined carbohydrates and added sugar.

The unified diet, a consensus of recommendations from several health organizations, calls for distributing your daily calories into 55 percent carbohydrates, 30 percent fat — no more than 10 percent saturated fat — and 15 percent protein.

**Don't underestimate the cost of overbuying.** A sale isn't always a bargain if it forces you to buy more. You can save more money by only buying what you need. Clutter consultant Jane Lawson points out the costliness of overbuying.

"Don't fall for these buy-one-at-full-price, get-one-at-half-price sales," Lawson says. "Basically, they give you 25 percent off each item if you buy two. They force you to buy two. That's too much. I would rather have 20 percent off one, period, no strings attached, better sale. But it's not as effective. People like that — half price, wow. But it's only one. You still have one body to cover and seven days to cover it in a week. Why do you need two? People don't think that way."

Another good guideline is to only buy an article of clothing if you're willing to purge your closet of a similar item. You'll have less clutter and less temptation to spend.

**Super shoe-shopping tips.** You may get your kicks shopping for shoes, but make sure you follow these sensible suggestions to find the best footwear.

+ Shop for shoes at the end of the day, when your feet are the largest. Your feet tend to swell during the day.

+ Shoes should be comfortable immediately. You shouldn't need to break them in.

+ Always try on shoes. A size 7 for one brand or style may not be the same for another.

+ Walk around the store for five or 10 minutes to make sure the shoes fit comfortably.

If you have arthritis, the right footwear becomes even more important. Poorly fitting or poorly made shoes can make you alter your way of walking to compensate, leading to other problems. They can also aggravate bunions or bone spurs, frequent byproducts of arthritis. You also need to pay special attention to your footwear if you have diabetes. Avoid high heels, slip-on loafers, and sandals with straps between the toes.

**Get two sizes for one low price.** Buying shoes can be tough if your feet aren't the same size. Whether it's because of injury, disease, genetic disorder, or just a fluke, your mismatched feet shouldn't burden your wallet. Instead of buying two full-priced pairs of shoes, shop at stores that split pairs or offer a discount on the second pair. If a store has a fitting service, it will be more likely to understand and accommodate your needs.

You can donate unworn mismatched pairs of shoes to the National Odd Shoe Exchange, a nonprofit group that provides shoes to amputees and people with significantly mismatched feet. Check them out online at *www.oddshoe.org*. You can send shoes or a letter requesting shoes to:

National Odd Shoe Exchange
P.O. Box 1120
Chandler, AZ 85244-1120

## Take a walk to jog your memory

Now that you have comfortable shoes, put them to good use. Start walking. A recent Italian study found that people aged 65 or older who regularly walk significantly lowered their risk for vascular dementia, the second most common form of dementia after Alzheimer's disease.

**Run away from expensive running shoes.** Don't pay more for high-end running shoes and expect better results. A recent Scottish study found that when it comes to comfort and shock absorption, $80 shoes were no different than those priced at $150.

Pay more attention to the way a shoe fits than the way it's marketed or priced. With the money you save, you could almost buy a second pair of cheaper running shoes. Or a nice outfit to wear while working out.

## Buy shoes with help from Medicare

If you have diabetes and certain foot conditions, Medicare will pay 80 percent of the cost of special shoes to prevent foot ulcers. These conditions include partial or complete amputation of the foot, previous foot ulceration, history of preulcerative callus, peripheral neuropathy with evidence of callus formation, foot deformity, and poor circulation. Ask your doctor about this program, which also requires a prescription for the shoes.

# Ins and outs of clothing care

**Bright ideas for button sewing.** When buttons fall off, use these helpful tricks to sew them back on.

+ Do you normally sew buttons on too tight? Next time, lay a pin across the top of the button before sewing it on. After you secure the button and knot and cut the thread, slip the pin out. Your button will have some give to it.

+ Reinforce a button by placing a small square of fabric between the button and the garment. It will put less strain on the button.

+ Paint some clear nail polish over the threads, both on the button and inside the garment, to seal them.

+ For garments that get a lot of rough use, like camping or hiking gear or clothes you wear for yard work, use something stronger than regular thread. Dental floss, carpet thread, embroidery floss, or fishing line all make great substitutes.

+ When sewing on a four-hole button, knot the thread after stitching through two holes. Then finish the job. If one thread breaks, the button won't come completely detached.

**Cut down on trips to the cleaner.** Your garment's label reads "dry clean only." But must you obey that command? Not always, according to clothing expert Steve Boorstein, whose wisdom can be found at *www.clothingdoctor.com*. But you have to be very careful.

"It's all based on fabric content, color, the quality of the dyes, the construction of it, and the personal ability of the person washing it, and the personal comfort level of going against the care label to do it at home," Boorstein says. "Many cotton, rayon, microfiber, polyester, some acetates — they can be washed."

But he stresses that all clothing may fade, shrink, or bleed in water. Stain removal, especially with oily and colored stains like mustard or soy sauce, may also be a problem. "There are those four major reasons — fading, shrinkage, dye bleed, and stain removal — that are concrete reasons not to wash something that's dry clean only," he says.

You also need to worry about ironing the garment. It could become stiff or lose its shape, and you may need a professional to steam and iron it properly.

Remember, just because it says "dry clean only" doesn't mean it is. Federal law only requires one care label, so manufacturers may not even test an item for washing as long as it can be dry cleaned. But sometimes it's best to play it safe. "Any item that you really care about and you don't want to take a chance on, dry clean it," Boorstein says.

You can also save money — and trips to the cleaner — by using home dry-cleaning kits, like Dryel, FreshCare, or Dry Cleaners Secret. But these in-dryer products have their limits. "If you get French fry grease or olive oil or any of those things — blood, ink, mustard, coffee — and you stick it in the dryer with your Dryel pack or one of the other brands, those stains are probably not coming out," Boorstein says. "They're very good for freshening and refreshening, they do remove some stains, and in a pinch, I think that they'd serve their purpose.

"But people should not be misled to believe there is a home dry-cleaning kit or something in a sealed package that you can put in your dryer and will do the work of a dry-cleaning plant that cost a million dollars to build and staff. That's just not a reasonable statement."

**Identify stains for easy removal.** It's important to know what type of stain you're dealing with if you want to remove it successfully. Here are some ways to identify the offender as well as advice on treating it.

| Stain | Description | Treatment |
|---|---|---|
| water–based | Stain has an obvious ring or outline and appears to be absorbed into the fabric. | If garment is washable, wash as soon as possible. |
| oil–based | Stain has no clear outline, but is still absorbed into the fabric. It may look like a cross because oil wicks out into the fabric along the weave. | Dry clean within 48 hours. |
| combination | Stains contain both oil and water. Things like butter, lipstick, makeup, paint, chocolate, icing, and salad dressing fall into this category. | Dry cleaning may be necessary. |

**Pay less for dry cleaning.** Not every garment needs deluxe treatment. You can save money by taking some of your clothes to a bargain dry cleaner rather than spending extra for specialty or custom cleaning. Steve Boorstein, clothing expert and star of the DVD "Clothing Care: The Clothing Doctor's Secrets to Taking Control," points out when it's safe to scrimp and when it's best to splurge on dry cleaning.

"You got blue jeans, you got a basic suit, you've got clothing that is soiled or you got a basic stain on it and you just want it cleaned," he says. "You don't need Liberace, you don't need Elton John for this job. All you need is for it to be dry cleaned and pressed so you can wear it the next day or the next week."

In those cases, a discount dry cleaner should be fine. But don't trust your everyday clothes to just anyone. Beware of shops with signs claiming "Not responsible for buttons, trims, zippers, this, that." Budget cleaners often handle a lot of volume and need to work quickly, so they don't have the time to dedicate to your clothing that a custom cleaner does.

"I would stress, if you're going to go to a bargain cleaner, ask them to show you some of their work before you drop your clothes off," Boorstein says. A little comparison shopping can help you find a quality discount dry cleaner. But you should spend the extra money to clean special fabrics or outfits. You'll want to take those to a custom cleaner for expert service and overall peace of mind.

## Sidestep disaster with simple test

Always test a small, inconspicuous area of your garment before attempting any do-it-yourself stain removal.

**6 ways to erase ink stains.** The following household items can come in handy for removing tough ink stains from your clothes.

- Hairspray. Spray the stain, let it sit for 30 minutes, and dab with a wet sponge.

- Toothpaste. Use plain toothpaste, not gel. Rub gently into the stain.

- Rubbing alcohol. Soak the stain, let sit for 30 minutes, and lift stain with a damp sponge.

- Shaving cream. Use the foaming kind, not the gel. Let sit for 30 minutes, then run under cool water and rub away stain with your fingers.

- Bar of Ivory soap. Run stain under cool water and gently rub soap into it. Rinse after 30 minutes.

- Buttermilk. Let garment soak in buttermilk for 24 hours, then rinse under cool water with some liquid hand soap.

**Defeat tough stains with dish soap.** Mama mia! You just spilled spaghetti sauce on your blouse. Squirt some liquid dish soap onto the stain to treat it. Or soak the entire garment in soapy water for hours. Liquid dish soap also works for grease, chocolate, baby formula, and perspiration stains.

**Smart way to save money.** When you get a new tie, apply a fabric protector right away. This will help repel stains and lower your dry cleaning bills.

**Lessen laundry costs.** Here are three easy ways to save money while doing laundry.

+ Use only half the recommended amount of laundry detergent.

+ Don't dry your clothes completely. Take them out after about 15 minutes and hang them.

+ Fill a cloth tea bag with dried lavender flowers. Use this instead of dryer sheets. It should be good for five or six loads before the flowers need replacing.

**Dry your sweater better.** Avoid unsightly clip marks when drying your sweaters on a clothesline. Simply put pantyhose in the neck of the sweater and pull the legs through the arms. Then clip clothespins to the pantyhose to hang your sweater.

**Boost laundry with baking soda.** Baking soda does more than keep your refrigerator smelling fresh. It also does wonders for your laundry — and costs much less than expensive laundry detergents. Add half a cup of baking soda to your wash to help your regular detergent work better. It helps by neutralizing the pH of the wash water. It also increases the effectiveness of bleach. Just mix half a cup of baking soda with half a cup of bleach for whiter whites. Of course, baking soda also helps with odors. Freshen stinky laundry by adding half a cup of baking soda in the rinse cycle.

334

**Trick helps towels absorb more.** Don't bother using fabric softener with towels. It makes them less absorbent. Instead, shake them once when wet and again when dry to fluff the fibers.

**3 ways vinegar helps with laundry.** Make vinegar part of your laundry routine. Here's how it can help.

+ Bleaches. Add a cup of vinegar to the presoak or rinse cycles when washing whites.

+ Fights odors. Deodorize your clothes by adding a cup of vinegar to the rinse cycle.

+ Removes stains. Use a half-water, half-vinegar mixture to treat perspiration, grass, urine, or pet stains.

**Iron out a new plan for an old bottle.** Thoroughly rinse out an empty squeeze detergent bottle. Fill it with either tap or distilled water, and keep it near your ironing station to fill your steam iron.

**Blow away wrinkles.** To get wrinkles out of your vinyl coat, put it on a hanger and use a hair dryer on the wrinkles until they disappear.

**Simple steps to spruce up your shoes.** Don't spend money on new shoes when your old ones still have miles of wear in them. Try these shoe-revitalizing ideas to breathe new life into old shoes.

+ Remove surface dirt from leather shoes with a leather cleaner. Then condition, polish, and weatherproof them. Use a mild cleaner and conditioner for exotic leathers, such as snakeskin.

+ For suede shoes, apply a water and stain repellant designed for suede. Regularly use a plastic or rubber-tipped brush to restore the nap and get rid of dirt.

✦ Perk up athletic shoes just by changing the laces. Get rid of odors with a deodorizing product that counteracts bacteria. Cornstarch also works well as a home remedy.

## *Breathe easier with common spice*

Instead of throwing away old clothes, save them to use as poultices or wraps when you're sick. Herbal healers suggest making a paste from powdered black mustard seeds and warm water, wrapping it in linen, and laying it across your chest for 10 to 15 minutes to relieve congestion. Mustard can irritate your skin, however, so think twice before trying this folk remedy. Rubbing olive oil onto your skin after removing the paste may ease the irritation. You don't have to put mustard on yourself to benefit from it. Cooking with this common spice may ease many respiratory problems, such as chest congestion, bronchitis, bronchial cough, and sinusitis.

**Smart way to recycle.** Pillowcase lost its pizazz? Give it a second life in the laundry room. You can turn an old pillowcase into a drawstring bag, and use it to hold dirty laundry. You can also wash your delicate items inside this homemade bag.

**Terrific trick to make your zipper unstick.** When your zipper's stuck, use a cotton swab to dab a drop of olive oil on it. This should lubricate the teeth so your zipper can move up and down like normal. Just make sure not to get the oil on the fabric.

**Break in blue jeans.** Soak your stiff jeans in fabric softener overnight, then wash them as usual. They should come out soft and comfy.

# Best-ever beauty tips

**7 secrets to staying young.** Follow these natural anti-aging tips. They're better than anything else you can do — and no pills or surgeries are on the list.

+ Surround yourself with friends and family. A large support group lowers stress levels, blood pressure, and your risk of heart disease and heart attacks.

+ Stretch. It's natural to get less flexible as you age, but stretching is a natural way to slow and even reverse this process.

+ Aim for more antioxidants. They put the brakes on free radicals, which cause cell damage and lead to over 200 diseases. Eat more fruits and vegetables to boost your levels.

+ Bolster your bones. Dairy foods like milk, yogurt, and cheese are good sources of calcium, which is a key to strong bones. You'll also get plenty of the critical nutrients phosphorus and vitamin D. Adding dairy to your diet helps shield you from osteoporosis.

+ Feast on fish. Eating fish at least twice a week could sink your risk for heart attack and stroke. Thanks to its omega-3 fatty acids, fish may also help fight arthritis, diabetes, cataracts, Alzheimer's disease, depression, and a host of other age-related illnesses.

+ Take a walk. Walking is an easy, cheap, safe, and effective way to exercise. You'll lose weight, have more energy, lower your blood pressure and cholesterol, think more clearly, have less anxiety, and sleep better.

+ Deal with stress. Finding ways to cope with daily stress is essential to staying and feeling young. Religion, exercise, laughter, and relaxation techniques can all help.

## The simple way to a natural 'face lift'

Don't spend big money on plastic surgery, Botox injections, or expensive creams. Just drink more water. It's a natural way to fight wrinkles. That's because water keeps your skin tissue firm and elastic. Without enough hydration, your skin looks brittle, flaky, wrinkled, and dry. So drink up. Even if you're not thirsty, your skin might be. Make sure to drink water with meals, snacks, and activities such as using a computer or watching TV. Eating water-rich foods like soup, fruits, and vegetables also helps.

**6 surprising head-to-toe remedies.** You don't have to spend a lot of money to look — and feel — better. Just try these low-cost beauty tricks.

✦ For cleaner teeth, use baking soda as a toothpaste. Just wet your toothbrush and dip it in the baking soda. "It has a little bit of grit to it, so it can scrub plaque off your teeth," says Dr. Frank Toton, a dentist in Shawnee-on-Delaware, Pa. "What causes tooth decay is bacteria in your mouth producing acid. If you brush with baking soda, it will neutralize acid. It's the same thing you do for indigestion."

✦ For shiny, dandruff-free hair, eat flaxseed. Like fish, these tiny powerhouses are a good source of omega-3 fatty acids, which keep your skin and hair healthy. Aim for 4 to 6 tablespoons of ground flaxseed a day. Toss them in yogurt, smoothies, cereal, or salad.

✦ To get rid of puffy eyes, apply a cold compress to the skin under eyes. You can also use chilled cucumber slices or damp tea bags.

✦ To keep yourself from biting your fingernails, dab a bit of aloe vera on them. The taste will make them less tempting.

✦ For softer hands, mix one tablespoon of sugar with fresh lemon juice to form a paste, then rub it on your hands.

✦ To cure dry feet, make a soothing foot bath using a cup of honey for every gallon of hot water. You can even add marbles to the bottom of the basin to massage your feet while they soak.

## Swap sticks for stones to save money

Spend less on deodorant by using a deodorant stone. These crystals, which eliminate odor–causing bacteria, usually cost less than $10 and can last up to a year. Just apply the deodorant stone right after a shower or bath, when you're still wet. Remember, these stones fight odor but don't stop perspiration.

**Better way to brush your teeth?** One recent study found that electric toothbrushes with circular bristle heads that rotate in alternating brushes work better than manual toothbrushes, slashing plaque by 11 percent and gingivitis by 6 percent. But that doesn't mean you need to run out and buy an electric toothbrush.

"It's not going to shake anything else off the teeth that a regular manual toothbrush won't get," says Dr. Frank Toton, a dentist in Shawnee-on-Delaware, Pa. "I just think it's hype. As a rule, I don't recommend electric toothbrushes because I feel they are an expensive toothbrush. But they do work if they are used correctly."

That means directing the brush at a 45-degree angle into the gums so the bristles will clean below the gums. And make sure to brush all sides of every tooth.

Electric toothbrushes may come in handy in some situations, though. "It usually has a bigger handle on it," Toton says. "Somebody with arthritis, if they try to grasp a toothbrush with a little handle, they may have trouble holding it, let alone do the correct motion."

Toton stresses that, no matter what type of toothbrush you use, you also need to floss. "If you have trouble manipulating regular floss on a spool, small plastic devices with a piece of floss can be used very efficiently with one hand," he says. He also recommends rinsing your mouth with an over-the-counter or prescription fluoride rinse to bathe the surfaces of your teeth after brushing and flossing.

## Beware of bacteria at the gym

Working out at the gym can keep you looking good — but you need to take some precautions. If you're not careful, you could pick up a skin infection from methicillin–resistant *Staphylococcus aureus* (MRSA). Protect yourself by not sharing towels, putting clean towels over workout mats, and wiping down equipment with the alcohol spray supplied by most gyms. If you notice boils or a localized, painful rash that doesn't heal, see your doctor.

**Brush up on toothpaste tips.** Don't spend too much money on fancy new toothpaste. Any brand with fluoride cleans teeth and prevents decay. You can also save money by squeezing less toothpaste onto your brush. A little dab works just fine.

**Pay less for pearly whites.** Getting your teeth whitened at the dentist's can be pricey. But you may brighten your smile for a fraction of the cost by using over-the-counter whitening kits.

**Make your hair color last longer.** You pay good money to get your hair colored. Keep your locks looking good — and the right color — in between trips to the stylist.

✦ Condition your hair a few days before you color it. Healthier hair holds color longer.

✦ Wait at least two days to shampoo your hair after it's been colored.

✦ Avoid chlorine, which can change your hair's color — even to green, if you're a blonde.

✦ Shield your hair from the sun if you don't want it to lighten. But, sometimes, the sun can help give your hair a brighter, warmer look.

✦ Beware of dry heat and hard water, which can change your color. You may want to use a filtered shower head attachment. Avoid curling irons, flat irons, and blow dryers as much as possible.

✦ Only wash your hair when it's dirty. The more you wash your hair, the quicker the color fades.

**Walk away from wrinkle creams.** Don't waste your money on costly wrinkle creams. Objective tests found no difference between expensive creams and cheap ones. In fact, even when wrinkle creams did smooth out some fine lines and wrinkles, the effect was barely noticeable.

## Shield your skin with laundry secret

Sometimes light clothes don't offer enough shelter from the sun's damaging ultraviolet rays. One cheap way to solve that problem is with SunGuard, a laundry additive that washes UV skin protection into your clothes. Just add a package of SunGuard, along with your detergent, to a warm or hot water load. Your clothes will block 96 percent of the sun's harmful rays, similar to a sunscreen with an SPF of 30. One box costs just $1.99, and the treatment lasts for up to 20 washings. You can order SunGuard at *www.sunguardsunprotection.com* or by calling 866-871-3157.

**Groom like a man to save money.** Women's skin care products typically cost much more than similar products for men — even though they have the same active ingredients. Save money by buying men's lotions, cleansers, and other grooming products.

**Toss old makeup to avoid infection.** Out with the old, in with the new. That should be your approach to makeup. If the color changes or develops an odor, get rid of it. Toss your foundation after a year, and ditch your mascara after three months. They may be harboring bacteria.

**Treat your feet right in the winter.** Dry, cold winter weather can take its toll on your feet. Wearing poorly fitting boots can make matters worse, as can sweating in heavy socks or walking through snow and rain. You end up with cracked heels, corns, calluses, odor, and bacteria. Here's how to take care of your feet during the winter.

+ Soak your feet once a week to get rid of dead skin and smooth rough surfaces. Lukewarm water and a few drops of skin-softening oil should do the trick.

+ Use a lightweight insole to keep your foot in place inside your boots or shoes. Moving around can cause friction, leading to corns and calluses.

+ Moisturize your toenails so they don't become dry and brittle.

### Take steps to spot skin cancer

You may wear hats, sunglasses, and sunscreen to guard against skin cancer — but don't forget your feet. Melanoma of the foot can be tough to spot. Regularly check your feet for moles, freckles, or spots that have grown or changed in appearance. Look at your soles, between your toes, and under your toenails.

# Travel steals and deals

**Where to look for special deals.** Senior travel discounts haven't disappeared. You just have to know where to look.

+ Airlines. Since September 11, 2001, airlines have dramatically cut back on their senior discounts, but you can still find them if you ask. Southwest offers Senior Fares, where people over age 65 qualify for discounted, fully refundable airline tickets. Other carriers, including United and American Airlines, also offer senior discounts, but you must ask for them when booking your ticket.

+ Hotels. Get a 15-percent discount or more at Marriott hotels around the world if you're age 62 or older just by asking for the senior hotel discount when you book. Hyatt hotels promises discounts up to 50 percent off the going rate of rooms in the continental United States and Canada. Other hotels also offer senior rates, so ask for them when booking.

+ Senior groups. There's power — and savings — in numbers. AARP members reap discounts of 10 percent or more on certain hotels, flights, rental cars, vacation packages, tours, cruises, and entertainment. Book these deals through *www.travelocity.com/AARP* or call 888-291-1757.

**Surf your way to low airfare.** If you want to find good travel deals on airfare, the Internet is the place to go. According to The New York Times editor Damon Darlin and Jay Cooke, editor for Lonely Planet travel guides, these Web sites can help you plan your trip and save money — to boot.

+ Farecast at *www.farecast.com* predicts the cost of airfare on particular routes. A new feature even tells you whether a particular fare is a real deal or not. Type in a departure city, and a list of deals will pop up with designations such as "record low" or "$105 less than the average low."

✦ Airfarewatchdog.com at *www.airfarewatchdog.com* digs deep for deals, according to Cooke, and includes listings for low-cost carriers Southwest and JetBlue. Most other travel sites do not.

✦ SmarterTravel at *www.smartertravel.com* offers consistent, steady deals, says Cooke.

✦ Southwest Airlines at *www.southwest.com* is well worth checking, if Southwest flies where you're going. They will likely offer a good bargain fare.

Don't forget to check other travel Web sites such as Orbitz *(www.orbitz.com)*, Travelocity *(www.travelocity.com)*, Expedia *(www.expedia.com)*, and more specialized sites including Kayak *(www.kayak.com)*, CheapTickets *(www.cheaptickets.com)*, and SideStep *(www.sidestep.com)*.

**Time your buying for super savings.** Snag the best price on flights just by booking on certain days and times. In general, you'll find the cheapest airfare early in the week. Airlines usually release new sales and fares Tuesday morning. By that evening, other airlines have matched the lower price with their own sales. Look for the best rates Tuesday evening and Wednesday morning. Prices start rising again Friday and through the weekend.

One exception — airlines typically work on their Web site late Saturday night and early into Sunday morning. Occasionally, they mistakenly list the wrong prices for airfares. These "oops" prices can be a fraction of the cost of a regular ticket, but don't expect them to last long. The bargain will disappear as soon as the airline notices the mistake. If you're fast and a bit of a night owl, you could cash in first.

**Expert advice about car rental insurance.** To buy, or not to buy? That is the question. This is the extra insurance rental companies try to sell you. Tom Schneider, a partner in Schneider Insurance Agency, says you may not need it if you already have auto insurance. Check with your agent. Your regular policy may offer plenty of coverage.

"Two questions to ask your insurance agent. First, 'does my policy cover the rental if it gets damaged or stolen?' Almost 99 percent of the time, the answer is yes," says Schneider. "Second, 'does my policy cover the "loss of use" the rental company will have if I wreck their car, and it's in the shop for a week?' Some policies do, and some don't," he warns.

Planning to travel internationally? Ask your agent if your policy covers a rental car in the country you're visiting, or if you can buy an endorsement that will, Schneider says. If you don't own a car or have auto insurance, then rental car coverage is a no-brainer. "Buy every damage waiver, loss waiver, and insurance you can get, because otherwise you do not have a policy to fall back on."

## Tips for travelers with special needs

New security rules may scare you away from traveling if you have a medical condition. But the Transportation Security Administration (TSA) makes exceptions for people with diabetes, pacemakers, defibrillators, and other special needs. When you get in the security screening line, tell the guard about any syringes, insulin, or medications you have with you. You can ask for a visual inspection of your items instead of an X-ray.

Make sure all your medicines are clearly labeled. Also, tell security if you have an implanted medical device, like a pacemaker. If you are worried about walking through the metal detector with an implant, ask for a pat-down inspection, instead. TSA suggests people with a pacemaker carry a Pacemaker ID Card when traveling.

**5 ways to lighten your load.** Packing light is not only smart, but it can save you money. Airlines that once allowed two checked bags per person now charge extra for more than one, not to mention the chances that checked luggage will get lost and cost a small fortune to replace. Lighten your load with these tips the next time you travel.

+ Pack a pair of long underwear if you chill easily or are traveling in winter. They double as sleepwear, so you won't need pajamas.

+ Roll up socks and stockings and place inside women's shoes. Then, place the shoes in a plastic bag, and tuck them inside the men's shoes to make the best use of suitcase space.

+ Wear your just-in-case sweater, jacket, and heaviest pants the day you travel instead of bulking up your suitcase. Airplanes tend to get cold anyway.

+ Save perfume samples from magazines and take these on trips instead of fragile perfume bottles. Do the same with shampoo and other samples. They take up less room, and you'll avoid the mess of squeezed bottles inside your suitcase.

+ Take old shoes you no longer want, and throw them away at the end of your trip. Do the same with worn out undergarments and socks. Toss them after wearing.

**Click your way to budget friendly airfare.** Hunting for deals through a budget air carrier can be an exercise in frustration. Not all airports have low-cost airlines, and some low-cost carriers fly only in certain parts of the country. Two Web sites — *www.lowcostairlines.org* and *www.cheapflights.co.uk* — make it easy to find a budget carrier at any airport, both in the States and abroad in Europe, Asia, and elsewhere. Just choose the city you're flying to or from, and the Web sites will tell you which low-cost airlines serve that airport.

**Never lose frequent-flier miles again.** Don't let frequent-flier miles and other loyalty-program points go to waste. Three simple computer programs will keep track of them for you so you can use points before they expire. Both MilePort at *http://mileport.com* and

MileTracker at *www.miletracker.com* are free. MileageManager at *www.mileagemanager.com* charges $14.95 a year but offers a few more bells and whistles.

## A healthy way to see the world

Walking 30 minutes a day, most days of the week — that's all it takes to lower your risk of Alzheimer's disease and heart disease, plus reduce your blood pressure. Hitting the road after retirement is no excuse for not exercising. Walking and biking are great ways to see the world, especially when visiting pedestrian friendly towns.

Retiree and avid 65-year-old runner John agrees. "Running is a great way to have a quick look around a new location. Also, it is much more acceptable now than 40 years ago when folks tended to stare in disbelief at an adult running through the streets. Or maybe just this adult."

**Save a bundle on credit card fees.** Credit cards are one of the safest, most convenient ways to pay when traveling abroad, but the costs can add up. Most banks and credit card companies charge a fee every time you make a purchase in a foreign country or use an out-of-network ATM. Most, but not all.

Discover card and the bank Capital One typically don't charge foreign fees, while American Express, Visa, Mastercard and the banks Citigroup, Bank of America, and Wachovia do. Total fees can ring up to 3 percent of the purchase price. Save your hard-earned cash for more vacations. If you travel abroad a lot or plan a big trip in the future, consider getting a card that does not charge foreign fees. Call your current bank and credit card issuer and ask about their policies, then choose a company that won't fleece you.

**See America for only $10.** Enjoying the natural beauty of your nation is a perfect way to spend your golden years. Now you can do it for just $10 with an America the Beautiful Senior Pass from the National Park Service. This lifetime pass entitles people over the age of 62 and three other adults — or a car full of people in a per vehicle fee area — free entrance to national parks and reduced fees for camping, swimming, boat launches, and other amenities. Disabled people of any age can get a lifetime park pass free. You can only get these passes on park grounds, so hop in your RV and start seeing America.

### No-hassle directions instantly

The Internet has revolutionized trip planning. Web sites, such as *www.maps.google.com*, *www.mapquest.com*, and *www.maps.yahoo.com*, can give you driving directions to almost anywhere, plus help you find the shortest routes and save fuel, or take the most scenic route. Just type in your starting point and your final destination. Keep in mind, sometimes these sites make mistakes, so it's always best to get directions from more than one to double-check them. Another Web site, Seeaarch at *http://directions.seeaarch.com*, makes it simple by doing this for you.

# Stay safe away from home

**Make your own "fast food."** Taking a trip is no excuse to take a vacation from good nutrition. Seniors need plenty of water, protein, calcium, and fiber while they travel, says Ruth Frechman, a registered dietitian and spokesperson for the American Dietetic Association. Take along these cheap, tasty, and nutritious choices.

- ✦ Trail mix for energy, calcium, and fiber. You can buy the prepackaged variety, but watch the carbohydrate content if you have diabetes. Or make your own from high-fiber cereal, unsalted nuts, and a few raisins or dried cranberries. Frechman points out almost any high-fiber cereal makes a nutritious high-energy snack. "As long as it's a whole grain, you're getting lots of nutrients," she says. "It's better than eating a piece of cake." Put some in a zippered bag and take it with you.

- ✦ Bottles of water or fruit to provide fluid. "Older adults are at risk of being dehydrated," Frechman says.

- ✦ String cheese for protein and calcium. Small cans of tuna also work.

- ✦ A peanut butter sandwich for protein. "The energy bars tend to be convenient, but they also tend to be a little on the pricey side," Frechman says. Instead, make this old standby using whole-grain bread. "That way you're getting a whole grain and protein."

## Protect yourself from easily ignored hotel danger.

Hotels must follow certain rules when it comes to providing working smoke detectors and fire alarms, but not for carbon monoxide (CO) detectors. You can't see or smell CO gas, but it can kill you if you inhale too much. You may be at risk of CO poisoning from a faulty furnace every time you're a hotel guest.

A 2007 study found 68 incidents of CO poisonings at hotels, motels, and resorts between 1989 and 2004 — including 27 people who died. Even after these tragedies, most of the hotels still didn't install CO detectors. Protect your family by carrying your own CO alarm when you travel.

**Hotel key card myth exposed.** Some people think personal information may be shared on a hotel key card. *Computerworld* magazine tested 100 key cards from various hotels in the United States to see if they contained personal or credit card information. They didn't. In fact, most of the cards couldn't even be read by a typical card reader. Most hotel key cards hold only the assigned room number, a code that refers to the guest, and the guest's checkout date. Your personal information — including your credit card information — is stored in a separate computer system.

**Clever solution for travelers with pet allergies.** Many hotels are attracting guests by letting them bring their pets. If you have allergies to dogs or cats, that's a problem. Even requesting a pet-free room when you make a reservation is no guarantee your room will be free of hair and dander. Some hotels don't actually track where pets stay. To be sure, find a hotel that doesn't allow pets in any rooms.

**Prescription drug safety for people on the go.** Pack your prescriptions the right way when you travel. Here's what you should do.

+ Use insulated, cooled packaging for prescriptions that need to be refrigerated.

+ Keep drugs in their original labeled containers in a carry-on bag if you're flying. It's best to check the latest restrictions for what you may take on an airplane.

+ Take more than you plan to need. Don't assume you'll be able to pop into a neighborhood pharmacy for a refill. The Institute for Safe Medication Practices issued a safety alert in 2005 about drugs sold in other countries that have different ingredients as U.S. drugs with the same names.

✦ Pack a list of all the drugs you take regularly — even over-the-counter medicines.

**Prevent theft with a $5 gadget.** Experienced travelers go prepared. The readers of *Budget Travel* magazine suggest these uses for a mountain climber's carabiner, also called a D-ring.

✦ Connect your suitcase to a chair leg while you're sitting in an airport.

✦ Clip your purse or camera to your belt for hands-free walking.

✦ Attach small bags to the handle of your rolling suitcase so you can pull just one bag.

### Help for frazzled airline passengers

When you fly, things can go wrong. Experts recommend checking in early to head off any problems. Just remember, there are no federal rules for exactly how airlines handle compensation for delayed flights and other problems. You can see the policies of major airlines, including Delta, Southwest, US Airways, and others, at *http://airconsumer.ost.dot.gov/*. Click the link for "Airline Customer Service Plans."

**Turn your cell phone into a travel assistant.** It's not just for calling a cab. Your camera cell phone has features that can make your trip safer and remove some of the hassles of navigating in a strange place. Try these tricks.

✦ Store emergency phone numbers and medical information in the notes section of your phone's address book. You'll have your doctor's name and telephone number handy, as well as a list of medications you're taking and any health conditions you have.

✦ Take a daily photo of your traveling companions. If you get separated, it's easier to explain who you're looking for — including what they're wearing that day.

✦ Snap a picture of your rental car and its license plate so you'll recognize it later.

✦ If you're in a city with posted maps, store a close-up photo of one in your phone. You can zoom-in on the map as you move around the city.

## What you should never drink on an airplane

Bring your own water next time you fly. Tests by the Environmental Protection Agency (EPA) found around 15 percent of airplanes had coliform bacteria in their tap water. Coliform bacteria are not dangerous, but they may be a sign that disease-causing bacteria are present. Airlines are working with the EPA to figure out how water was contaminated and keep it from happening again. For now, you may want to bring bottled water onboard. Just be sure you buy it after you go through the security checkpoint. Better yet, ask for drinks in cans or bottles when you fly.

**2 ways to stay healthy on a cruise.** You can pick up the norovirus, which causes severe vomiting and diarrhea, anywhere people come into close contact. But getting it on a cruise will sure put an end to your fun. Norovirus can spread through food, on surfaces you touch, or directly from another person. To avoid it, wash your hands often with soap and water — not alcohol-based sanitizers — and avoid shaking hands. All ships that sail from a U.S. port get health inspections twice a year. Check on your ship's report at *wwwn.cdc.gov/vsp/*.

# Free-time fun

**Explore new books for free.** It's hard to find something good to read, and buying a book you later decide you don't like is a waste of money. Skip that hassle and expense by joining a Dear Reader book club. Pick from nearly a dozen clubs, like mysteries, nonfiction, science fiction, and romance. Each week you'll sample short selections from a different book — sent directly to your e-mail every day. If you don't like that week's book or you don't have time to read it that day, just delete the message.

Suzanne Beecher, founder of DearReader.com, writes a short column to go with each day's passage. She says she started the book clubs to help busy people get back into the habit of reading. "I felt reading was starting to take a back seat to all of the other activities that are offered to someone, and reading had a lot of competition," she says. But with the five-minute-a-day reads, there's no commitment. You can try out a new title and decide if you want to buy the book or borrow it from your library. Sign up for free at *www.dearreader.com* or at your local public library.

"I like it when people become part of their library's book clubs because — not only are they part of an online club and group of people worldwide — but they are also a part of the group in their own community," Beecher says. Her column makes you feel like a part of the online reading community, with some 350,000 people reading through Dear Reader every day.

**Clever way to swap old books for new.** Clean out your bookshelves and get new books through the Web site *www.paperbackswap.com*. Just sign up and list at least 10 books you're willing to give away. If you receive a message that a member wants your book, mail it at inexpensive Media Mail rates. You earn credits for giving away your books. Then when you see a book you'd like posted on the Web site, request it. The owner will send it to you — for free. You can also swap music CDs and video DVDs for a small fee.

## Beware drugstore reading glasses

You can buy over-the-counter (OTC) reading glasses for a few dollars at the supermarket or drugstore. But use this inexpensive option only in an emergency. Eye specialists say OTC glasses are fine for a little while — if you break your good glasses or leave them at home. But they're not as durable or accurate as prescription lenses. Also, if you don't pick just the right pair, they may cause eyestrain. For long-term wear, it's best to be examined and fitted by a professional. She'll also check for silent eye problems, such as cataracts or glaucoma.

**Save money on magazine renewals.** When your subscription is over, the price to renew could go way up. Instead, resubscribe at the original lower rate. You can find that price in a magazine insert card or online at a Web site like *www.magazines.com*. To be sure you don't end up with two subscriptions, include your address label from the magazine when you renew.

**Reliable rules for "regifting.** Giving away something that was given to you — regifting — saves money and avoids waste. Follow these rules to avoid hurting someone's feelings or looking just plain cheap.

✦ The item must be new and in its original package.

✦ Wrap it with new wrapping paper and discard any signs of the original gift. A tag with your name on the "to" line is a dead giveaway.

✦ Don't regift anything that's monogrammed, handmade, or an obvious freebie. You're likely to get caught.

✦ Have good intentions. It's fine to regift when you know the recipient will truly love the item — not just so you can cross a name off your list.

**Reap the benefits of little-known discounts.** Savvy seniors can save a bundle of money on recreation. Movie theaters, museums, amusement parks, ski resorts, national parks — they all want to get seniors in the door by offering a price break, often around 20 percent off the regular cost.

Bill H., 67 years old, always asks about senior discounts when he golfs. He finds that some city park and recreation departments offer an annual card for public courses. Seniors pay $31, for example, while other users pay $39. And some courses offer seniors a deep discount on a certain weekday, when other golfers are working. He also finds great deals when he shows his AARP membership card.

"At some point, maybe after 55 years old, you're no longer embarrassed to ask for a senior discount," says Bill. He even gets a break at some fast-food restaurants near his seniors-only neighborhood in northern California. "I went through the drive-through at Wendy's, and just by chance I asked, 'Do you have a senior discount?' And by golly, they did!"

### Best time to rent a movie

Hit the video-rental store early on a Tuesday afternoon. Morning returns should be back on the shelves, and you can take advantage of middle-of-the-week deals.

**Join the club for movie savings.** Don't spend $30 every time you take your honey to the theater. AMC Theatres offers a free MovieWatchers reward card. Show it every time you buy movie tickets and you can earn points for free concessions and tickets later on. Sign up online at *www.moviewatcher.com*. Regal Cinemas has a similar program, the Regal Crown Club. You can get your free membership card at *www.regalcinemas.com*. Check your local theater to see if it's owned by Regal, AMC, or another company.

**Discover a better way to watch TV.** Make the most of your television-viewing time by recording your favorite shows using a digital video recorder (DVR). It's much simpler than programming a VCR. With a DVR, you use your remote control to search for and select your favorite show by name, without knowing when it's on or how long the show lasts. You can also pause live TV — a great feature when the phone rings.

A DVR also saves you time viewing, explains Donald A. Norman, professor of computer science and psychology at Northwestern University and the author of books on good design. "Suppose there's a two-hour show you want to watch when it's really showing, like a football game," says Norman. "I know people who won't watch it when it starts. They'll wait for 30 or 40 minutes, and then they'll go and watch it." The DVR allows people to easily fast-forward through commercials without missing a single play, seeing the game's end in real time. "But they saved themselves a half hour." You can rent a DVR from your cable company or buy a machine such as the TiVo brand.

**4 easy tips for great digital photos.** Switching from a camera that uses film to one that's digital may make you feel like a beginner. Digital cameras can be complicated, but these tips can help you shoot like a pro.

+ Get close to your subject. You can use the manual zoom feature if you're far away, but turn off the digital zoom.

+ Hold down the shutter button halfway for a second to let the camera prefocus. Then there won't be a delay when you're ready to click.

+ Try a tripod to avoid the blur that can come from shaky hands. Or turn on your camera's image-stabilization feature.

+ Remember to recharge the battery between uses.

**Can't-miss idea for music lovers.** Classical or country, blues or big band — preview new music before you plunk down $18 for a compact disc. Many chain bookstores, including Borders and Barnes & Noble, offer free listening stations in the store. Put on headphones and scan the CD you want to hear. You can also hear short clips of songs online, at a bookstore Web site like *www.amazon.com* or at the iTunes store. Navigate to *www.apple.com/itunes/store/*, then search for the song or artist you want to hear.

### Eat out for less

Eating in a restaurant doesn't have to be expensive. Here are eight ways you can dine for less.

* Clip a coupon.
* Go out for lunch rather than dinner.
* Find an early-bird special.
* Drink water — it's free.
* Share the entree.
* Order food to go and skip the tip.
* Search out a kids–eat–free night.
* Try a hospital cafeteria.

**Chill warm soda in 5 minutes.** Put the cans or bottles of soda into a large stockpot and cover with ice. Fill the pot with water, and pour in 2 cups of table salt. Stir it up to help the salt dissolve. Place the pot in the freezer for 5 minutes, and your soda will be ice cold and ready to enjoy.

**Tips for a terrific toast.** You've heard plenty of well-meaning speakers fall flat while giving a toast. Don't be one of them. Remember these basic rules from Toastmasters International.

+ Be brief — a couple minutes or less. That way you won't lose your audience.

+ Practice beforehand, and speak clearly and loudly during the toast.

+ Say something personal, heartfelt, and tailored to the occasion.

+ You can be funny, but keep it clean and positive.

Even if you don't drink alcohol, you can still participate in a toast. It's better to politely sip soda than to refuse offering your good wishes.

---

### Finger friendly tricks for knitters with arthritis

Try these small changes to make your painful fingers feel better while you knit.

* Avoid cotton yarn. Wool and wool blends are more elastic and easier to work with.

* Use a circular needle — even if you're knitting a flat piece. The weight of the item you're knitting then rests on your lap instead of pulling on your wrists.

* Try knitting with needles made of lightweight birch, bamboo, or plastic instead of cold metal.

---

**Arrange your workspace to avoid injury** Dr. Christopher P. Andreone, of Andreone Sports and Family Chiropractic in Peachtree City, Ga., sees people with overuse health problems from a number of hobby- and work-related activities.

"Typically, both hand and machine sewers show up with more neck, arm, and upper-back issues, either from sitting with their head in a downward position for long periods of time, or from working on a machine that is either too tall or too short," he says. "Low-back issues tend to rank higher in the hand sewers due to sitting consistently for longer periods of time." To avoid injuries, follow basic principles of ergonomics, or arranging your workspace to fit the way your body works. Dr. Andreone has this advice.

"Look to simple geometry for the answers," he says. "Ideally, your head should be straight versus head down or leaned forward, arms should hang straight down at your sides, and then elbows should be at 90-degree angles, making the tops of the forearms parallel to the floor. Your seat height is important, too. Your back should be straight, and the tops of your thighs should be parallel to the floor with your knees at 90-degree angles and your feet flat on the floor."

Dr. Andreone says these changes will soon become habit. "If you can't lower your chair, put some books under your feet. If you're bending to use your machine, put something under the legs of the machine so you can sit up straighter."

**Frugal storage ideas for savvy crafters.** Spend your limited craft budget on supplies — not on containers to store these treasures. Longtime sewer and quilter Alice Jewell saves money by inventing new uses for old items. "I like clear shallow boxes that are sold to fishermen," she says. "The small compartments can be customized for almost anything. I use one for various machine needles. Another is set up with the supplies I carry to workshops. One division is large enough for scissors and rotary cutter. Handles make it easy to carry." Jewell points out these fishing tackle boxes are cheaper than similar organizers made just for crafts and sewing.

Don't throw away candy boxes with dividers — they work to separate small items in a drawer or on a table surface. "Reusing a bedroom chest of drawers for sewing-room storage works well," Jewell says. Other great organizing items come from the hardware store and office-supply store.

"I use a desk organizer carousel to separate pencils, marking tools, seam rippers, and other items I want to reach from my sewing machine but have out of the way," she says. "By far my favorite organizer is a pegboard hung within easy reach of my chair. I like this especially for hanging my scissors and having easy access to them."

## Turn a short table into an elevated cutting table.

Whether you're cutting fabric, paper, or plastic while you stand, the job is more comfortable at a table that's countertop height. You can spend $300 or more on an elevated cutting table, or you can modify a table you already have for about $20. Here's how.

Decide how high you want the table to be. Commercial tables are about 35-inches high, but pick a height that's comfortable for you. Have four pieces of 3-inch PVC pipe cut to about that length. All must be exactly the same length. Place each leg of your table inside a PVC pipe. To keep the table from wobbling, use shims inside the PVC to make the pipes fit snugly. No more stooping over to cut or mark.

**Get creative with bubble blowing.** One-size-fits-all bubbles get old fast. Give your grandchildren an affair to remember using items you have around the house.

+ Try a clean, plastic fly swatter dipped in bubble solution. You'll get a gaggle of different-size bubbles.

+ Reuse a plastic strawberry basket for a huge herd of bubbles.

+ Shape pieces of floral wire into circles for unique bubbles. Or bend a wire coat hanger for one really big bubble.

### 5-minute homemade ice cream

Thrill your grandkids by helping them make ice cream from milk — with no mess. Put ice cubes and some salt or rock salt in a one-gallon plastic zip-lock bag. Don't fill it more than halfway. Then place one-half cup milk, a tablespoon of sugar, and a bit of vanilla in a sandwich-size plastic zip-lock bag and seal. Put the small bag into the large bag, seal it, and shake it up. Keeping shaking until it turns into ice cream.

# Index

speeding tickets, dealing with 307
supplies, for emergencies 303
Carbon monoxide, and hotels 349
Carpet
  cleaning 67, 87
  dents, fixing 88
CDs
  caring for 112
  music listening stations 357
Cell phones. *See also* Telephones
  and cancer 236
  and pacemakers 234
  buying online 234
  cancellation fees 235
  cleaning 111
  text messages, blocking 235
  travel safety 351
Charitable donations
  and tax deductions 135
  avoiding scams 177
Check fraud, 123, 176
Chimney sweeps, hiring 85
Christmas lights, storing 77
Chrome, cleaning 61
Cleaning products
  safety 65, 67, 72
  saving money 59
Closets, organizing 80
Clothing, buying
  discounts, asking for 324
  secondhand stores 125, 133, 325
  shoes 327-329
  vanity sizing 325
Clothing care
  button sewing 330
  dry cleaning 330, 332, 334
  hair dryer, for wrinkled vinyl 335
  jeans, softening 336
  shoes, cleaning 335

stain removal 331-334
washing and drying 334, 341
zippers, unsticking 336
Coffee
  filters, clever uses for 58
  preparing 26-28
Colds and flu, preventing 65, 219
Computers
  and high blood pressure 284
  and neck strain 184
  bill paying, online 181
  browser and cookies 186
  buying 125
  e-mail 182, 183
  file wiping 186
  Internet access, free 181
  password precautions 181
  safety online 183, 184
  social networking 185
  trip planning 348
Concrete cracks, patching 93
Cookies 34
Copper, cleaning 56, 60
Countertops, cleaning 64
Credit cards
  and traveling abroad 347
  cash back rewards 119
  convenience checks, disadvan-
    tages of 122
  late fees 121
  virtual numbers 180
Credit counselors 116
Credit reports
  false information 185
  freezing 175
  ordering a copy 116
Credit score, boosting 115
Crockpot cooking 32, 33

HEPA filters, for allergies 223
Herbs and spices
   buying in bulk 43
   freezing 40
   garlic, chopping 22
   growing indoors 251
   mustard seeds, for respiratory
      problems 336
High blood pressure, and
   computer use 284
HMOs
   disadvantages of 195
   shopping for 191, 193
Home improvements
   decorating diary 86
   for seniors 98
   hiring a contractor 85
   upgrades, dollar-wise 85
Homeowners insurance 145, 146
Humidifiers, caring for 106

## I

Ice cream, homemade 361
Identity theft 172-176, 179
Injuries, preventing 66, 266, 359
Inkjet printers, cleaning 112
Insurance
   car 143, 144
   car rental 344
   filing a claim 148, 149
   flood 147
   fraud 179
   health. *See* Health insurance
   homeowners 145, 146
   life 141, 147, 148
   pet 149
   renters 146
   unneeded coverage 141

Internet. *See* Computers
Ivory soap, for ink stains 333

## J

Jewelry
   buying 125, 129
   cleaning 63
Junk mail, stopping 75
Jury duty, scam 178

## K

Keogh plans 164
Kitchens, organizing 79
Kitchenware
   buying 53
   cast iron, caring for 54
   enamel cookware, cleaning 56
   nonstick pans 51, 56
   pastry slab, homemade 58
   stainless steel, cleaning 57
Kitty Litter, for oil spills 93

## L

Ladybugs, allergy to 69
Lawn care
   and drought 271
   grass varieties 271
   leaf-bagging 270
   mowers 272, 273
   mowing mistakes 270
   watering a slope 274
Lead contamination
   avoiding 96
   test kits 97
Lemon pledge, for spider control
   279

online pharmacies 210
pill organizers 212, 213
storing 81
traveling with 350
Probiotics, and diarrhea 218

# R

Real estate
  and market value 322
  buying tips 309
  environmental checkups 312
  for sale by owner 322
  foreclosures 311
  fraud 309
  home inspectors, choosing 312
  moving companies 323
  open house safety 321
  rental property, buying 314
  renting 310, 311
  selling tips 320
  value, maximizing 313
Rebates
  for electronics 111
  how to obtain 127
Rechargeable batteries 113, 114
Refrigerators
  boosting efficiency 226
  caring for 104
  troubleshooting 105, 225
Renters insurance 146
Respiratory problems, and
  mustard seeds 336
Restless legs syndrome, and cast
  iron 55
Restocking fees, avoiding 128
Resumes, updating 167
Retirement
  adjusting to 166

and money management 156-164
and second careers 167, 168, 170
best places to settle down 171
long-distance learning 170
scholarship programs 169
volunteering 169
Roth IRA 160
Rubbing alcohol, for ink stains 333
Rust, WD-40 for 92

# S

Safety
  break-ins, surviving 94
  burglars, deterring 94, 110
Salmon, preparing 22
Scholarship programs for
  seniors 169
Scuff marks, removing 65
Seafood. See Fish
Septic tanks, caring for 239
Shaving cream, for ink stains 333
Shoes
  buying 327
  cleaning 335
  organizing 80
Shower curtains, cleaning 62
Shower heads, unclogging 61
Showers, cleaning 63, 64
Sinks, cleaning 61, 62, 64
Skin cancer 145, 342
Sleep, better quality 71, 318
Slow cookers. See Crockpot
  cooking
Social Security
  and federal income tax 160
  benefits, delaying 158, 164
  payment errors 165, 166
Space heaters, and house fires 99

# Index

Squeeeeek No More, for carpeted
floors 89
Stain removal 331-334
Sterling silver, cleaning 60
Stocks, playing it safe 117
Storage options, inexpensive
cardboard tubes 77
cup hooks 82
filing cabinets 78
for crafters 359
hanging shoe bags 77
magnetic strips 82
pegboards 81
shower rings 81
tie racks 79
Stress
and tea 317
work burnout 167
Stroke, and omega-3 fatty acids 38
Sunburn relief 99
SunGuard, for clothes 341
Sunscreen, and Mexoryl SX 273
Surge protectors 112

## T

Taxes
and audits 136, 138, 140
and small businesses 137
and Social Security benefits 160
deductions, itemizing 135
estate 138, 154
property 139, 140
Roth IRA and 160
Tea, for stress 317
Tea bags, for puffy eyes 338
Teeth, cleaning 338-340

Telephones. *See also* Cell phones
411 calls, free 233
billing fraud 232
long-distance calls 121
slamming scams 233
telemarketers, stopping 232
Television-shopping networks 133
Tile, cleaning 60, 61, 62, 65
Toastmasters International tips 358
Toilets, cleaning 61, 62
Tools
cleaning 64, 92
storing 91
Toothpaste
baking soda as 338
for ink stains 333
Travel safety
cell phones and 351
hotel key card myth 350
hotels and carbon monoxide 349
medical conditions 345
norovirus, preventing 352
nutritious snacks 349
pet allergies 350
prescription drugs, packing 350
preventing theft 351
Travel savings
America the Beautiful Senior
Pass 348
delayed flights 351
discounts, for seniors 343
driving directions, and the
Internet 348
Elderhostel 171
low airfare 343, 344, 346
loyalty programs 346
packing light 345

373